Freud the Man

Freud the Man

An Intellectual Biography

Lydia Flem

Translated by Susan Fairfield

OTHER

Other Press
New York

Copyright © Editions du Seuil, 1991
Collection La Librairie du XXe siècle, sous la direction de Maurice Olender
Originally published as *L'Homme Freud: Une Biographie Intellectuelle*

Translation copyright © 2003 Other Press

Production Editor: Robert D. Hack

This book was set in 11 pt. Berkeley by Alpha Graphics of Pittsfield, New Hampshire.

10 9 8 7 6 5 4 3 2

Library of Congress Cataloging-in-Publication Data

Flem, Lydia.
    [Homme Freud. English]
    Freud the man : an intellectual biography / Lydia Flem ; translated by Susan Fairfield.
        p. cm.
    Includes bibliographical references and index.
    ISBN 1-59051-037-2 (alk. paper)
    1. Freud, Sigmund, 1856-1939. 2. Psychoanalysts—Austria—Biography.
    3. Psychoanalysis—History. I. Title.
    BF109.F74 F4813 2003
    150.19'52'092—dc21
                                                            2003007466

To my mother
who gave me an interest in words
and to my father
who handed down the pleasure of storytelling

Contents

Introduction

Who has not wanted to penetrate into the intimacy of the creator—into the painter's studio, the scientist's laboratory, the writer's notes? Who has not dreamed of understanding what lies behind the gesture and the thought, seizing the moment when something comes into being? How does someone become a genius? What is the secret of the making of a work?

Freud was well aware that psychoanalysis cannot offer an answer to the riddle of creation, but he still kept examining the lives of exceptional people: Leonardo da Vinci, the man Moses, the great Goethe. In his youth, he bitterly regretted "that nature had not, in one of her benevolent moods, stamped my face with that mark of genius which now and again she bestows on men."[1] But in adulthood he was able to define his creative experience as a combination of imaginative boldness and strictly realistic self-criticism.

In his own eyes, Freud is not a therapist but a conqueror, an archeologist, a detective of the human soul. As he explores the unconscious and puts it into words, he is not afraid to go forward, to immerse himself more and more deeply, to be on familiar terms with the object of his conquest. There is something downright concrete, sensual, even sexual in his connection to his research. He is prepared to "put his hand in his own store-cupboard"[2] in order to feed his powers of invention.

A double union, confirmed by his father from childhood on, weds Freud to knowledge: in one and the same affective movement, games of knowing are both authorized and erotized. What is written is sexual. Texts both respect and transgress one another. Freud belongs to the book and the book to him.

In order to bring to light a knowledge of what is invisible, accessible by indirect pathways, he dares to rely not only on his patients' stories but also on his daily life, his dreams, his journeys, his readings, the fertile tensions he encounters with his Judaism, his love of friendship, and his ambivalent fascination with images.

What I shall be sketching out here is the way Freud invents psychoanalytic theory on the basis of his intimate metaphors. Imaginary cities, the railway, ruins of the past, optical machines, figures of the devil, civilizing heroes, plots from novels or detective stories: Freud multiplies comparisons in trying to define a psychic object that resists representation. Careful not to "mistake the scaffolding for the building,"[3] he is still concerned, every step of the way, to perceive the unconscious.

On the construction site of his oeuvre, constantly revised, reworked, and always open, self-analysis and theory beget one another. Knowledge of the unconscious and the writing of this knowledge come from the same place: Made in Unconscious.

Beyond science and fiction, with writers as allies (and also as disturbing doubles), and by means of analogies drawn from every domain of culture and civilization, what is most intimate becomes the property of each and every one of us.

To show how much he loves to link his own words to writers' words, I have included excerpts from Freud's readings throughout this book. This is the way their dialogue is held: the singular opens out into the universal.

After my book on the daily life of Freud and his patients,[4] there is no further need to describe the history of Vienna between two analytic sessions or to recall the first disciples and the first patients who lay down on the couch of this unlikely doctor who made an interest in the past his healing principle. There is no further need, then, to leaf through an old album of yellowed photographs in which we think we can recognize the faces of our own cultural memory. At this time, perhaps because the wish for filiation has been satisfied, what will be found here is the novel of the unconscious told "live" by its author Freud: the way his writings give birth to an interior discovery called psychoanalysis.

Between the visible and the invisible, figures and words, Freud moves forward along oblique pathways without trying to sidestep doubt or vagueness. He takes pleasure in collecting pieces of the unconscious puzzle, and equal pleasure in setting them forth in their scenarios. He knows the art of gradually unfolding a story, placing the primary and secondary characters, and making his reader want to turn the page. He invites us to reconstruct his discovery step by step, to take a direct part in creating his work.

What I wanted to do is to follow Freud's trail, to accompany him in his voyages to the land of nowhere, to read over his shoulder the strange and fabulous tale he brought back with him. I have tried to get to know the man together with the work, the underlying passions inextricably linked with his theoretical fiction. I slipped into the witch's kitchen to see whether I could recognize the ingredients, the spices, that go into the brew of his pact with the unconscious. But the unconscious always escapes, putting on masks and disguises like Casanova in Venice. Unique and multiform, it is what we know without knowing it, what emerges and takes us unawares: most alien and at the same time most intimate.

In two or three centuries, when psychoanalytic treatment will have long disappeared, there will no doubt remain on the shelves of libraries, alongside the names of Shakespeare, Dante, Sophocles, Goethe, Proust, Borges, Perec, and Celan, the name of Sigmund Freud.

With him, I have come to understand that barbarity is part of being human, and that civilization is a ceaseless task, never achieved, like love or writing.

NOTES

1. Letter to Freud's fiancée Martha, February 2, 1886 (Freud 1960, p. 202).
2. Letter to Wilhelm Fliess, October 31, 1897 (Freud 1954, p. 227, translation modified).
3. Freud 1900, p. 536.
4. Flem 1986.

Creation Day by Day

Each morning as he comes into his office, Freud waves a friendly greeting to the statue of a Chinese sage with a slightly inclined head and a beatific smile on his lips. At his side Imhotep, an Egyptian deity of knowledge and medicine, holding a papyrus scroll on his knees, welcomes him.

On his desk or behind his couch, everywhere his gaze falls, Freud converses with the traces of the past. One and the same search for origins, a patient and infinite quest for archaic history, links his archeological collection and his psychoanalytic approach. As in the night of the unconscious, yesterday and today overlap, what was dead returns to life, memory prevails over the pain of forgetfulness, the invisible finds a face.

For Freud, the ancient figurines surrounding him with their motionless gaze recall the immortality of our emotions. These fragments of long ago embody his wish to find intact what has disappeared, to reconstruct everyone's childhood past and connect it to a general law of the human soul.

His intellectual procedure is a twofold movement: opening individual singularity out to the universal through cultural references and revealing the subjectivity of cultural figures. The characters of myths, legends, tales, plays, or novels emerge in their uniqueness and, once again connected to their carnal origins, speak for human desire.

The distinction between the normal and the pathological vanishes as the work of art bears witness to the subjective and the everyday.

The Freudian concept of the psychic apparatus is not a system enclosed within itself, dogmatic. On the contrary, Freud is constantly trying to expand his investigations to other domains of knowledge. His multiplicity of comparisons define the soul's polyphony; he weds infinitely unfolding associations of thought to those of affectivity. The unconscious never stops bringing forth new networks of linkages. In one and the same place several registers are in play at the same time, as in his consulting room where suffering and laughter, childhood and death, dream and silence, the forbidden and the impossible are woven together—all the mirrors of the self, disturbing and familiar.

> No mortal, if the course of his life is followed, can be congratulated before he has crossed the finish-line without having known suffering.
> —Sophocles, last words of *Oedipus the King*[1]

The stage is set. Once the visitors step across the threshold, the deities of long ago invite them to seek their memories, their origins, their buried emotions. More eloquent than the fundamental rule of saying everything, the ancient statuettes lead them to ask questions about themselves in a gripping encounter with no possibility of escape.

When he receives his patients, often as early as eight in the morning and up to one in the afternoon, the narratives Freud hears blend together with the myths, tragedies, and novels he has read. From the past of humanity to the past of his analysands, and to his own past, he constructs a theoretical bridge. In discovering the unconscious, he discovers himself. The words of his patients are linked to those of writers and poets: across the images offered by the culture, both sets of words recognize a single humanity. In the footsteps of Oedipus, everyone must confront his destiny.

On the couch covered with an Oriental carpet, through the magic of words each patient is transformed into a tragic hero: Hamlet, Lady Macbeth, Doctor Faustus or the Witch, or into a character

from Schnitzler, Anatole France, or Maupassant, but also into a
Roman or Pompeian archeological dig, a detective story, a river hard
to navigate, a dark continent, archives, hieroglyphics, clay, or gold.
In a dazzling carnival, Freud himself plays with all these identifications. To get closer to the disguises of the soul, he turns detective,
explorer, archivist, sculptor, chemist, chess player, jigsaw-puzzle
solver, gambler, surgeon, writer, or archeologist—always the iconoclast. Through the threefold path of the personal, the pathological,
and the cultural, what he is trying to do is interpret the unknown of
the human soul.

> The fabric of thoughts is like a weaver's craft, in which a movement
> of the foot moves thousands of threads, in which the shuttle cease-
> lessly rises and falls, in which the threads glide invisibly, in which a
> thousand knots form at once.
>
> —Goethe, *Faust*

Five minutes after the last patient leaves, the clock strikes one
in the afternoon. Two doors open into the dining room, where Martha
and their six children are already seated: from one side, the maid enters
with the steaming soup tureen, from the other, always on time, the
head of the family. Freud is an attentive father and proud of his little
troupe, as he is fond of calling it. During the week he does not have
much time to spend with them, but day by day, at meal time, he follows their progress, is concerned about their illnesses, rejoices in their
pleasures and successes, is amused by their childish sayings. On Sunday, and especially during vacations, he likes to go on walks with them,
take them to the museum, on fishing trips, strawberry or mushroom
hunting. He teaches them to play cards and thoroughly enjoys the
party game Hundred Journeys across Europe.

His family life is not essentially different from his intellectual life;
although he keeps them separate for those close to him, he himself
experiences them on a continuum. Thus, in a single sentence, he writes
to his friend Wilhelm Fliess that his son Oliver has lost a tooth and
that he himself, that evening, has brought into the world some new
theoretical ideas. Everything is mixed together and takes on mean-

ing: the carnal and the abstract, the trivial and the sublime, play and seriousness.

"Stories about the devil, the vocabulary of popular swearwords, the rhymes and habits of the nursery," he explains, "all are gaining significance for me."[2] All human productions present formations of the unconscious for him to explore. He finds a resemblance between the confessions extorted from suspected witches by the ecclesiastical tribunals of the Middle Ages and the accounts given by his female patients during psychoanalytic treatment. He compares the mechanics of poetic creation to those of hysterical fantasies: "Goethe [lent] Werther something he had experienced. . . . So Shakespeare was right in his juxtaposition of poetry and madness." He dreams "over-affectionately" about his oldest daughter Mathilde and infers that this dream fulfills his wish to prove that the father is the "originator of neurosis."[3]

During the period of gestation of *The Interpretation of Dreams* (1900), and hence of the birth of psychoanalysis, Freud writes at length to Fliess about the interweaving of his creative life and his personal life. He goes to the opera to hear Wagner's *Meistersinger* and is deeply moved: "Real ideas are put into music as in no other opera through the association of feeling-tones to meaning."[4] Six weeks later, it is Zola who keeps him in suspense at the time of the Dreyfus affair: "He is a fine fellow, a man with whom one could get on."[5]

He reads extensively, especially literature; scientific publications leave him numb: "Reading is a terrible infliction imposed upon all who write."[6] He offers Fliess his first analysis of a literary work, Conrad Ferdinand Meyer's *Die Richterin*; shortly thereafter he analyzes his forgetting of the name of the painter Signorelli. He makes careful note of all the new theoretical ideas that seem to him to be worthy of his friend's attention, so as to submit them to him in their "Congress" à deux. He needs to rekindle his "flickering light" at Fliess's "steady flame," and the latter helps him find "eyes to see" once again.[7] He also asks Fliess to reread the proofs of his book on dreams, as they become available, and to critique them. He does not think he is obliged to render Fliess the same service (his friend is writing a book on biology), for, he explains, "You deal in light, not darkness, with the sun and not the unconscious."[8]

In his free time he reads Burckhardt on the history of Greek civilization and finds some "unexpected parallels" with his own theories: "My predilection for the prehistoric in all its human forms remains the same."[9] He plays chess, reads English novels, and especially admires the adventures of Sherlock Holmes written by his colleague, Conan Doyle.[10] He leads the life of a "pleasure-seeking Philistine," explaining to his correspondent: "You know how limited my pleasures are. I must not smoke heavy cigars, alcohol does not mean anything to me, I have finished with begetting children, and I am cut off from contact with people."[11] Still, every Saturday he happily immerses himself in games of tarok with a few old friends and, every other Tuesday, spends the evening with his "brothers" of the B'nai B'rith, secular Jews like himself.

In each of his letters to his friend in Berlin we can see how his ideas are connected to his daily activities, his readings to his clinical experience, his journeys to his self-analysis, his dream life to the development of his theory, his friendship to the writing of his oeuvre.

> Sometimes Pangloss would say to Candide: All events are linked in the best of all possible worlds. For, in the last analysis, if you hadn't been chased from a fine castle with big kicks in the behind for the love of mademoiselle Cunégonde, if you hadn't been sent to the Inquisition, if you hadn't run all across America on foot, if you hadn't given the baron a good swordthrust, if you hadn't lost all your sheep from the good country of Eldorado, you wouldn't be eating preserved citrons and pistachios here.—Well said, replied Candide, but we must cultivate our garden.
> —Voltaire, Candide[12]

After lunch, he walks for about an hour, measuring in long strides the streets of Vienna. After heading back up Berggasse he circles Ringstrasse, going through the Old City where he visits his bookseller and antique dealers, drops off or picks up proofs at his publishing house, stops in at his barber and certainly at his cigar dealer.

Then Freud sees patients without appointments from three to four in the afternoon, as the sign on his door indicates. The income from his practice goes to the purchase of antiques. Twice a month, a merchant comes to show him items sought out for him at second-hand shops. And Freud often brings back objects from his own travels in Italy and, over the years, receives some from friends and disciples. When she was very young, his daughter Anna once called a Roman figurine her father had bought in Innsbrück an "old child." The remark amused Freud. On the other hand, he had to resent Fliess's calling his cherished treasures "disgusting" deities.

Between four and seven, sometimes even later, he takes his customary place behind the couch. He devotes fifty-five minutes to each patient and spends the five-minute intervals between sessions resting, checking up on his family, drinking a cup of tea, or scribbling down a few words. After dinner with the family he goes for another walk, often with his wife, his sister-in-law, or his daughters. He sometimes takes them to the theater or comes to pick them up there; sometimes, too, they stop at one of those great cafés where Viennese artists and intellectuals are inventing our modernity.

Back home again, he retreats into his office. On his desk he always keeps a large sheet of paper on which, under the date of that day, he notes letters received on the left side, letters sent on the right. He writes them all by hand. Even his family doesn't understand how he can write so many, so quickly: he goes into his office, they say, and an hour later brings us ten letters to be mailed.

From time to time he receives friends or disciples, often ones who have come from foreign countries to meet him. While speaking with them, Freud is in the habit of picking up one or the other piece from his archeological collection, handling it, and looking at it carefully as though it had the power to inspire him. When listening, however, he remains motionless, his gaze turned inward, only playing from time to time with his wedding ring or a small Roman stone mounted in a ring, representing a bearded man delicately sculpted—no doubt Jupiter.

On Saturdays, Freud gives a two-hour lecture at the University. He prepares by taking a long walk, during which he ponders his subject and lets himself be guided by the associations of his unconscious. He likes to begin his talks with statements that may seem implausible to his listeners. He then defends them by quoting a scene from *Hamlet* and announcing, "So I too shall ask you first to give welcome to the things that here rise so strangely from the tomb of the past."[13]

As in his writings, he uses a number of metaphors to illustrate his theories. The most common ones are often the clearest. Thus, for example, one day he shows a postcard depicting a country bumpkin in a hotel room trying to extinguish an electric bulb as though it were a candle. This is what you are doing if you address the symptom directly, Freud comments; what you have to do is look for the light switch.[14]

An extraordinary matter described in ordinary words.

> Now, reader, do not leave your bench, but stay
> to think on that of which you have foretaste;
> you will have much delight before you tire.
> I have prepared your fare; now feed yourself,
> because that matter of which I am made
> the scribe calls all my care unto itself.
> —Dante, *Paradiso* X.22–27

Between eleven at night and two in the morning, Freud puts together, imagines, seeks, guesses, builds, composes, fixes on paper his ideas, his intuitions, his readings, his clinical experience, his dreams. Ever since he was a young man, his dearest wish has been to disturb the sleep of the world. A therapist against his will, a poet of the unconscious in spite of himself, he has aspired all his life to philosophical knowledge. In order to bear his everyday cares and efforts, he muses that, if a few years of work still remain for him, he will surely leave behind "something which will justify our existence,"[15] new truths about the human condition.

Under the pressure of an inner dictation, he writes in one sitting a text that was often composed mentally beforehand. If the manuscript does not please him, he throws it away and begins again another

evening, guided by an irresistible internal force. Freud likes to aban-
don himself to the twists and turns of his thoughts, extending as far
as possible a bold speculation, an idea still vague but completely new.
He usually begins with some precise elements but gives up the attempt
to make the whole coherent, so as not to distort what he is seeking to
discover: "I know that in writing I have to blind myself artificially in
order to focus all the light on one dark spot."[16] Little by little he tries
to draw maps of the psyche, always more vast, more detailed.

He moves forward and, as he proceeds, does not obliterate his
footsteps; on the contrary, he calls attention to their imprints. He not
only shows his ideas but reveals them to us, his readers, as though he
were unfolding them as we read. Always it has been the other, the
distant friend, the imaginary interlocutor, to whom Freud is speaking. When he writes, as when he travels, he needs a witness—a guide,
too, who will permit him to defy the prohibition of knowledge that
has weighed on the West since Eden and Olympus. From Athens, to
Rome, to Jerusalem, Freud walks with the freedom of a man who is
not afraid to look squarely at his contradictions and his doubts. He
does not resolve the tensions that animate him. He draws his creative
strength from them.

Freud needs only a little sleep and has the useful ability to fall
asleep instantly, without continuing to entertain thoughts or cares in
his head. According to Martha, he awakens at exactly the same time
each morning. He himself admits that it is often hard to get up after
getting too little sleep.

His time is precious. Unable to wait, he very often celebrates the
birthdays of his children the day before. He does not put up with
patients who come late for their appointments. In railway stations,
however, he can't stop himself from wasting time; he invariably arrives over an hour before the train is due to depart.

All year long he is nostalgic for travel. He dreams of going to Italy
at the end of the summer, ascribing to this country the power to stimulate his creative activity and calm his agitated feelings. Nor has he ever
forgotten his stay in Paris; he cherishes many stirring memories, like
this one: "I remember how, on a spring day on the Boulevard Michel,
a group of young men and girls walked in front of me. Every now and

then they stopped walking and fell spontaneously into a few dance steps without any apparent cause or motive, just because they were young and in Paris and it was springtime."[17]

His suitcases are quickly packed, since he has few clothes: usually three suits, well tailored and of good cloth, as is appropriate for physicians of that time. He sometimes takes along a silk suit when he travels in the South. Despite all his precautions, at the last minute he is seized with fever, and it is not uncommon for him to lose his luggage in his confusion, or miss his train. After this perturbation, all is calm once again. Freud takes his seat. The psychoanalytic voyage can begin. Through the window of his railway compartment, under his gaze, the unconscious files past endlessly.

NOTES

1. Unless otherwise noted, translations of the epigraphs are by S. F.
2. Letter to Fliess of January 24, 1897 (Freud 1954, p. 189).
3. Letters to Fliess of January 17, 1897, May 31, 1897 (Draft N), and May 31, 1897, respectively (Freud 1954, pp. 188, 206, 208).
4. Letter to Fliess of December 12, 1897 (Freud 1954, p. 239).
5. Letter to Fliess of February 9, 1898 (Freud 1954, p. 239).
6. Letter to Fliess of December 5, 1898 (Freud 1954, p. 270).
7. Letter to Fliess of January 3, 1899 (Freud 1954, p. 272).
8. Letter to Fliess of September 6, 1899 (Freud 1954, p. 295).
9. Letter to Fliess of January 30, 1899 (Freud 1954, p. 275).
10. Freud identifies with the English detective in a letter to Jung on June 18, 1909, in connection with a reply to Sabina Spielrein: "[I] was ever so wise and penetrating; I made it appear as though the most tenuous of clues had enabled me Sherlock Holmes-like to guess the situation" (Freud and Jung 1974, pp. 234–235).
11. Letter to Fliess of March 11, 1900 (Freud 1954, pp. 311–312).
12. Encouraging himself to pursue his investigations despite all the obstacles, Freud was fond of quoting, in French, this last sentence of *Candide* as well as another one: "To work without reasoning is the only way to make life bearable" (trans. S. F.).
13. Reik 1940, p. 13.
14. Sachs 1944, p. 45.
15. Letter to Fliess of April 2, 1896 (Freud 1954, pp. 161–152).
16. Letter to Andréas-Salomé, May 5, 1916 (Freud and Andréas-Salomé 1985, p. 45).
17. Sachs 1944, p. 46.

2

Through the Train Window

A window, a train, the countryside filing past from Freiberg to Vienna, the description of some traveling companions: an old Jewish man, very dignified, a little girl drooping apathetically, a brazen boy, a cook from Bohemia who is the spitting image of a bulldog, soldiers taking a madman to the asylum, an anxious mother, and a little girl with intense eyes. Time stands still, the shade of a subtle nod. This is how a first Freudian novel is written.

Freud is 16 years old on this eighteenth of September, 1872. In the small room on Pfeffergasse (Pepper Street), by the light of a shabby oil lamp that damages the eyes, he writes the promised letter to a friend who had remained behind in the country of their childhood:

> I stayed at the window and watched for the moment when the blond head with the big questioning eyes would appear. I soon caught sight of it, and, even amid the deafening noise, I never took my eyes off it. The breeze merrily rumpled her short, curly hair. Two hours flew by like one minute. But then the head drew back, and I didn't see it again until a station appeared on the side where both of us were seated at the window. For me, the time didn't pass less pleasantly. I waited, I hoped, and meanwhile I thought of Freiberg. Thus I arrived at Vienna. Once again, I saw the nervous mother and the blond child, and I promised myself to make a note

of where, in the Viennese crowd, I shall meet up with them again.
And that is the end of my little novel.[1]

Long before extending his invitation to the psychoanalytic journey through a railway metaphor, Freud himself had behaved like a
traveler who, seated by the window of his railway compartment, would
describe, to a friend who had stayed home, the landscape passing
before his eyes.[2] Sketched from life or memory, the happiness of the
journey is inextricably mingled with the pleasure of recounting it.
Describing the valleys, mountains, stations, the glimpse of mushrooms, the transient encounters between two railway stops (a shy
blond head with beautiful eyes), the incidents,[3] the fears, the hesita-
tions, the concern about being late: the least detail becomes the pretext for a letter, the occasion to consolidate memories, prolong sensations, deepen feelings. Writing duplicates the journey.[4] Writing is
journey, memory in motion, work of the past.

Beneath recent turmoil float ancient impressions: his father's
failure; the final departure from the Moravian countryside; the trip
during which, as a very young child, Freud had turned toward his
pregnant *matrem nudam*[5]; the gas jets in the Breslau station like the
fires of hell after the death, wished for, of his little brother Julius.
Naked mother and dead brother, the disappearance of the happiness of childhood: trains will remain synonymous with catastrophe,
antisemitism, poverty and hunger, the sudden loss of the maternal
breast, guilt feelings, forbidden transports, excitations, uncanniness,
and death. Writing, friendship, and analysis will be inscribed in this
way: displacements, transferences, and free associations.

Freiberg-Leipzig-Vienna and Vienna-Paris-London: Freud's life
could be written between two railway lines. The long detour from
Moravia to England through the Austrian capital: seventy-eight
years of waiting for a train taken too soon—and the invention of
psychoanalysis.

On April 21, 1896, Freud gives a lecture, "The Aetiology of Hysteria." To illustrate the link between a hysterical symptom and a trau-
matic scene from the past, he gives the example of an episode of vom-

iting in connection with "a great fright, e. g. from a railway accident" and "the sight of a decomposing dead body." A patient's history? Not at all, Freud explains to his audience; he invented them. And the author of this fiction adds that real observations are too complex, in the manner of genealogical trees.[6]

A brief railway genealogy in the Freud family:

Alexander Freud, Jacob's last son, became the primary Austrian expert on transportation, receiving government commendation for the services he rendered during World War I.

Emmanuel, Jacob's first son, died on October 17, 1914, at age 24, of injuries incurred when he fell off a moving train.[7]

Sigmund suffered from a longstanding railway phobia. Fear of a train accident accompanied him all his life. He would arrive at the station early lest he miss the departure and, during family vacations, would always travel alone while his wife and children took a different train. He was unwilling to let his anxiety about traveling be seen.[8]

His niece Anna from Odessa married an engineer with the Russian railroad, "and everyone over there agrees on the suitability of the match."[9]

> I was sitting alone in my *wagon-lit* compartment when a more than usually violent jolt of the train swung back the door of the adjoining washing-cabinet, and an elderly gentleman in a dressing-gown and a traveling cap came in. I assumed that in leaving the washing-cabinet, which lay between the two compartments, he had taken the wrong direction and come into my compartment by mistake. Jumping up with the intention of putting him right, I at once realized to my dismay that the intruder was nothing but my own reflection in the looking-glass on the open door. I can still recollect that I thoroughly disliked his appearance.
>
> —"The 'Uncanny'"[10]

In the fall of 1897, Freud returns from Berlin, where he visited Fliess. His self-analysis is absorbing all his psychic energy. It is not the countryside he sees through the window of his railway compartment but his own face superimposed on it. Eyes closed. Eyes open.

Trains offer travelers their windows as mirrors in which the inner gaze is sharpened.

Thus the image of the train comes to represent the analytic situation, and the landscape in motion the rule of free association. First connected with the erotic and destructive agitations of early childhood, at the time of Freud's self-analysis and his friendship with Fliess the railway metaphor is expressed in calmer terms. Then, in 1913, it takes the form of a technical rule.[11]

In 1920 the image is still there. This time, however, the entire analytic process is included in a comparison with "two stages of a journey." "The first," Freud explains,

> comprises all the necessary preparations, today so complicated and hard to effect, before, ticket in hand, one can at last go on to the platform and secure a seat in the train. One then has the right, and the possibility, of traveling into a distant country, but after all these preliminary exertions, one is not yet there—indeed, one is not a single meter nearer to one's goal. For this to happen one has to make the journey itself from one station to another, and this part of the performance may well be compared with the second stage of an analysis.

During this second stage, Freud had explained, "the patient himself lays hold of the material put before him, works on it, recollects," and so on.[12]

The train journey holds an unfailing fascination for Freud. The railway metaphor for analytic treatment is not its only appearance: it persists throughout his theoretical writings. The train, the station, and railway accidents make their way across the unconscious landscape to indicate Eros and Thanatos. Modern technology joins up with immemorial fantasies and intensifies them. Madness, death, love, and sex encounter each other there.

1905. Three Essays on the Theory of Sexuality

> The shaking produced by driving in carriages and later by railway-travel exercises such a fascinating effect upon older children that

every boy, at any rate, has at one time or another in his life wanted to be an engine driver or a coachman. It is a puzzling fact that boys take such an extraordinarily intense interest in things connected with railways, and, at the age at which the production of phantasies is most active (shortly before puberty), use those things as the nucleus of a symbolism that is peculiarly sexual. A compulsive link of this kind between railway-travel and sexuality is clearly derived from the pleasurable character of the sensation of movement. In the event of repression, which turns so many childish preferences into their opposite, these same individuals, when they are adolescents or adults, will react to rocking or swinging with a feeling of nausea, will be terribly exhausted by a railway journey, or will be subject to attacks of anxiety on the journey and will protect themselves against a repetition of the painful experience by a dread of railway-travel.[13]

1916–1917. Introductory Lectures on Psycho-Analysis

An example of a dream in which he kills everyone on a train in order to escape from an accident reminds him of an account of an incident in which a madman killed a traveler in the same train compartment.[14]

1929. Civilisation and its Discontents

If there had been no railway to conquer distances, no child would ever have left his native town and I should need no telephone to hear his voice.[15]

1936. Letter to Georg Hermann

All these dreams of journeys, missed trains, etc. have to do with death, seek to defend against the expectation of death. You recall what people customarily say to children when someone is not going to come back because he is dead: he left on a journey. You also remember the traveler setting out for the land from whose borders no one returns (or something of the sort), the final voyage, the other side (of a river), the detailed Baedeker for this journey in the Egyptian Book of the Dead, etc. . . . The fact that we missed the train is actually the consoling assurance that we are not dead either.[16]

"Can we see the trip yet?"
—Question asked by Sophie Freud to her father[17]

What does it mean to travel? Curiosity, escape, a search for the forgotten, a feeling of conquest. Also a dream: of going away and coming back.

At the end of his life, Freud relates that, in his adolescence, the hopes for travel expressed the wish to flee the family atmosphere and live independently: "When one first catches sight of the sea, crosses the ocean, and experiences as realities cities and lands which for so long had been distant, unattainable things of desire—one feels like a hero who has performed deeds of improbable greatness."[18]

The dream of travel often does duty for the journey itself. In his youth, Freud experiences that irresistible longing for a place one cannot yet reach. Thus, at age 17, he writes to Silberstein: "I'm reading English history, writing English letters, declaiming English poetry, hearing accounts of England. The essential thing, alas, the trip to England, is beyond reach."[19] To console himself, he scales the mountains around Vienna, alone, gathering strawberries and blackberries.

During another Viennese summer, Freud enlivens his days with vicarious escape, devouring books on exploratory voyages to Africa. He reads Baker, Schweinfurth, and Stanley, enticing accounts that remind him of fairy tales in which the king's son takes up his sword and kills horrible dragons and invincible magicians one after the other. Yet he regrets that none of these modern travelers, "each of whom slays a hundred or two pieces of game, is not so much as wounded by an arrow. It seems that there is a God in heaven after all." Having learned that some of these present-day adventurers got themselves killed nevertheless, he ends on a note of amusement: "This introduces a serious note into history."[20]

Nearly fifty years later, Freud will remember Stanley's books in particular: *How I Found Livingstone* (1872) and especially *Through the*

Dark Continent (1881). In 1926 the bold explorer of human sexuality had to admit humbly: "The sexual life of adult women is a 'dark continent' for psychology."[21]

Throughout his life Freud remains an enthusiastic traveler, diving into his impressions with the amazement of a young man. When circumstances and lack of money force him to stay in Vienna for too long, he suffers, like an adolescent, from a great thirst for "the spring, and sun, and flowers, and a stretch of blue water"[22] and needs to regain his strength and peace of mind on Italian soil. If the wait is prolonged, he pines and tries to distract himself by playing chess, studying the street map of Pompeii, and reading English novels or new accounts of expeditions such as Fridtjof Nansen's to the North Pole. The same complaint recurs as a leitmotiv in his letters to Fliess: "I am not in a state to do anything else, except study the topography of Rome, my longing for which becomes more and more acute."[23]

When summer comes, Martha and the children set out on vacation. Freud often joins them later in the season, carrying on as best he can behind the couch and in his Vienna office.

Returning from Paris in 1886, Freud had announced to Martha that, after they were married, they would practice together the art of traveling. In September, they left for a honeymoon on the Baltic coast; for many years afterward they would spend family vacations in the Austrian Alps, not very far from Vienna, in the Semmering and then in Reichenau and Aussee.

After 1895 Freud has an annual appointment with Italy, but Martha almost never accompanies him. After an extended period of walks and other family pleasures in July and August, he usually sets off alone to enjoy the beauties of the Mediterranean. Everything enchants him, from antique jewelry to the flowering of the olive, orange, and magnolia trees.

Venice, the first of the Italian cities visited in the footsteps of Goethe and Heine, intoxicates him. To his wife he writes about the *vaporetto* that takes him to the Lido, where, early every morning, he bathes before strolling through the squares and alleyways around San

Marco. He visits the churches; feasts his eyes on the works of Tintoretto, Titian, and Canova; visits the Café Quadri four times; and throws himself into negotiations over various purchases.

In the course of his travels, Freud finds it remarkably easy to go from a high level of activity to just idling around and is happy to give up cultural pleasures for the joys of the sea, or vice versa. Thus he writes from Rapallo: "I realize that the only thing that has hitherto kept us going has been that remaining sense of obligation to identify—Baedeker in hand—new regions, museums, palaces, ruins; since this obligation does not exist here I am simply drowning in a life of ease." And he goes on to describe at length the beach of fine silt and the flat rocks onto which he jumps "like a monster in one of Böcklin's pictures, completely alone and losing all account of time."[24] Freud teases the octopus, gets stuck by the sea urchins, chases after wicked little crabs, and spends the whole morning bathing.

The descriptions of these moments of happiness are often interspersed with regret that his large family is unable to share them. He cannot help thinking that another profession, very different from his, might have been more lucrative: "a manufacturer of something useful such as toilet paper, matches, shoe buttons."[25] And, when he has spent all the money he got from his books, he goes back home.

> I saw things that he
> who from that height descends, forgets or can
> not speak; for nearing its desired end
> our intellect sinks into an abyss
> so deep that memory fails to follow it.
> —Dante, *Paradiso* 1.5–9

Railroad or mountain road: the metaphor of the path opened out, the trail that marks landscape, water, soil, and subsoil, permeates Freud's writings. A tireless walker with a galloping stride, he likes to present his theoretical progress as though it were a ramble over hill and dale. Thus, in *The Interpretation of Dreams*, written during dreams and walks, he suddenly marches in place, speaking to his reader as to a fellow traveler apparently out of breath from trying to follow him, and takes stock of the situation: "When, after passing through a narrow defile, we suddenly emerge upon a piece of high ground, where the path divides and the finest prospects open up on every side, we may pause for a moment and consider in which direction we shall first turn our steps. Such is the case with us, now that we have surmounted the first interpretation of a dream. We find ourselves in the full daylight of a sudden discovery."[26]

His analogy with walking, like all his metaphors, helps to describe his ongoing theoretical trajectory and also to define the object of his research: the mechanisms of the unconscious. Thus, for example, still in *The Interpretation of Dreams*, Freud compares the dream process of the displacement of normal, serious thoughts by others that are more superficial and seem absurd with the various pathways that mountain climbers may take: "Superficial associations replace deep ones if the censorship makes the normal connecting paths impassable. We may picture, by way of analogy, a mountain region, where some general interruption of traffic (owing to floods, for instance) has blocked the main, major roads, but where communications are still maintained over inconvenient and steep footpaths normally used only by the hunter."[27]

Archeologist, detective, interpreter, and poet of the unconscious, Freud is also its surveyor. The psychoanalytic hypothesis is worked out in the form of a spatial proposition. In the letter to Fliess of December 6, 1896, the topographical theory takes shape; the psyche is seen as a threefold system: conscious, preconscious, unconscious. Freud offers an analogy with certain regions of Spain that, from time immemorial, had enjoyed special privileges thanks to ancient laws, the *fueros*, that were still in effect: "Thus an anachronism remains: in a particular province *fueros* are still in force. Relics of the past still survive."[28]

At the other end of his journey, in 1933, writing the *New Introductory Lectures on Psycho-Analysis* to present his structural theory with its topography of ego, superego, and id, Freud advises the reader not to imagine that these three realms of the personality are separated by clear boundaries, such as are artificially drawn in political geography, but to think instead of fields of color shading off into one another as in modern painting. He feels obliged to go on to ask for his public's indulgence, pleading the need for his metaphorical elaboration, his theoretical fiction, in depicting the psyche.

Freud presents himself as a pioneer, an explorer, and a civilizing hero, and the geographical metaphor suits his adventurous intellectual approach just as it corresponds to the therapeutic efforts of psychoanalysis, which, in a celebrated metaphor, he compares to the building of a dike on an inland sea in the Netherlands: "Where id was, there ego shall be. It is a work of culture, not unlike the draining of the Zuider Zee."[29]

This image of new lands won from the water recurs several times, as do ocean and river images, as, for example, when he speaks of the history and life of his patient Dora: "The first account may be compared to an unnavigable river whose stream is at one moment choked by masses of rock and at another divided and lost among shallows and sandbanks."[30]

The topography of the psyche includes more than landscapes and seascapes. Freud also uses analogies with the interior of a house or the place where he is giving his lectures. For example, he imagines someone beginning to chatter, laugh, or tap his feet in such a way as to prevent him from teaching; after a brief struggle several brawny listeners throw the troublemaker, thus "repressed," out the door. But so as to make sure that the same disturbance does not recur, several chairs are piled against the door to form a "resistance." And Freud concludes that, if the lecture hall is consciousness and the hallway outside is the unconscious, this would be a rather good image of repression.[31]

The psychic apparatus is territory: province, kingdom, new land, promised land, land won from the sea. The soul is a city: Pompeii, Troy, or Rome. In an extraordinary comparison of unconscious memory to the Eternal City, Freud imagines that Rome has kept all the traces of its past without anything from previous eras being destroyed:

In the place occupied by the Palazzo Caffarelli would once more stand—without the Palazzo having to be removed—the Temple of Jupiter Capitolinus; and this not only in its latest shape, as the Romans of the Empire saw it, but also in its earliest one, when it still showed Etruscan forms and was ornamented with terracotta antefixes. Where the Coliseum now stands we could at the same time admire Nero's vanished Golden House. On the Piazza of the Pantheon we should find not only the Pantheon of today, as it was bequeathed to us by Hadrian, but, on the same site, the original edifice erected by Agrippa; indeed, the same piece of ground would be supporting the church of Santa Maria Sopra Minerva and the ancient temple over which it was built. And the observer would perhaps need only to change the direction of his glance or his position in order to call up the one view or the other.[32]

Freud's geography is a geography of the gaze, associating movement with vision, the foot with the eye. In order to measure the curves of the landscape, the course of streams, and the lines of buildings, and to travel among new thoughts and ideas, he must dare to penetrate the unknown, allow himself to overcome some prohibition, some transgression.

> I have always read that the world comprising the land and the water was spherical, and the recorded experiences of Ptolemy and all others have proved this. But I have now seen so much irregularity that I have come to another conclusion respecting the earth, namely that it is not round as they describe, but of the form of a pear . . . or like a round ball, upon one part of which is a prominence like a woman's nipple.
>
> —Christopher Columbus[33]

As he maps out the unknown lands and seas of the unconscious,[34] he compares himself to Columbus, to Stanley, or to Nansen crossing Greenland and exploring the glacial Arctic Ocean. Freud is confident. "We shall not be shipwrecked," he writes to Fliess. "Instead of the passage we are seeking, we may find oceans, to be fully explored by those who come after us; but, if we are not prematurely capsized, if our constitutions can stand it, we shall make it."[35]

This conqueror's feeling, this assurance of success, "which not seldom brings actual success along with it," is, Freud believes, owing to the unconditional love of his mother, whose "undisputed darling" he was.[36] This does not shield him from discouragement, however, and in one of his moments of doubt and guilt he likens himself to Moses, who can only see the promised land from afar but not rule there: "It will be a fitting punishment for me that none of the unexplored regions of the mind in which I have been the first mortal to set foot will ever bear my name or submit to my laws."[37] He uses the same geographical and Biblical image with Jung: "If I am Moses, then you are Joshua and will take possession of the promised land of psychiatry, which I shall only be able to glimpse from afar."[38]

Writing the history of the psychoanalytic movement, he notes that, if some people compare him to Columbus, Darwin, and Kepler, others consider him simply "a general paralytic."[39] And he explains to Marie Bonaparte that Einstein had the advantage of a long series of predecessors, beginning with Newton, whereas he himself had to open out a pathway, alone and step by step, through a dense jungle: "No wonder that my path is not a very broad one, and that I have not got far on it."[40]

> Journeys end in lovers' meeting,
> Every wise man's son doth know.
>
> —Shakespeare, *Twelfth Night*

But what is the meaning of the countryside, the mountain, the water? Of the forest, the city, the station?

When he sets himself the task of discovering the symbolism of dreams, Freud notes that the complex topography of the female genitalia often lends itself to being represented as a landscape with rocks, forest, and water, while the imposing mechanism of the male genitalia is symbolized in the form of all kinds of complicated machines that are hard to describe. With the aid of mythology and poetry, he associates to representations of the female a fortress, castle, and city, but also a room, open or locked.[41]

In German as in French, means of transportation evoke displacement and, at the same time, sexual pleasure. In a note to "Fragment of an Analysis of a Case of Hysteria," he explains that "a 'station' is used for purposes of *Verkehr* ['traffic,' 'intercourse,' 'sexual intercourse']: this fact determines the psychical coating in a number of cases of railway phobia."[42]

In a dream, Dora saw herself walking in a city, looking for the station, penetrating into a thick forest, returning home, and then having to go back to the cemetery. The forest in the dream reminds her of the scene at the lake with Herr K. and also of a picture she had seen the day before, in which there were "nymphs," confirming Freud's suspicion that Dora's dream journey through station, cemetery, and vestibule comprise a symbolic sexual vocabulary.

Freud is surveying the soil of the earth mother, but he is also willing to penetrate into the subsoil of the past. Like geography, archeology presents us with a metaphor for the unconscious and, simultaneously, with a Freudian passion.

NOTES

1. Letter to Emil Fluss of September 18, 1872 (Freud 1990, pp. 229–230). All translations from this volume are by S. F.

2. "Act as though, for instance, you were a traveler sitting next to the window of a railway carriage and describing to someone inside the carriage the changing views which you see outside" (1913a, p. 135).

3. Thus, for example, in a letter to Martha of December 16, 1883, Freud describes an antisemitic incident (Freud, 1960, p. 78).

4. See the letter to Martha of July 16, 1882, written on the way to Hamburg: "All the beautiful things I still have to say will have to be left unsaid. But we are going to compete as to who will set eyes on Martha first: I or this scribble. We will be traveling by the same train" (Freud 1960, p. 17).

5. At the time of this journey from Leipzig to Vienna, which took place in the winter of 1859–1860, his mother was pregnant with Rosa, who was born in Vienna on March 21, 1860. Jean Starobinski (1954, p. xxxv) points out that only a term taken from a dead language could give Freud's mother a mythic image.

6. 1896a, p. 194.

7. Krüll 1983, p. 342, n. 98. The death certificate in the General Register Office in London indicates: "Cause of death: accidental injuries received through falling from Manchester to Southport Express, in which he was a passenger, whilst in motion on date of death."

8. Martin Freud (1957, p. 45) describes how his mother used to organize the way her children and servants sat in the train while her husband traveled alone.

9. Letter to Eduard Silberstein, January 24, 1881 (Freud 1992, p. 181). The niece has not been identified.

10. 1919a, p. 148, n. 2.

11. See note 2.

12. 1920a, pp. 208-209.

13. 1905a, p. 202.

14. 1916–1917, pp. 399-400.

15. 1929, p. 88.

16. 1936a, p. 261, trans. S. F.

17. Martin Freud (1957, p. 45) recalls that this question was part of the family tradition and that, many years later, his father used it in a letter written to his son Ernst several days before beginning his final journey from Vienna to London.

18. 1936b, p. 247.

19. Letter of August 6, 1873 (Freud 1990, p. 63).

20. Letter to Silberstein of August 14, 1878 (Freud 1990, p. 64).

21. 1926a, p. 239.

22. Letter to Fliess of March 11, 1900 (Freud 1954, p. 311).

23. Letter of October 23, 1898 (Freud 1954, p. 269).

24. Letter to Alexander Freud of September 17, 1905 (Freud 1960, p. 248).

25. Letter from Palermo to Martha of September 15, 1910 (Freud 1960, p. 281).

26. 1900, p. 122.

27. 1900, p. 530. Martin Freud (1957, p. 75) tells how his father made the difficult ascent of the southern face of the Dachstein alone, probably in 1891, and also how, during a family vacation in the mountains, when a flood made the usual supply routes impassable, he put his biggest knapsack on his back and set out along steep roads to get new provisions. His children retained the memory of his bag, full to bursting, from which there emerged a huge salami.

28. Freud 1954, p. 175.

29. 1933, p. 80. In 1932 the Zuider Zee was enclosed by a thirty-kilometer dike separating it from the sea and transforming it into a freshwater lake. The entire project included placing new land into cultivation.

30. 1905b, p. 16.

31. 1910a, p. 41.

32. 1929, p. 70.

33. Cited in Boorstin 1983, p. 242.

34. In his dream book, he says, he is drawing "the first crude map" of the psyche. Letter to Fliess of February 9, 1898 (Freud 1954, p. 245).

35. Letter of January 9, 1897 (Freud 1954, pp. 182–183).

36. 1917a, p. 147; cf. 1900, pp. 192–193.

37. Letter to Fliess of May 7, 1900 (Freud 1954, p. 318). I shall return to this quotation and the following one in the final chapter, where I discuss Freud's friendship with Fliess and Jung.

38. Letter of January 17, 1909 (Freud and Jung 1974, pp. 196–197).

39. 1914a, p. 43.

40. Letter of January 11, 1927, quoted in Jones 1957, p. 131.

41. 1916–1917, pp. 155–158.

42. 1905b, p. 99, n. 2.

3

The Archeologist

On his work table, upright, in a half circle surrounding him, the ancient gods of Greece, Rome, Egypt, and India are present as he writes his theoretical works and personal correspondence. Among the hundreds of antique treasures that cover the tables, walls, display cases, and even the floor of his office, Freud has chosen twenty or so and placed them right near him—to support his strange meditations on sexuality and death, to embody the unconscious and the power of the past, to dream of the immortality of human emotions.

Seated at his desk-sanctuary, against the background of the books of his library, he can contemplate the statuettes at leisure and also touch them lovingly—in the center, a very beautiful object presented by his Indian students: a delicate ivory Vishnu crowned with a canopy of serpents' heads. On either side, in an order designed to please the eye and the hand, chosen for their mythological and historical evocativeness, there stand Osiris, god of death and resurrection; his wife Isis suckling Horus; a winged goddess; another with a lion's head; Ptah and his son with the lotus headdress; the head of an Egyptian sparrow-hawk; a clay funerary figure from China; a Greek terra cotta; two small Roman bronzes (Jupiter and Mercury?); the goddess Aphrodite; and, at the edge of the desk, a small Athena.

This last is his favorite, Freud tells his patient, the poet H. D., one day as he hands it to her. It is a little bronze statue without a scratch, helmeted, clothed in a chiseled robe down to her feet, her upper body draped in an engraved peplum, one of her hands extended as if to hold a stick or wand. She's perfect, Freud adds, except that she has lost her lance.

H. D. does not reply, but she recalls the small temple on the right-hand side as one climbs the steps leading to the Propylaea on the Acropolis at Athens. She imagines that Freud, too, mounted these steps to take in at a glance the glory of Greece, and that here, in his office that is also a temple and a museum, he enjoys the perfection of a sculpted image like a man ardently in love with beauty.[1]

Freud always meticulously observes the objects he chooses, assesses their artistic value, and attaches great importance to their authenticity, to the possibility of a forgery. Like a true collector, he attends to every detail: the patina, the restored sections. He checks to see whether any dent on the surface, any stain on the metal, any wearing down of the fold of a garment might mar his pieces. If he is in any doubt, he has them examined at the Kunsthistorisches Museum of Vienna. Despite his precautions, he cannot avoid some imitations or counterfeits.

From the end of the century up to the last years of his life, he pursues his treasure hunt, his quest for beauty, his hope to see art as a safeguard against death and the excess of the passions. Freud confesses to the writer Stefan Zweig that, despite the much vaunted modesty of his way of life, great sacrifices had to be made for him to form his collection of antiquities, that he has read more works on archeology than on psychology, and that, almost every year, he could not help going to Rome or at least to Italy.[2]

Many years earlier he had pointed out to his friend Wilhelm Fliess that, when an old maid has a dog or an old bachelor collects snuff-boxes, the former is compensating for her need to be married and the latter for his wish for multiple conquests. His conclusion leaves no doubt: "Every collector is a substitute for Don Juan Tenorio."[3] Is he one himself, then, carnal and sublimated at the same time?

> If I begin this book with my autobiography, it is not from any feeling of vanity, but from a desire to show how the work of my later

life has been the natural consequence of the impressions I received in my earliest childhood, and that, so to say, the pickaxe and spade for the excavation of Troy and the royal tombs of Mycenae were both forged and sharpened in the little German village in which I passed eight years of my earliest childhood. I also find it necessary to relate how I obtained the means which enabled me, in the autumn of my life, to realize the great projects I formed when I was a poor little boy.
—Heinrich Schliemann[4]

When Freud reads these opening words of the autobiography of Heinrich Schliemann in May 1899, he immediately sends a paper to the printer: "Screen Memories" conceals his recollections of his childhood at Freiberg, for which he felt lifelong nostalgia.

Perhaps encouraged by this reading, he writes to Fliess about his decision to reveal his self-analysis and his resolve to finish *The Interpretation of Dreams*, the publication of which will be postponed one year. He confides in his friend: "I have bought myself Schliemann's *Ilios* and enjoyed the account of his childhood. The man found happiness in finding Priam's treasure, because happiness comes only from fulfillment of a childhood wish."[5]

In the course of spring 1899, Freud is happy. Two dreams of this period, concerning the dissection of his own pelvis and an Etruscan funerary urn, represent his wish to become immortal through his work.[6] In this same letter, he announces proudly to Fliess: "I cannot afford to keep to myself the finest—and probably the only lasting—discovery that I have made."[7]

In reaction to the death of his father on October 23, 1896, Freud undertakes an intense investigation of his past, trying to bring repressed fragments from his childhood into the light of his memory. It is at this very time that he begins to collect antiquities. Less than six weeks after his father's burial, he tells Fliess: "I have now adorned my room with plaster casts of the Florentine statues. It was the source of extraordinary refreshment to me."[8]

His dreams and his self-analysis his only tools, he explores the lands of the unconscious. The only evidence he has of the existence of this invisible continent are the archeological fragments and the verses of the poets who made this attempt before him.

The conqueror of the human imagination, Freud can only be seduced by Schliemann, who, against the advice of all the scholars, had been able to prove the existence in earth and in gold of places that had been thought to live only in Homer's mind. For Freud, sole party to the victory over an invisible psychic space, archeology offers a grasp of the visual, the representational.

While he has always intensely invested the eye and the gaze, he is now bidden to close his eyes to listen to the unconscious. Yet he never gives up his wish to see it. He surrounds himself with antiquities, mute but visible traces of the past of civilizations. It is as though his statuettes with their fixed smiles are inviting him to lend the vestiges of the individual past the most tangible of incarnations. This wish remains with him throughout his life: in 1930, in a letter to Arnold Zweig, he even writes that "through the opening of the retina we can see deep into the unconscious."[9]

Another connection between the archeology of the period and the psychoanalysis that was coming into being is that archeology had not yet crossed the threshold between poetic intuition and scientific technique. Schliemann was a heroic figure of nineteenth-century archeology for whom digs were often synonymous with treasure hunts. What was important at the time was to clear the ground, to open deep trenches and bring to light the greatest possible number of impressive ruins. It was not yet known that an archeological site is like a book that can be read only once.

The irony of the unconscious: in his enthusiasm, Schliemann destroyed many fragile signs of the past of the heroes he wanted to revive: "At last I was able to realize the dream of my whole life, and to visit at my leisure the scene of those events which had such an intense interest for me, and the country of the heroes whose adventures had delighted and comforted my childhood."[10]

Schliemann is concerned with a text. His digs in Mycenae and Asia Minor are a living illustration of the *Iliad* and the *Odyssey*. He verifies history, exhuming the mask of Agamemnon, the Troy of

Homer, the palace of Ulysses.[11] As an archeologist, he proves the truthfulness of an ancient tale. Freud uses archeology to confirm the basis of a narrative that is in the course of being written. Like the stories, plays, novels, and poems he cites abundantly in all his theoretical pieces, the archeological metaphor serves as cultural warrant for his highly unique discovery. Freud likes to illustrate his own texts with allusions to the work of antiquarians and especially enjoys his collection of antiquities when he can mention his clay and bronze figurines in support of his theories. Thus he shows the Rat Man[12] the ancient objects on his desk in order to explain the psychological differences between conscious and unconscious and the deterioration undergone by everything that is conscious, whereas the unconscious remains relatively unalterable.

And above all there is this declaration to Fliess, one that has all the hallmarks of a declaration of victory:

> Buried deep beneath all his phantasies we found a scene from his primal period (before twenty-two months) which meets all requirements and into which all the surviving puzzles flow. It is everything at the same time—sexual, innocent, natural, etc. I can hardly bring myself to believe it yet. It is as if Schliemann had dug up another Troy which had hitherto been believed to be mythical.[13]

> I just had time for a fleeting glance at the Assyrian and Egyptian rooms, which I must visit again several times. There were Assyrian kings as tall as trees and holding lions for lapdogs in their arms, winged human animals with beautifully dressed hair, cuneiform inscriptions as clear as if they had been done yesterday, and then Egyptian bas-reliefs decorated in fiery colors, veritable colossi of kings, real sphinxes, a dreamlike world.
>
> —Letter to Martha, October 19, 1885[14]

As a passion, archeology inhabits Freud's thoughts, journeys, walls, and heroic identifications throughout his life. This "dreamlike world," fostered by childhood wishes, offers him "as much consolation as anything else in the struggles of life."[15] The archeological metaphor traverses the Freudian library from 1896 to 1939, the year in which he publishes *Moses and Monotheism*.

As early as *Studies on Hysteria* (1893–1895), Freud speaks of layers and stratifications in psychic material, but he compares them to archives to be gone through, as opposed to a field of archeological investigations. It is in his lecture "The Aetiology of Hysteria" that he introduces the archeological analogy:

> Imagine that an explorer arrives in a little-known region where his interest is aroused by an expanse of ruins, with remains of walls, fragments of columns, and tablets with half-effaced and unreadable inscriptions. He may content himself with inspecting what lies exposed to view, with questioning the inhabitants—perhaps semi-barbaric people—who live in the vicinity, about what tradition tells them of the history and meaning of those archeological remains, and with noting down what they tell him—and he may then proceed on his journey. But he may act differently. He may have brought picks, shovels, and spades with him, and he may set the inhabitants to work with these implements. Together with them he may start upon the ruins, clear away the rubbish, and, beginning from the visible remains, uncover what is buried. If his work is crowned with success, the discoveries are self-explanatory: the ruined walls are part of the ramparts of a palace or a treasure-house; the fragments of columns can be filled out into a temple; the numerous inscriptions, which, by good luck, may be bilingual, reveal an alphabet and a language, and, when they have been deciphered and translated, yield undreamed-of information about the events of the remote past, to commemorate which the monuments were built.[16]

Freud uses this parable to explain to his colleagues that, in place of traditional medical anamnesis, which is unable to go back to the cause of hysteria, he is proposing to substitute another method, one that can make hysterical symptoms speak. When his audience expects him to reveal this personal method of his, he introduces the metaphorical passage in which he implicitly identifies with an archeologist whose efforts are crowned with success. He goes on to liken this method to Breuer's, announcing that he does not intend to discuss this therapeutic method, after which he pursues the slow development leading to the revelation of his hypothesis: the sexual etiology of hysteria. What he sees here is the discovery of a "*caput Nili*," the source of the Nile of neuropathology.[17]

The archeological metaphor here is inserted in an ellipsis of Freud's scientific demonstration. He calls on it to illustrate a new technique for the discovery of buried material, but, having made the comparison, he can presume on the attention of his listeners and goes on his way as if the aesthetic argument made further statements unnecessary.

Freud's artistic imagination and literary knowledge enabled him to give a shape to his introspective intuitions.[18] But what if the archeological metaphor operated in the reverse direction, and psychoanalysis were the scientific displacement of what is obvious poetically?

Be that as it may, Freud is always fascinated by men who found immortality in the area between art and science. He devotes works with similar titles to two of them: "Leonardo da Vinci and a Memory of His Childhood" (1910b), particularly rich in allusions to past civilizations and their vestiges, and "A Childhood Recollection from *Dichtung und Wahrheit*" (1917a), about Goethe.

When Freud writes "Fragment of an Analysis of a Case of Hysteria" and must admit that he was unable to understand the transference soon enough, he consoles himself over this incomplete treatment that Dora prematurely interrupted, likening his work to that of the archeologist for whom the smallest shard or fragment of pottery or wall conceals precious signs for the reconstitution of the hidden past. For the first time, he spells out the analogy to the archeologist:

> In face of the incompleteness of my analytic results, I had no choice but to follow the example of those discoverers whose good fortune it is to bring to the light of day after their long burial the priceless though mutilated relics of antiquity. I have restored what is missing, taking the best models known to me from other analy-

ses; but, like a conscientious archeologist, I have not omitted to mention in each case where the authentic parts end and my constructions begin.[19]

This is the first allusion to the task of reconstruction shared by psychoanalysis and archeology, a comparison he will develop in "Constructions in Analysis" (1937a). But in the Dora study, in contrast to the later paper, where the psychoanalyst fails the archeologist enjoys success.

Like psychoanalysis, archeology digs up the past: a buried past that, when restored and reconstructed, gives rise to a present that is less mutilated, more authentic. For the archeologist, a truth presumed to be hidden can be recovered by digging deeper and deeper, going further and further down beneath the surface of the present. The archeologist supposes that there was something that can be brought to light again. The origin takes on the form of memory here, of a reality lost for a time but really experienced long ago, of a cause bringing about the present. The other aspect of the origin is the narrative into which it can be made, the presentation and interpretation it calls for. Freud never renounces this double reading: he gives the origin the two faces of Janus, one side turning to fantasy and the other to reality.

Although he stops believing in the seduction theory and discovers the role of fantasies, he nevertheless pursues a quest for the real, verifiable archeological event transcending psychic reality. His search for an initial foundation leads him to assume the existence of phylogenetic scenes anchored in the individual psyche from the time of the primal horde.[20]

With the force of an epistemological dam, the archeological metaphor channels Freud's approach, in which can be found the alibi of his desire, never given up, to dig ever more deeply into the chronological succession of strata in the unconscious so as to discover the core, the bedrock, of the past, its originary and original version.

The unconscious is a constantly elusive object, and yet Freud cannot stop hoping to give form to the formless. The comparison with archeological work convinces him of the objectivity of origins. In a regressive movement entailed by the interest in the primordial, he can assume that, by going deeper, he will reach the ultimate cause of the neuroses, the final reality of originary scenes. It is very tempting, here, to speak of a screen metaphor.

> It is more than India, gentlemen, it is a page from the origins of the world, from the primitive history of the human species, that we shall attempt to decipher together.
> —Eugène Bernouf[21]

Freud's fascination with the past and the origin is characteristic of his time. In 1749, Rousseau had stated that man's true progress was not ahead of him but behind him, and ever since then, each time buried cities were revealed or lost writings deciphered, people exclaimed that the cradle of the human race had been found.

And there was a spate of archeological digs. Antiquity arose from the earth. Pompeii reappeared in 1748; the ruins of Palmyra were made known in 1753. In 1754, Anquetil-Duperron set out for India, the Englishman Stuart and the Frenchman Leroy explored Greece, and Winckelmann founded art history in Rome. The discoveries at Herculaneum were published in 1757.

For the first time, the West could read a great text translated from the Sanskrit, the *Bhagavad-Gita*; other linguistic breakthroughs followed. Paleontology and geology were born as sciences. Bonaparte's expedition in Egypt opened the world of the pharaohs to the curiosity of the West as teams of scientists traversed it, drew it, picking up and carrying away whatever they could. They published the *Description of Egypt*, and Rosellini presented his *Monumenti Storici*.

In 1808, Friedrich Schlegel's *On the Language and Wisdom of the Indians* posited a single primitive language and claimed that the original is in no way the simplest but in fact the most complex. In 1816, classical Greek art appeared; the Parthenon marbles, first catalogued as a Roman fraud contemporary with Hadrian, were exhibited in the British Museum thanks to Lord Elgin. Soon the Venus of Milo was acquired by the Louvre. On the morning of September 14, 1822, Champollion, who lived in Rue Mazarine, rushed across it into the library at the Institute, where he found his brother, announced the deciphering of the Rosetta Stone, and fell into a faint.

Halfway through the nineteenth century, pre-Columbian America and prehistory appeared at the same time. Max Müller published his study of comparative mythology in 1856 and Darwin *The Origin of Species* in 1859.

Germany was filled with pride when Schliemann, after discovering Troy in 1871, uncovered the ruins of Mycenae four years later. It already had ten chairs of archeology at a time when there was still only one in Great Britain and France. Little by little archeology gained standing as a science. The last quarter of the nineteenth century was the Golden Age of Greek archeology: German digs at Olympia and Pergamon, Austrian at Ephesus. The stratigraphic method began to be applied to the Near East. Palestine, Babylonia, the Hittites, and others entered into the history of archeology. At the turn of the century, Sir Arthur Evans discovered Crete and its refined civilization.

Throughout the end of the classical era, one and the same prejudice had ascribed unseemliness to whatever was "archaic," "Gothic," "Oriental," or "barbaric." Origins were proscribed or mocked. From now on, however, an ancient object was seen to hide another, still older one; people sought to go further and further back to the original darkness. As Raymond Schwab puts it, the pejorative prejudice was inverted, so that it became possible to speak of a Renaissance of the archaic.

> Which of the two, it may be debated, walked up and down his study with the greater impatience after he had formed his plan of going to Rome: Winckelmann the vice-principal or Hannibal the Commander-in-Chief?
>
> —*The Interpretation of Dreams*[22]

Freud is no exception to the enthusiasm for origins that has suddenly become obligatory in his time. His lifelong fascination with archeology and ancient studies is no doubt nourished by the drive sources of his childhood wishes, as we see in the dreams he reports in *The Interpretation of Dreams*.

Associated with his four Roman dreams are Hannibal, his childhood hero, and Johann Joachim Winckelmann, who, after an inter-
val of medical studies, became the father of art history and had a
profound influence on the aesthetic awareness of the West. Freud
connects the Carthaginian general with his own promise to avenge
a Christian's affront to his father.[23] The Rome of his childhood is to
be conquered politically, but that city as it is imagined in his mature
years belongs to the universe of Winckelmann, the peaceful scholar
of archeology and ancient art.

In identification with the unlucky warrior, between 1895 and
1899 Freud visits the museums and churches of Italy without reaching Rome, the archeological paradise and unique object of his longing. But in the "Count Thun" dream of August 1898 and the dream
of "Father on his death-bed like Garibaldi" of February–March 1899,[24]
he manages to discharge his political mission[25] and acquits himself
of the debt he had contracted with regard to his father. Instead of tri-
umphing politically, he triumphs over politics. Instead of undertaking a career as a jurist, he legislates in discovering the universal laws
of the human soul.

Thus the curse of Hannibal's oath is undone, and, when his
Roman dream is finally fulfilled in 1901, the Catholic city casts a
shadow over him once again but does not prevent him from finding
pleasure in the ancient sites.

In disclosing his childhood dream, "My beloved mother and
people with birds' beaks," at the conclusion of *The Interpretation of
Dreams*,[26] Freud is perhaps revealing to us his most intense ties to
archeological images. Here is the account:

> It is dozens of years since I myself had a true anxiety dream. But I
> remember one from my seventh or eighth year, which I submit-
> ted to interpretation some thirty years later. It was a very vivid one,
> and in it I saw *my beloved mother, with a peculiarly peaceful, sleep-
> ing expression on her features, being carried into the room by two
> (or three) people with birds' beaks and laid upon the bed.* I awoke in
> tears and screaming, and interrupted my parents' sleep. The

strangely draped and unnaturally tall figures with birds' beaks were derived from the illustrations from Philippson's Bible. I fancy they must have been gods with falcons' heads from an ancient Egyptian funerary relief.[27]

The backdrop to this anxiety dream is the death of his maternal grandfather, Jacob Nathansohn, in October 1865. Thus Freud was not 7 or 8 years old, but rather 9½. It was in the course of his seventh year that his father gave him biblical history to read in the bilingual edition of the *Israelitische Bibel*, with illustrations and commentary by Rabbi Philippson, the subtitle of which is *Der Heilige Urtext*, the sacred primordial text.

The exegeses in these volumes reflect the philosophy of Moses Mendelsohn, who emphasized the universal nature of the Jewish message, while at the same time attempting to preserve its originality. Each passage of the Bible is placed in its historical context: linguistics, anthropology, geography, and above all archeology are called on to prove the historical truth of the sacred book. The reader is invited to visualize the places and actions of the men of the Bible and especially to become aware of the polysemy of the text. Philippson stresses the inherent conflictuality of the human being: "In the beginning, man lived . . . psychologically in a state of innocence. . . . Aroused by an external stimulus, the bodily element in man awakened the appetitive faculty. . . . Man's conscience awoke and an ethical feeling was set against the appetive faculty, thereby assuming in man the form of a struggle between good and evil."[28]

At a number of points Philippson emphasizes the importance of dreams. Thus, for example, he speaks of Joseph, "who has a colorful depth to his dreamlife, [which] enables him throughout his lifetime to claim a high position in a foreign country,"[29] or "Nevertheless, no one can escape the mysterious weaving of the dreamworld. . . . At important moments of life, everyone has felt within himself dreams that are full of meanings but for which we lack a guiding thread."[30]

As a child, Freud quenched his thirst for knowledge in this Bible, a true encyclopedia with 3,820 pages and 685 illustrations. Most of the engravings depict the ancient Mediterranean region: its temples, walls, tombs, funerary barks, ruins. From one page to the next, there unfolds a landscape of archeological monuments that have recently emerged from the ground. In 1838 the publisher, Baumgärtner in Leipzig, had bought in England the most beautiful engravings available at the time, taken from the British Museum, the *Description of Egypt*, or Rosellini.

In going through this book of images and readings, Freud could dream as he contemplated the figures of the Egyptian pantheon, the bas-reliefs of Pompeii or Thebes, the Athenian Acropolis, Nero's palace in Rome, the profile of Alexander the Great, the statue of Diana of Ephesus, the account of Hannibal crossing the Alps, and, at the head of the volume, the man Moses.[31]

When he is 35, his father dedicates a copy of the Philippson Bible to him. Did Freud, like the Wolf Man, find his image of anxiety here? In the dream about his mother and the people with birds' beaks, "anxiety can be traced back, when repression is taken into account, to an obscure and evidently sexual craving that had found appropriate expression in the visual content of the dream."[32] But, behind the oedipal agitation revealed by this dream, we can already see at work the renunciation of incestuous fulfillment in favor of an intellectual passion promoted by Freud's father. In making the Philippson Bible available to him, hadn't his father offered him "the sources of wisdom, of knowledge and understanding"?[33]

Thus, from childhood to the autumn of his life, the gods of Egypt and all the other representations of antiquity retain a great deal of affectively charged evocative power. Since archeology extends its roots into the soil of drives, of childhood wishes, and offers a sublimated fulfillment of them, it always represents happiness for Freud.

> There is one misreading which I find irritating and laughable and to which I am prone whenever I walk through the streets of a strange town on my holidays. On these occasions I read every shop sign that resembles the word in any way as "Antiquities." This betrays the questing spirit of the collector.[34]

The beginning of the twentieth century coincides with the height of Freud's "questing spirit." His library is full of works on art, linguistics, history of religions, and archeology.[35] His tables and display cases disappear beneath ancient faces: "a ring of bronze statuettes and terra cotta figures," "a beautiful little marble Venus," "a handsome glazed Egyptian figure."[36] All around him, wherever he looks, his eyes encounter nothing but the past, but it is a past that is always quivering with life. In Burckhardt's *Cicero* Freud underlines this eloquent passage: "What the eye perceives, in one or the other of these Greek buildings, are not mere stones but living beings."[37]

His journeys draw him to three sacred sites of archeology: in 1901, eternal Rome welcomes him to its heart; in 1902, Freud, accompanied by his brother, has "a ravishing experience" at Pompeii[38]; in 1904, with Alexander once again, he finds himself unexpectedly on the Acropolis in Athens. A feeling of alienation comes over him, as does a magical preoccupation regarding the date of his death.

In his personal copy of the second edition of *The Psychopathology of Everyday Life* (1901) he notes that his superstitiousness, "which he links to suppressed ambition (immortality), [reflects] 'anxiety about death, which springs from the normal uncertainty of life.'"[39]

During the sunny days of summer 1906, Freud takes great pleasure in using "a bit of news, without great value in itself" as a basis for writing an "archeological" essay, a "Pompeiian fantasy" revealing personal concerns of his, with the scientific pretext of analyzing dreams and delusions as imagined in literature.[40]

In a style more literary than academic, he slips in several notes on immortality and phantoms. Freud is familiar with the belief in the ghosts of heroes. In the interpretation he gives of his own *non vixit* dream,[41] he likens his friends to ghosts, successive incarnations of an original figure he recognizes as his nephew John, his childhood friend in Freiberg. But John may well conceal the figure of Freud's dead brother, Julius, whose disappearance evoked a sharp sense of guilt in the survivor. With the help of his childhood nurse, a Catholic who had filled him with ideas of heaven and hell, and no doubt also ideas of redemption and resurrection of the dead, Freud was able to transform his guilty death wishes into a wish for reparation.[42]

"[T]he most important of all the explanatory and exculpatory factors remains the ease with which our intellect is prepared to accept something absurd provided it satisfies powerful emotional impulses."[43]

With this reflection, Freud moves on to the memory of having seen a girl come into his office one day, someone he had believed was dead. The only thing that occurred to him was "after all it's true that the dead can come back to life."[44] The visitor was the sister of a former patient who was deceased.

On his archeological vacations Freud is often accompanied by his brother Alexander, whose Greek name he chose, while his dead brother Julius had a Roman one. Archeology has every reason to be haunted by ghosts—and likewise by a particular ghost, his nude mother, glimpsed when he was a child by gaslight, a memory that, more than twenty years after he had admired them, leads him to state that "the amber-colored columns of the Acropolis were the most beautiful thing he [has] ever seen in his life."[45] His mother's unclothed body remains associated with the exile from Freiberg. All his life Freud longed for the lost paradise of his childhood and the feeling of having been the favorite child of a young, beautiful mother, a longing that always remained with him and fostered his great interest in the past.[46]

With the charm of a fairy tale, the plot of Jensen's *Gradiva* (1903) unfolds in the joy of a fantasy come to life: the young archeologist in search of a lovely stone wins a living woman who has come from his own distant past, a dear childhood friend whose memory he had repressed. In identifying with the hero, seeing him as he would see his own double in a mirror, Freud tries to suspend for a moment the longing for every "Gradiva" who is not *rediviva*.

As he closes this book, with its image of Zoe Bertgang crossing the street, does Freud recall that, during their engagement, he had compared Martha's foot to that of the Venus de Milo? "Do you remember how in our walks with Minna along the Beethovengang you kept going aside to pull up your stockings?"[47]

Freud shares with Jensen the hope that Eros will finally triumph. He compares the method used by Gradiva to cure the delusion of her childhood friend to psychoanalytic investigation, which is an attempt to free up repressed love. With regret, he must acknowledge the difference: "Gradiva was able to return the love which was making its way from the unconscious to consciousness," something the physician cannot do.[48]

Against the backdrop of the intact ruins of Pompeii he easily forms his concept of the unconscious as consisting of structures hidden and immortal until dug up into awareness by the psychoanalytic pickax: "There is . . . no better analogy for repression, by which something in the mind is at once made inaccessible and preserved, than burial of the sort to which Pompeii fell victim and from which it could emerge once more through the work of spades."[49]

He also uses this plot to state the analogy between ontogenesis and phylogenesis: "The young archeologist was obliged in his phantasy to transport to Pompeii the original of the relief which reminded him of his youthful love. The author was well justified, indeed, in lingering over the valuable similarity which his delicate sense had perceived between a particular mental process in the individual and an isolated historical event in the history of mankind."[50]

The archeological argument from history facilitates his demonstration of the importance of the past. The power of the past, supposedly vanished but in fact perfectly preserved, is its ability to repair a destroyed present. The origin is not only a matter of romantic nostalgia; it carries within it a principle of cure.

In this small work for which Freud thinks he deserves praise,[51] psychoanalysis and archeology walk hand in hand, a companionship in which he takes great pleasure. He will always have a special fondness for *Gradiva*, and, in Rome in 1907, he finds her with great emotion: "Just imagine my joy when, after being alone so long, I saw today in the Vatican a dear familiar face! The recognition was one-sided, however, for it was the 'Gradiva,' high up on a wall."[52]

He takes her with him in the form of a plaster cast that he hangs above the foot of his couch and sets off with a dried papyrus. Above his armchair he hangs two large Pompeiian frescoes, one representing a centaur, the other the god Pan who rules over Arcadia, the land of the archaic for the Greeks.

If Freud's archeology were to take on a shape, it would surely be that of Gradiva, whose step was of such singular grace that it still fascinates us centuries later.

> I recall as one of my very earliest memories that while I was in my cradle a vulture came down to me and opened my mouth with its tail, and struck me many times with its tail against my lips.[53]

On the archeological loom of Freud's texts, "Leonardo da Vinci and a Memory of His Childhood" weaves the most sparkling cloth. With the art of the storyteller and the scholar, Freud intertwines the "remarkable smile, at once fascinating and puzzling," with which Leonardo animated the lips of his female figures with another smile: "The connoisseur of art will think here of the peculiar fixed smile found in archaic Greek sculptures."[54]

He combines his reflections on the thirst for knowledge and infantile sexual theories with references to Greek and Egyptian mythology and the history of the religions of antiquity. For his analyses, he calls on Champollion's hieroglyphics, the divinities Isis and Hathor. He associates Neith[55] with the fantasy of the phallic mother and homosexual object choice with the Greek legend of the young Narcissus. And, to shed light on the psychic life of children, he turns to the primitive epochs of humanity and, in particular, the cults of the Phallus.

Here the archeological analogy appears in its most complex workings, revealing Freud's never-ending quest for an ultimate truth beneath psychic reality. His passion for origins could explain the persistence of this metaphor of antiquity.

He gives the memory reported by Leonardo the status of a fantasy constructed later on and projected back into childhood, comparing this psychic process to the writing of history by a nation that has become rich and powerful and is searching for its origins: what motivates it is not objective curiosity but the wish to have an effect on its present-day population, to exalt them. Still, fantasies should not be discredited: "In spite of all the distortions and misunderstandings, they still represent the reality of the past."[56] Beneath the legendary or fantasmatic material lies historical truth.

Confident in his success in the archeology of the psyche, Freud adds that, since psychoanalytic technique has "excellent methods for helping us to bring this concealed material to light, we may venture to fill the gap in Leonardo's life story by analysing his childhood phantasy."[57]

If archeology was the image of his tenacity as a detective and puzzle solver, of his wish to follow memory down to its last traces, there was something beyond archeology: at the point where individual memory disappears there arise the unforgettable recollections of humanity.

The sole childhood memory of Leonardo da Vinci evokes the sole childhood dream related by Freud: the flight of a bird—a kite or vulture—in the former corresponds to the birds—sparrowhawks or falcons—in the latter. *Vögeln* and *ucello* are disguises for sexual desire, and, by association, the bird equals maternal presence: "In the hieroglyphics of the ancient Egyptians the mother is represented by a picture of a vulture."[58] It seems that the Philippson Bible never stopped orienting Freud's interests.

Alongside Minerva, Athena, Brünnhilde, and Neith, another goddess held Freud's attention: Artemis-Diana, whose cults and temples are found across the centuries, from earliest antiquity to the Christian era itself. "Great Is Diana of the Ephesians," appearing in 1911, once again illustrates Freud's curiosity about mythology, history of religions, and archeology. This brief note, based on a chapter from Sartiaux's book on the ancient cities of Asia Minor, emphasizes the perseverance in history and the immortality of the fantasy of an archaic mother, untouchable and invulnerable.

A similar "mythological parallel to a visual obsession" associates a clinical case of obsessional imagery to the figure of the goddess Baubo. Citing a work by Salomon Reinach, Freud mentions the digs at Priene in Asia Minor: "Some terracottas were found which represented Baubo. They show a body of a woman without a head or chest and with a face drawn on the abdomen: the lifted dress frames this face like a crown of hair."[59]

This last point recurs in the short 1922 paper entitled "Medusa's Head." In this trio of articles we find the same use of archeological findings to relate the archaic fantasies of men.

Freud is always searching for a clear view of the psychic domain, always trying to deprive the unconscious of its opacity. In 1929 Freud uses Rome as an example of the way the intrapsychic past is preserved:

> Let us, by a flight of imagination, suppose that Rome is not a human habitation but a psychical entity with a similarly long and copious past—an entity, that is to say, in which nothing that has once come into existence will have passed away and all the earlier phases of development continue to exist alongside the latest one. This would mean that in Rome the palaces of the Caesars and the Septizonium of Septimus Severus would still be rising to their old height on the Palatine and that the castle of S. Angelo would still be carrying on its battlements the beautiful statues which graced it until the siege by the Goths.[60]

Freud's desire has always effortlessly included the desire of the archeologist, who, like him, is above all a collector. Both seek to rediscover what has disappeared, to repair and preserve what has been destroyed, to conquer death by digging up the past from the earth so as to set it up triumphantly in the showcases of immortality.

But Freud has to yield to reason. Although archeology can serve as a metaphor for mental functioning, it is still only a metaphor: despite the analogy, archeology and psychoanalysis do not coincide. The archeologist is fascinated more by objects and sites than by texts and words. And, despite his nostalgia, Freud cannot make the archeologist's deafness his own.

The unconscious speaks, and the analyst's task is to find its voice in the fragile treasures of speech and the unsayable. Yet Freud cannot resign himself to being merely a blind psychoanalyst: "mastering the characteristics of mental life by representing them in pictorial terms"[61] is a goal that never vanishes, though it is a dream whose object is always beyond reach. The unconscious cannot be grasped with hands or eyes.

In the last of the papers in which Freud calls on the archeological metaphor, he does so in order to point out its limits. Can it be that, at the end of his life, despite his identification with Schliemann, Winckelmann, or Jensen's Hanold, he finally admits that his discoveries have not made him an archeologist of the unconscious? Or is it just one last trick he plays on himself, an attempt to overcome his disappointment in the face of the impossible fusion of the archeologist and the psychoanalyst in himself, when he writes in "Constructions in Analysis" that the analyst's "work of construction, or, if it is preferred, of reconstruction, resembles to a great extent an archeologist's excavation of some dwelling-place that has been destroyed and buried or of some ancient edifice. The two processes are in fact identical, except that the analyst works under better conditions."[62]

To support this idea, he adds that the psychoanalyst is concerned not with what has been destroyed but with what is still alive, and that, above all, he benefits from something that has no equivalent in archeological digs, namely the material that emerges in the transference. The essence of the psychic object is preserved, even if it is hidden and inaccessible to the subject, which is the case in archeology only in exceptional situations, as in Pompeii or the Tomb of Tutankhamen.

As he explains with pride, "[i]t depends only upon analytic technique whether we shall succeed in bringing what is concealed completely to light." He grants that "there are only two other facts that weigh against the extraordinary advantage which is thus enjoyed by the work of analysis, namely that psychical objects are incomparably more complicated than the excavator's material ones and that we have insufficient knowledge of what we may expect to find, since their finer structure contains so much that is still mysterious."[63]

And he concludes as follows: "But our comparison between the two forms of work can go no further than this; for the main difference between them lies in the fact that for the archeologist the reconstruction is the aim and end of his endeavours while for the analyst the construction is only a preliminary labour."[64]

After these preambles, the archeologist and the psychoanalyst should go their separate ways, but Freud the man continues to seek in the living ruins of the past the unsurpassed consolations he has drawn on all his life.

> Though the universe collapses around him,
> the falling ruins leave him undismayed.
> —Horace, *Odes* III.3.6–7[65]

On the eve of his death, though ravaged by cancer of the jaw and by the collapse of European civilization, Freud does not give up: he still wagers on Eros against Thanatos. Deprived by the Nazis of the archeological treasures that have sustained both his pleasure in life and his intellectual research, he hopes to undo this damage and re-constitute the world of his former dreams. In these "sad days," await-ing authorization to leave Austria, he writes to his son, Ernst, who is already in London:

> If I were to arrive as a rich man, I would start a new collection with the assistance of your brother-in-law [Hans Calmann, a Lon-don art dealer]. As it is I will have to be content with the two small figures which the Princess [Marie Bonaparte] rescued on her first visit, and those which she brought during her last stay in Athens and is keeping for me in Paris. How much of my own collection I can have sent on is very uncertain. The whole thing reminds me of a man trying to rescue a bird cage from the burn-ing house.[66]

After leaving Vienna for Paris, thanks to Marie Bonaparte Freud finds one of the favorite pieces from his collection, a statuette of Athena that had stood on his desk. To ease the journey into exile, Marie also gives him some Greek terra cottas. Arriving in London on June 8, 1938, he thanks her heartily: "The one day in your house in Paris restored our good mood and sense of dignity; after being surrounded by love for twelve hours we left proud and rich under the protection of Athena."[67]

NOTES

1. See Engelman 1998 and H. D. (Hilda Doolittle) 1994. The present chapter is a modified version of Pontalis 1982.

2. Freud 1960, p. 403.

3. Freud 1954, p. 112.

4. Schliemann 1880, p. 1.

5. Letter of May 28, 1899 (Freud 1954, p. 282).

6. Anzieu 1959, pp. 543–558.

7. Letter of May 28, 1899 (Freud 1954, p. 281).

8. Letter of December 6, 1896 (Freud 1954, p. 181).

9. Letter of September 10, 1930 (Freud and Zweig 1970, p. 190). This letter is written in response to Zweig's account of his eye problems and of the grimacing heads he sees day and night before his open or closed eyes.

10. Schliemann 1880, p. 8.

11. Schnapp 1982.

12. Freud 1909.

13. Letter of December 12, 1899 (Freud 1954, p. 305).

14. Freud 1960, pp. 173–174.

15. Freud 1914b, p. 245.

16. Freud 1896a, p. 241.

17. Freud 1896a, p. 203.

18. Wolf 1976.

19. Freud 1905b, p. 12.

20. Laplanche and Pontalis 1985.

21. Bernouf was Professor of Sanskrit in the Collège de France. This excerpt from his opening lecture in 1832 is taken from Schwab 1950, p. 24. The following paragraphs are based on this fine book, where further references can be found. On the life and work of Champollion, see Lacouture 1988.

22. Freud 1900, p. 196.

23. Freud 1900, p. 197. See also Chapter 4, this volume.

24. Freud 1900, pp. 208–218 and 427–429, respectively.

25. Schorske 1981.

26. Freud 1900, pp. 583–584.

27. P. 583, emphasis in original.

28. These paraphrases from the Book of Genesis are taken from Pfrimmer 1981, p. 107 (trans. S. F.). With regard to the Philippson Bible, see also Pfrimmer 1982.

29. Pfrimmer 1981, p. 134 (trans. S. F.).

30. Pfrimmer 1981, p. 138 (trans. S. F.).

31. Translator's note: *The Man Moses (Der Mann Moses)* is the German title of *Moses and Monotheism*.

32. Freud 1900, p. 584.

33. E. Freud et al. 1978, p. 134.

34. Freud 1901, p. 110.

35. Trosman and Simmons 1973. Beside the work of his friend, Emmanuel

Löwy, and those of Schliemann, Freud had guides to the British Museum and works on the recent discoveries in the Roman Forum and on Pompeii and Nineveh. There were also several books in French, including *Ruines et Paysages d'Egypte* by Gaston Maspéro, Jean Capart's *Abydos: Le Temple de Seti I*, and Emile Bourget's *Les Ruines de Delphes*.

36. Freud 1901, pp. 167, 169, and 170, respectively.
37. Cited in Spector 1976, p. 99 (trans. S. F.).
38. Jones 1955, p. 23.
39. Schur 1972, p. 239.
40. Freud 1984, p. 111.
41. See the analysis in Schur 1972.
42. Suzanne Bernfeld (1951) understands Freud's wish to keep his collection of precious objects intact as his need to master his destructive fantasies. Freud gives examples of this double movement of aggression and reparation associated with his collection in *The Psychopathology of Everyday Life*. For example:

> I had once seen fit to reproach a loyal and deserving friend on no other grounds than the interpretation I placed on certain indications coming from his unconscious. He was offended. . . . While I was writing [my reply], I had in front of me my latest acquisition, a handsome glazed Egyptian figure. I broke it in the way I have described and then immediately realized that I had caused the mischief in order to avert a greater one. Luckily it was possible to cement both of these together—the friendship as well as the figure—so that the break would not be noticed. [1901, pp. 169–170]

43. Freud 1907a, p. 71.
44. Freud 1907a, p. 76.
45. Jones 1955, p. 56.
46. Lou Andréas-Salomé thought that it was the archeologist in Freud that made the physician into a psychoanalyst.
47. Jones 1953, p. 128.
48. Freud 1907a, p. 90.
49. Freud 1907a, p. 40. See Kahn 1986.
50. Freud 1907a, p. 40.
51. Letter to Jung of May 26, 1907 (Freud and Jung 1974, p. 51).
52. Letter to Martha of September 24, 1907 (Freud 1960, p. 167).
53. From "Leonardo da Vinci and a Memory of His Childhood" (Freud 1910b, p. 82).
54. Freud 1910a, p. 102 and p. 107, n. 2.
55. Freud owned several versions of this Egyptian goddess, who represented the primordial water from which every creature arises. She is both the vault of heaven and the protector of sleep. The Greeks identified her with Athena.
56. Freud 1910a, p. 84.
57. Freud 1910a, p. 85.
58. Freud 1910a, p. 88.

59. Freud 1916a, p. 338. On the figure of Baubo, see Olender 1990.
60. Freud 1929, p. 70.
61. Freud 1929, p. 71.
62. Freud 1937a, p. 259.
63. Freud 1937a, p. 260.
64. Freud 1937a, p. 260.
65. Quoted in a letter to Stefan Zweig of October 17, 1937 (Freud 1960, p. 438).
66. Letter of May 12, 1938 (Freud 1960, p. 298).
67. Cited in Jones 1957, pp. 227–228.

4

The Conquistador: Athens, Rome, Jerusalem

Freiberg, Vienna, and London are the landmarks of Freud's official biography, but his interior geography takes him to the three sacred places of the West: Athens, Rome, and Jerusalem. Mirrors of his gaze, they link words with the unutterable, images with the invisible, totems with taboo. From Freiberg to London, Freud speaks to us in a language in which Yiddish mingles with Greek and Latin.

Hannibal and his father Hamilcar, Oedipus and Laius, Aeneas and Anchises, Joseph and Jacob weave the journeys of his lineage.

Behind the hero, warrior, legislator, archeologist, or poet stands the humble and fundamental figure of Freud's father, to whom all the heroic identifications lead back without his ever being able to rub the mud off his cap.

> I may have been ten or twelve years old, when my father began to take me with him on his walks and reveal to me in his talk his views upon things in the world we live in. Thus it was, on one such occasion, that he told me a story to show me how much better things were now than they had been in his day. "When I was a young man," he said, "I went for a walk one Saturday in the streets of your birthplace; I was well dressed and had a new fur cap on my head. A Christian came up to me and with a single blow knocked off my cap into the mud and shouted, 'Jew, get off the pavement!'" "And what did you do?" I asked. "I went into the roadway and

picked up my cap," was his quiet reply. This struck me as unheroic conduct on the part of the big, strong man who was holding the little boy by the hand.[1]

At the bidding of a Christian, Jacob Freud stepped off the sidewalk to pick up his brand-new fur cap that he was wearing to celebrate the sabbath. The child Schlomo/Sigismund[2] cannot forgive this resignation so wounding to the omnipotence he has ascribed to his father and to his own narcissism. He makes up his mind to counter meek obedience with a visible vengeance. His father's humiliation and the desire for revenge that it arouses will narrate and organize his imaginative life and his biographical reality.

He tries to contrast this first masochistic identification with a heroic one. To avenge his father, he will become a great man, someone who will be spoken of. Ambition consumes him.[3] "I could gladly sacrifice my life for one great moment in history."[4] He will be a conqueror or a minister, as a café poet had predicted for him.[5] He will make law so as not to be subject to law. No one will force him—or his children—to step down off the sidewalk into the mud. The wish to make his way leads him to join the closed circles of the Christian aggressor, to identify socially with those who make graven images and those who adore them.[6]

In the Austro-Hungarian Empire of the nineteenth century, in the brilliant university world of Vienna, not always exempt from ingrained antisemitism, all the pathways of ambition pass through Rome to lead to eternal glory.

For Freud, Athens, Rome, and Jerusalem are bound up with the ambiguous combination of his vengeful ambition and the oedipal guilt it arouses in terms of both superiority to his father and the transgression of the Jewish heritage that it entails.

Freud never resolves these tensions in which he is simultaneously the son of a humiliated Jew and the father of a Western oeuvre. A secular Jew, assimilated into classical and Germanic civilization, he always refuses the temptation, as Heine put it, to pay the price of admission to European culture: the act of baptism. He lives in the midst of these fertile and subtle contradictions, finding in them a

creative power and sensitivity: "The fact that things will be more difficult for you as a Jew will have the effect, as it has with all of us, of
bringing out the best of which you are capable."[7]

The nouns Athens, Rome, and Jerusalem are declined around
gaze and words, seeing and saying. Freud's cultural memory, his work
instruments, are in Greek and Latin. In Hebrew he is silent. Jerusalem is not part of his education.[8] In order to belong to the West and
inscribe his name there, he rewrites its legends and myths. He makes
the letters φ, ψ, and ω the initials of his psychic apparatus. He offers
Narcissus an auto-erotic libido and Oedipus the tragedy of a complex.

With a troubled gaze, troubled from gazing, he sees Athens and
Rome. His first view of the latter appears in a dream, half hidden by
fog and "so far away that I was surprised at my view of it being so
clear."[9] He will have to undergo a long self-analysis before he can look
at it directly. As he stands before the Acropolis, his vision is disturbed.
He is amazed to behold Athens with his own eyes. Sites of a dream
geography, objects of daytime journeys, Rome and Athens are visible,
but the sight of them is hard to sustain for Jacob's son. Freud looks at
Athens and Rome with the eye of Jewish heritage, but these cities also
provide the backlighting for the silhouette of his Jerusalem. Jerusalem is his dark continent, his blind spot, his "wife."[10] It is associated
with intimacy, with the invisible: "The historians say that if Jerusalem had not been destroyed, we Jews would have perished like so
many races before and after us. According to them, the invisible
edifice of Jerusalem became possible only after the collapse of the
visible Temple."[11] "You are requested to close the eyes," commands
Jerusalem the iconoclast.[12]

Athens, Rome, and Jerusalem are joined in a letter from Freud's
adolescence that reveals his great familiarity with the texts of antiquity.
For his school-leaving certificate he had to translate a passage from Virgil
that, as it happened, he had already read for pleasure, along with thirty-
three lines of *Oedipus Rex*. In the privileged and conspicuous position
of a postscript he adds that a sage from Czernowitz makes daily visits
to his family: "He really is a sage; I have enjoyed him very much."[13]

Freud, who was not born in the cradle of Greco-Roman civilization, would like to make that noble genealogy his own. His belonging to the cultured West is demonstrated to others by his knowledge of the great books (Homer, Virgil, Cervantes, Dante, Goethe, all read in the original languages), his interest in archeological excavations, his passion for ancient art objects and his collecting of them, his Roman dreams and journeys, and his disturbance of vision on the Acropolis. He borrows a great many quotations from the knowledge base of the respectable nineteenth-century gentleman: epigraphs, literary interpolations in a scientific argument, evidence of solid membership in the majority culture.

But Freud is not a gullible self-deceiver. He is fully aware that his family romance cannot alter the historicity of his origins. All he can do, if he wishes to belong to the European family, is to locate his works in an intellectual heritage, becoming for the future a son of the West by placing a Jewish name on the cover of a book fundamental to European thought.

He has no doubt that another surname would have facilitated his access to the university and the traditional intelligentsia and decreased the resistance to psychoanalysis: "I think that we as Jews, if we wish to join in, must develop a bit of masochism, be ready to suffer some wrong. Otherwise there is no hitting it off. Rest assured that, if my name were Oberhuber, in spite of everything my innovations would have met with far less resistance."[14]

Joseph, interpreter of Pharaoh's dreams, and Solomon, to whom he owes his Hebrew given name, are familiar to him. Moses enriches his work twice. As a postscript to a long life, Freud writes in 1935: "My deep engrossment in the Bible story (almost as soon as I had learnt the art of reading) had, as I recognized much later, an enduring effect upon the direction of my interest."[15]

Freud has a lifelong fascination with this text, though he is unable to read it in the language of his ancestors. His living Jewish wisdom is oral: "those facetious Jewish anecdotes which contain so much profound and often bitter worldly wisdom and which we so greatly enjoy quoting in our talks and letters."[16] About the contents of Jerusalem Freud can say nothing, but in its form his Judaism is rooted in a stirring joy (*Freude*). This is what he presents along with his name to his future bride: "Even if the form wherein the old Jews were happy no longer offers us any shelter, something of the core, of the essence of this meaningful and life-affirming Judaism will not be absent from our home."[17]

On the Greco-Roman side of his life there is a claim, an ambition, a wished-for intellectual assimilation. Here words are his best allies. On the Jerusalem side there is a deep emotional attachment that has no need of words: he tells his brothers of the B'nai B'rith that his attraction to Judaism has to do with "many dark emotional powers all the stronger the less they could be expressed in words."[18] At the end of his life he states once again that his sense of being Jewish is made up of something very slight, a "miraculous thing" that is "inaccessible to any analysis."[19] These phrases may seem surprising from a man who, in all his works, has sought the latent beneath the manifest so as to put it in words, and whose approach has always been to analyze and explain what up to then had remained inaccessible to men: their unconscious.

What if, indeed, words could not reveal the essence? The unconscious also contains originary fantasies[20] that cannot be reduced to words, a storehouse inaccessible to awareness and to human knowledge. And what if something of the human mystery, of its very substance, always had to remain unknown and unpronounceable, like the Hebrew tetragrammaton whose lost vowels are silent among four voiceless consonants: "Among the ancient Hebrews the name of God was taboo; it might neither be spoken aloud nor written down. . . . This prohibition was so implicitly obeyed that to this very day the vocalization of the four consonants in God's name . . . [YHVH] remains unknown."[21]

Freud does not need words in order to experience his Jewish identity: he does not have to speak it, attain it, or justify it. It is an internal perception, a "joie de vivre," a private matter. He gives his three daughters names borrowed from Jewish friends from his circle, Aryan names to his three sons.[22] From the outset he makes it possible for the males to hold up their heads in public and succeed there; to the girls he offers the intimacy of the home.

His life is bilingual: he speaks German for business and Yiddish for personal pleasure. About to publish, and hence to make public, the royal road to the unconscious, he begins *The Interpretation of Dreams* with a phrase from the *Aeneid*, but it is with a Jewish anecdote that he tells his friend Fliess that his self-analysis is "all written by the unconscious, on the well-known principle of Itzig, the Sunday horseman. 'Itzig, where are you going?' 'Don't ask me, ask the horse!'"[23]

The invisible Jerusalem for which Freud has neither content nor words is illuminated by the way he sees Rome and Athens. These are the mirrors of his silent identity.

> All the dreams of my youth have come to life; the first engravings I remember—my father hung views of Rome in the hall—I now see in reality, and everything I have known for so long through paintings, drawings, etchings, woodcuts, plaster casts, and cork models is now assembled before me. Wherever I walk, I come upon familiar objects in an unfamiliar world; everything is just as I imagined it, yet everything is new.
>
> —Goethe, *Italian Journey*[24]

In the geography of his gaze, Rome is the city most intensely invested. He dreams of it urgently at night in January 1897, and it forms the Ariadne's thread of his epistolary (self-) analysis with Wilhelm Fliess. The Eternal City is the theater in which occur the completion of his mourning for his father, who died in October 1896, and the ambivalent and therapeutic friendship with Fliess, in which he experiences a "transference neurosis" that enables him to reorganize his oedipal positions (from approximately 1897 to 1899).

Rome is associated with his personal history via the scene with the cap in the mud that his father describes to him when he is 10 or 12 years old. He imagines that his father asks him to avenge this humiliation as Hamilcar asked his son Hannibal to undo the Roman insult. This childhood wish is strengthened in adolescence, when antisemitism reminds him that he is still part of a minority, a sort of outlaw. When he studies the Punic Wars in high school, he sides with the Carthaginians against the Romans.[25]

The Semitic warrior leads the adult Freud on the path to Italy. Freud wants to march triumphantly on Rome, but three times, like his ill-fated hero, he cannot get past Lake Trasimeno. He first has to get beyond his identification with the tragic hero. For, after brilliant military actions, Hannibal spoils his victory: he fails, losing an eye in the Etruscan marshes and, having given up his attempt to seize Rome, commits suicide, like the Jews of Massada two centuries later, so as not to be handed over alive to the Romans.

To Freud's adolescent eyes, Hannibal symbolized Jewish tenacity. But the will to victory is not enough, since Rome also represents the Catholic Church for him. A deep oedipal guilt keeps him far from this city, twice the persecutor in Jewish history. In 70 A.D. Titus had the temple at Jerusalem destroyed and thereby caused the exile without return. The tyranny of the Roman Empire was followed by the anti-Judaism of the Church. Ancient or Catholic, Rome was at all times the enemy of Jerusalem. Freud is ambivalent toward this mother-city of Christianity, as he is toward his Jewish father humiliated by a Christian. He collects Greco-Roman antiquities and wants to see in them only the origins of European civilization. But this splitting of the visible and the invisible solves nothing. For in his father's Jewish tradition, the cult of graven images is the first of the ten transgressions of the divine law. And so there is no escape from guilt.

What he needs is a permissive guide. He must ask a certain Herr Zucker the way to the city, so that his "zest for martyrdom"[26] can disappear and the imaginary Rome be incarnated.

Along the way he recounts his dreams, his self-analysis, the transference to Fliess, and the writing of *The Interpretation of Dreams*, and, after accepting the contradictory movements animating his unconscious, after this invisible journey, he will be able to see and penetrate the city of his dreams. In addition, he thinks, the journey to Rome will bring "the realization of a secret wish" to become a university professor.[27]

Freud has good reason to believe that the Eternal City could advance his "secret wish." He knows what a profound effect it had on Goethe's life and work, and that Winckelmann, whose name comes to him as he associates to his Roman dreams, converted to Catholicism in order to carry out the first major archeological investigations into ancient Roman art. But "we are not in Rome yet."[28]

Freud is aware of the "deeply neurotic" nature of his longing.[29] Nevertheless, to satisfy it he studies the topography of Rome, where one and the same place was the site of the Rome of the most ancient times, followed by Virgil's Rome, the Rome of Titus, Catholic Rome, and Italian Rome. He casts this same archeological gaze onto his psychic apparatus, where in a single internal space are anachronistic traces of experiences in which all the layers of an individual history are set down without erasing one another. Present and past are bound together there.

He knows that he is the archeological site of a plural Rome: fragments of memories and dreams, wished-for and guilty. He studies his dream topography.

Through the window of a railway car he sees the Tiber and the bridge leading to Sant' Angelo. The train begins to move, but, he says, "it occurred to me that I had not so much set foot in the city. Another time someone led me to the top of a hill and showed me Rome half-shrouded in mist; it was so far away that I was surprised at my view of it being so clear."[30]

Like Moses who will never enter into the Promised Land, Freud can still only catch a glimpse of the distant object of his desire: the eternal mother-city, *Roma aeterna*, the promised and incestuous discovery of the mechanisms of neurosis that mingle scandalous fantasies with castration anxiety.

Freud knows that he is the object of his discovery: at the origin of his creation are the warp of his dreams and the weft of their theoretical elaboration. He is writing a text of which he himself is the fabric. Psychoanalysis is a work written in the first person very singular. Discovering in himself what he hopes are the eternal laws of the human psyche, he dreads having to atone for this sin of knowledge, for, ever since Eden, Oedipus, or Teiresias, to know is always to transgress. The will to know is rooted in the difference between the sexes: what the gaze wants to fix on is "that."[31] This knowing, this erotized vision, aroused the fear of punishment. The law of the talion calls for visual castration, blindness. Freud intensely wishes to conquer and possess this eternal knowledge, to penetrate the human enigma, but, alone, he is not yet strong enough to violate the prohibition, say the unsayable, cross the bridge. For the moment, then, he is content to see from afar.

Seeing . . . , as when he was about 3, between Leipzig and Vienna, in a state of turmoil at the sight of his naked mother.[32] Seeing without touching, without crossing the bridge or getting off the train in the city, at a safe distance from the forbidden curiosity and the dreadful punishment (represented by the prison of Castle Sant' Angelo on the other side of the bridge): this is the phobic compromise Freud makes. In order to try, nonetheless, to approach this "promised land," he asks Fliess to play the role of the counterphobic object in accompanying him to Rome. "I noticed a Herr Zucker . . . and determined to ask him the way to the city. . . . 'Asking the way' was a direct allusion to Rome, since it is well known that all roads lead there."[33] The question contains the answer: what he is really asking Zucker/Fliess for is permission to penetrate the sacred city, or at least that Fliess follow him there so he will not risk being imprisoned: "What would you think of ten days in Rome at Easter (the two of us of course) if all goes well, if I can afford it and have not been locked up, lynched or boycotted on account of the Egyptian dream book? I have been looking forward to it for so long. Learning the eternal laws of life in the Eternal City would be no bad combination."[34]

But Fliess refuses to be Freud's guide and calm his fears of violating the prohibitions of his father, an uncultivated little Jewish merchant, humiliated and unlucky in business. Instead of Rome, Fliess suggests Prague. Freud's response is a fourth dream that once again takes him to Rome: "I saw a street corner before me and was surprised to find so many posters in German stuck up there."[35]

German substitutes for the expected Latin inscription. In the Austro-Hungarian Empire, this language is imposed on all minorities. At the University of Prague, in particular, instructors had to give up Latin for German. Freud himself went from Czech and Yiddish to German when he left Freiberg for Vienna. His father had him take Hebrew lessons from Professor Hammerschlag, but he learns Greek and Latin at school. He knows English, the language of his half-brother who emigrated to Manchester, and also French from his stay in Paris with Charcot, Spanish learned with Silberstein, and Italian perfected in the land of Dante.

The multiplicity of languages tells the story of his cultural migrations. Just as the Jews of the diaspora were obliged to learn the foreign languages of exile even as they sought to preserve the Hebrew of their origins, Freud adds on languages without forgetting any of them. Only the Czech of his Catholic nursemaid has faded until it is no more than a few lines of verse.[36] The contrast of languages also relates back to the contrast between Judaism and Christianity. In a family where Jewish law was observed, Freud was looked after as a child by a nanny who took him to church and talked to him about heaven and hell.

When Jacob Freud's family emigrated in 1859, Sigismund took the train for the first time. "At the age of three I passed through the station [of Breslau] when we moved from Freiberg to Leipzig, and the gas jets, which were the first I had seen, reminded me of souls burning in hell. . . . The anxiety about travel which I have had to overcome is also bound up with it."[37]

From then on, the train links the glimpse of his mother's nudity and the hell of guilty souls with separation from the lost paradise of a pampered and happy childhood, the path of exile, and various antisemitic incidents.

From Vienna to Rome "the journey is long, the stations at which one can be thrown out are very numerous, and it is still a matter of 'if I can last out.'"[38] These words allude to an anecdote Freud associates with his Roman dreams:

> An impecunious Jew had stowed himself away without a ticket in the fast train to Karlsbad [the city in which diabetes, the sugar disease,[39] is treated]. He was caught, and each time tickets were inspected he was taken out of the train and treated more and more severely. At one of the stations on his *via dolorosa* he met an acquaintance, who asked him where he was travelling to. "To Karlsbad," was his reply, "if my constitution can stand it."[40]

Freud wants to travel in the West without paying the price of a "ticket," without converting, the possibility of which was a constant temptation for the Jews of his time. His wife's family is an interesting example: his uncle by marriage, Jacob Bernays, a renowned classical philologist, remained faithful to the strictest Jewish orthodoxy, whereas his brother Michael left Judaism to launch himself on an even more brilliant career in the field of Germanic studies and Goethe criticism.[41] Freud stands outside these two poles. He hopes to assimilate a culture of reference without losing the landmarks of his culture of origin, to speak a new language without denying his mother tongue. But to travel without a ticket is to risk paying with one's own person, being merely a secret passenger, an unwanted guest. Like Christ handed over to the Romans, Freud follows the *via dolorosa* of his deep convictions. He takes the Western train but renders unto Caesar only what belongs to Caesar: he does not renounce the part of himself that is intimate with Jerusalem. He is prepared to pay the price for the guilt of transgression but will not engage in "undignified" and "foolish" denial.[42]

When he writes to his friend Fliess: "If I closed [my letter] with 'Next Easter in Rome,' I should feel like a pious Jew,"[43] he achieves a remarkable condensation of his contradictory wishes. In a few words he expresses both the Christian vow to spend Holy Week in Rome in a pilgrimage to the Catholic holy of holies and the ritual phrase with which Jews end the Passover seder: "Next year in Jerusalem." For the Jews of the diaspora, ever since Rome destroyed Jerusalem and the architecture of its visible temple, all that is left is "the invisible edifice of Judaism."[44] From now on, Jerusalem is as invisible as it is desirable: it remains desirable at the very price of its evanescence, the promised land and a promise whose fulfillment is always postponed. It is as though the solidarity of the Jews dispersed in exile could be expressed only by fidelity to a promise and not by attachment to a visible geography.

Rome and Jerusalem, assimilation and exile. These two cities are combined in the dream "my son the Myops."[45] Here Freud is alluding to his half-brother, who moved to England, safe from the mud of antisemitism, instead of staying in Austria.

With this dream a change of feeling with regard to Fliess becomes evident. Freud is distancing himself from his "transference neurosis," allowing himself to show more openly his disapproval of the theories of bisexuality put forth by his friend in Berlin. He will soon be ready to do without this counterphobic relationship. "As you say, I have become entirely estranged from what you are doing."[46] In connection with his latest book, *The Psychopathology of Everyday Life* (1901), he writes to him: "It is full of references to you: obvious ones, where you supplied the material, and concealed ones, where the motivation derives from you. . . . Apart from any permanent value that its content may have, you can take it as a testimonial to the role you have hitherto played in my life."[47]

In September 1901 he finally realizes the "long-cherished" Roman dream.[48] At the end of a long inner journey, the affective process becomes tangible and visible at the very moment when it loses its fantasmatic underpinnings. Freud undoes the ties that bound him to the guide he had chosen to travel with him through the subtle meanders of his unconscious terrain. The conqueror of this internal land that had never—except by poets—been explored before him, he has escaped the evil spell cast by Hannibal. He can now pay a friendly visit to his dear Rome.

Concerning this city, the symbol of an inner victory, he writes to the man who made it possible for him to go there: "It was a high spot in my life."[49] And his last epistolary message to Fliess/Zucker is: "Cordial greetings from the culminating point of the journey."[50] Thus there ends a slice of life and of self-analysis: one and the same journey. From now on, Freud is able to walk freely among Rome, Jerusalem, and Athens . . . and beyond, wherever the unconscious geography of his lineage leads him.

> Voice of Athena, dearest to me of the
> Immortals, how clearly, though thou be
> unseen, do I hear thy call and seize it in my
> soul, as when a Tyrrhenian clarion speaks
> from the mouth of bronze!
>
> —Sophocles, *Ajax*, 14–17

In Freud's gaze, Athens represents the primal scene of the West, the birthplace of the language and reason of Europe: its foundational myths, its ideal values. He is caught up in the frenetic passion to which his contemporaries are devoting themselves: the obsession with origins and genealogies. Researchers are looking into the substructures of their civilization. Between 1850 and 1890 European universities become filled with chairs of comparative mythology, history of religions, and the science of myths.[51] Archeological excavations and discoveries are on the increase. Laistner publishes *The Riddle of the Sphinx*, (1889), Gomperz *Greek Thinkers* (1896–1902). Schliemann discovers Troy, and the Englishman Evans unearths the Palace of Minos on Crete. "For relaxation I am reading Burckhardt's *History of Greek Civilization*, which is providing me with unexpected parallels. My predilection for the prehistoric in all its human forms remains the same."[52]

Athens forms an important chapter in his Western memory, a significant stage of the journey of his impossible lineage. When he stands before the Acropolis after a series of unforeseen circumstances, he doubts the reality of his perceptions: "So all this really *does* exist, just as we learnt at school!" Before the temple of Athena, Oedipus, and Eros the son of Abraham, Solomon, and Jacob is troubled; his vision blurs, his memory wanders: "What I see here is not real," it is "too good to be true."[53]

The traditional contrast between Hellenism and Judaism is played out in him, disturbing and tormenting him. Ernest Jones reports a conversation he and Freud had one day on the beautiful harmony among spiritual and physical activities characterizing the Greek ideal. "Yes," Freud replied, "that combination is certainly preferable. For various reasons the Jews have undergone a one-sided development and admire brains more than bodies, but if I had to choose between the two I should also put the intellect first."[54] On another occasion, however, Freud writes: "My attention has repeatedly been called to the observations in the Talmud about the problem of dreams. But I must say that the approximation to the understanding of the dream among the ancient Greeks is far more striking."[55]

For the heir of the people of the Torah—a text whose very name faded away beneath the Greek word *biblos* (the book, the Bible) "intellect" is inevitable associated with the corpus of all the other books, the books of the "others," the gentiles. But at Athens it is Freud who feels that he is the barbarian of a culture that his family did not promise he would attain and make his own. Moreover, it is by a curious historical circumstance that he finds himself on the Acropolis on September 4,1904, dressed in his finest shirt for the occasion.[56]

Five days earlier, he had met up with his brother Alexander in Trieste, from which they planned to set out to spend a few days on Corfu. A business acquaintance of his brother's dissuades them: it is much too hot; why not visit Athens, taking the boat leaving the next day? The two brothers are hesitant, see only obstacles and difficulties with this plan, are in a low mood. Nevertheless, at the last minute they get on board. On this boat taking them to the Piraeus is an archeologist, the assistant to the famous Schliemann. But Freud is intimidated and holds back from speaking to him: this 48-year-old man, the father of six children, a university professor and the author of revolutionary works, is as silent as a teenager in awe of his teachers.

His desires take him where his father never could or would go, arousing guilt that distorts his gaze. He had to doubt that he would discover Athens with his own eyes: "It seemed to me beyond the realm of possibility that I should travel so far—that I should 'go such a long way.'"[57] The feeling of uncanniness that comes over him on the Acropolis and makes it seem unreal to him can be understood as a twofold response to the guilty rivalry confronting him with his father internally and, what is more, with his father's Judaism.[58] In his imagination, Athens is the shrine of Western civilization, the wished-for place, if there ever was one, of an ambitious intellectual, and now "the distinction between imagination and reality is effaced, as when something that we have hitherto regarded as imaginary appears before us in reality."[59]

Despite all his successes, in front of the temple that is the symbol of his accomplishment he reproaches himself for seeing what his father never saw:

> It seems as though the essence of success was to have gotten further than one's father, and as though to excel over one's father was still something forbidden.

As an addition to this generally valid motive there was a special factor present in our particular case. The very theme of Athens and the Acropolis in itself contained evidence of the son's superiority. Our father had been in business, he had had no secondary education, and Athens could not have meant much to him. Thus what interfered with our enjoyment of the journey to Athens was a feeling of *filial piety*.[60]

Thirty-two years after this pilgrimage to the origins of Western thought, he analyzes the feeling of strangeness that overcame him on the Athenian Acropolis in a letter honoring Romain Rolland on the occasion of his seventieth birthday, the same age as Freud's brother Alexander, while he himself had just turned 80.

Like Oedipus, right up to the time of his death he investigates the human enigma, and, like the riddle-solving hero, he is ready to pay with his sight for his wish to see clearly: "A study of dreams, phantasies, and myths has taught us that anxiety about one's eyes, the fear of going blind, is often enough a substitute for the dread of being castrated. The self-blinding of the mythical criminal, Oedipus, was simply a mitigated form of the sole punishment that was adequate for him by the *lex talionis*."[61]

Oedipus's error was not killing his father and loving his mother but the desire for knowledge. Oedipus is the man with the swollen foot, the mark of his accursed birth, but also "the man who knows"[62] and always wants to know, even at the cost of his own destruction. A plaything in the hands of the fate that the Olympian gods had in store for him, he fulfills their curse unbeknownst to himself. He suffered his crimes; he did not commit them. It is in legitimate self-defense that he kills an old man; the victory over the Sphinx offers him the bed of a queen in whose country he believes he is a foreign guest. Patricide and incest are perpetrated with closed eyes. And it is his eyes that reveal the final knowledge: the blindness of King Oedipus is the price he has to pay for his insight. His crime, his unforgivable error for the city, is his stubborn will to discover the truth, his wish to solve the enigma whose enigmatic object he is. Oedipus is double: "The Corinthian stranger is in reality a native of Thebes; the solver of riddles is a riddle he himself cannot solve; the dispenser of justice is a criminal; the clairvoyant, a blind man; the savior of the town, its doom."[63]

Man is a riddle for himself, and it is not without risk that he seeks to solve it. Whoever is brave enough to persevere to the end in his discovery will be endowed with second sight, with an inner eye. He will have "acceded to the other light, the blinding, terrible light of the divine,"[64] he will be a prophet like Teiresias, who was able to experience sexual pleasure as both a man and a woman,[65] to the great wrath of Hera, who took away his eyesight.

Because he dared to see his incestuous and patricidal hands in Thebes, Oedipus can become the prophet of another town, the Athenian suburb Colonus. Whoever can take on the fate of his erotic and murderous drives on the stage of the unconscious, going beyond the ordeal of the oedipal drama, becomes the benefactor of his conscious life. Because he refused to close his eyes to the riddle of humanity, Oedipus blinds himself, but he then becomes endowed with insight for all men.

Freud sees dimly on the Acropolis; his father had lowered himself to pick up his hat from the mud and he, the son, holds his head high at the summit of Greece. What he sees blinds his memory: as a child he glimpsed his mother's bare body and his father laid bare. The one experience moves him, the other enrages him. As an adult he finds that these feelings are still there; they are part of human destiny, his and every other man's. Like the hero of the Greek tragedy, he sees in himself what human beings would rather not know about themselves. All they can do is banish, exile, or resist whoever escapes the prohibition against knowing, a prohibition that links the wish to know—in the biblical sense—one's own mother with the knowledge deep within oneself of the mystery of origins, the difference of the sexes, and the secret of their pleasure.

If the hero does not fear the pain of his truth, and if he finds sanctuary in a space less resistant to his clear vision, his insight will illuminate future generations. Oedipus speaks of his time in Colonus as "conferring benefit on those who received me,/A curse on those who have driven me away."[66] Taking the tragic path of Sophocles,

Freud the King promises to bring the plague to every Thebes, American and otherwise. Colonus is still very distant.

> As God is my witness, Doctor, I sat by Salomon Rothschild, and he treated me just like one of his equals—quite famillionarily.
>
> —Heine[67]

Athens, Rome, and Jerusalem form a triangular landscape in which Jerusalem is the outside-place, the invisible region, the empty temple that is materialized only in the field of literature.

"Needless to say, my idea of enjoying spring with you on Mount Carmel was a mere phantasy. Even supported by my faithful Anna-Antigone I could not embark on a journey."[68]

Jerusalem reveals a desert, fertile with words, that Freud crosses in the company of Joseph and Moses. As with them, the desert separating Egypt and Canaan entwines the reality of exile, its cows lean or fat according to the seasons, with the fantasy of a land always filled with milk and honey. Wandering in this intermediate cultural space can give rise to the interpretation of dreams and the tables of divine or unconscious laws.

A long line of Josephs runs through the fabric of *The Interpretation of Dreams* and weaves the "Egyptian dream book": his friend Paneth; the doctor one-eyed from birth; the Emperor Franz Josef; the teacher Breuer; and even Giuseppe Garibaldi, who all, like the uncle with the yellow beard, conceal Jacob, Freud's recently deceased father. In 1900 Freud can still believe that he is not Joseph, the oldest son of the patriarch, but just the protégé of the Austro-Hungarian pharaoh, "as if the role of sexuality had suddenly been recognized by His Majesty, the interpretation of dreams confirmed by the Council of Ministers, and the necessity of the psycho-analytic theory of hysteria carried by a two-thirds majority in Parliament."[69]

Moses is the ambiguous figure of his Judaism, at the juncture of the visible and the invisible, of idolatry and the iconoclastic temple: an entirely atheistic Jew,[70] he has never lost his sense of solidarity with his people,[71] but despite this membership, despite a conflict, he seems to want to deprive Moses of his place of honor[72] and prove that this greatest son of his people is not Jewish but Egyptian, thereby trying to push back to the last pages of his last book the moment when the repressed father will inevitably return.

Neither blind nor even one-eyed, Freud came to Rome to look at a sculpture by Michelangelo: a marble Moses carved as though he were one of the people, devoting himself to the adoration of the golden calf. But what he sees is the wrath of the hero, who, with "wrath and indignation,"[73] seems to reproach Freud for violating his first commandment. Isn't it the height of transgression of the law of the Jewish father to admire the image of the one who formulated the law prohibiting idolatry, to become entranced by the statue of the man who ordered the children of Israel to break their images, who demanded that they renounce the world of illusory sense perceptions in favor of abstraction and invisible spirituality? What are we to think of a Jew, even an unbeliever, who disdains his thousand-year-old heritage of iconoclasm before a fragment of the colossal mausoleum that was to be erected in honor of Pope Julius II in a Roman Catholic church?[74]

And yet Freud holds firm: he manages an amazing compromise, looking at Moses without seeing him. What interests him is the "meaning" of this statue, not its formal, technical qualities: "Some of the grandest and most overwhelming creations of art are still unsolved riddles to our understanding."[75]

But why, he wonders, can't the artist's intention be determined, formulated in words? For it is only the translation of the image into verbal language that allows him to enjoy it. Even in his dream life he favors words over images. In his dreams he does not paint or sculpt. He writes words, reads them: a chemical formula, names of streets, posters. In the dream preceding or following his father's burial he found himself in a shop where he read the following inscription: "'You are requested to close the eyes'" (or "'an eye'").[76]

This sentence, so often examined and interpreted,[77] is to be taken literally. Freud hopes to respect the wish of the dying man—that he not go over to the side of the Western makers of graven images—and, at the same time, he begs for the indulgence of his wish to glance at them nonetheless, to realize his ambition for glory and revenge.

Although at the time of his death Freud numbered as many years as his father, he is aware of his special destiny as innovator,[78] conqueror of a new realm of human knowledge. But, despite the temptation to be only the father of his works, he cannot escape his fateful lineage. From Hannibal, to Oedipus, to Aeneas, to Moses, his identifications with vanquished heroes have faded. Now he can no longer evade the final confrontation, the ultimate rendezvous of a son with his father, the encounter with death before accepting death.

When he failed, Hannibal committed suicide to escape revenge at the hands of the Romans; Moses, guilty four times over before God, was unable to reach the Promised Land; Oedipus, the scapegoat of Thebes, had to go into exile as bearer of the plague. Freud himself will not escape exile, forced by "the new enemy,"[79] the Nazis, to leave Vienna for the England to which his father had not taken him at the right time.

Up to the very end he hopes that the Church will be a solid bastion against Hitler's antisemitism; out of a sense of prudence, not at all out of cowardice, he hesitates to do anything that might arouse the hostility of the Church, that is, publish the "legend"[80] he is putting together around Moses, the father of the scrolls of Jewish law. Beneath the features of Moses is Freud's own father, who, "like an unlaid ghost,"[81] keeps on haunting him.

As the drama of his life comes to a close, and he waits for "the curtain to fall,"[82] Freud understands that he is both the father of a Western oeuvre and the son of a Jewish father, that intellectual, cultural identity does not undo the fact that he belongs to a family. His work has been serious, but his name retains its tone of joyful derision.[83]

In his concern to avenge his father he struggles for glory all his life, but his official success does not compensate for his parent's lack of heroism. Although he is an adoptive son of the West, he can still take his place in his own genealogy and be the son of a minority people that drew "this undying hatred" to itself.[84]

"Even the great Goethe, who in the period of his genius certainly looked down upon his unbending and pedantic father, in his old age developed traits which formed a part of his father's character."[85] The example of Goethe suggests to him that a son, no matter how renowned, must rework his paternal identification throughout his life; he cannot escape it. Before he can meet up with death, Freud must come face to face with the figure of the dead father.

With the boldness of someone who no longer has much to lose,[86] he contemplates this riddle of destiny: his father, in mourning for whom he had undertaken his self-analysis and set out on the royal road of *The Interpretation of Dreams*, Jacob Freud, whom he thought he was avenging and redeeming in his own eyes when he became famous, returns at the end of Freud's life like the return of the unthinkable. His final work is the site of a final encounter with his Jewish father.

Freud recognizes that he has not managed to eradicate the traces of oddness in his Mosaic essay. Throughout the book, he writes about how hard it is for him to write. First published in bits and pieces, the three sections that comprise *Moses and Monotheism* were brought together in 1939, but he does not smooth over the seams. He apologizes but defends the repetitions: "There are things which should be said more than once."[87] This involuntary return to the same point, this disturbing repetition of the identical, is the unavoidable reminder of the impossible filiation.

The question of identity keeps coming back in order to be resolved, or it remains indefinitely closed in on itself and cannot be gotten past. Like all those who, following in his footsteps, will take the dark path of desire, Freud tries to rewrite his story, to fashion it in such a way as to escape the sterility of repetition, the constraint of the eternal recurrence.

On the eve of his emigration to London he comes to terms with his genealogy, writing to his son Ernst: "I sometimes compare myself with the old Jacob who, when a very old man, was taken by his children to Egypt."[88]

Although he adds a "legend" to the Biblical text, up to its final page Jerusalem and the uniqueness of Jewish destiny remain unexplained. Jerusalem is still invisible, silent, and unsigned.[89]

> A man like you does not stay stuck at the same point where he was cast by the accident of birth.
>
> —Lessing, *Nathan the Wise*

Athens, Rome, and Jerusalem mark the boundaries of a cultural tradition and space peculiar to the nineteenth-century West. Freud approaches it with a trilingual gaze—Judaeo-Greco-Latin—so as to delineate his own heritage and territory there.

He custom-tailors a Western text for himself, cutting it in the Romanticism of Goethe and Schiller, the wisdom of Lessing, and the fantasies of Hoffmann, basting it with great dramas by Shakespeare and Ibsen, and adding fine embroidery with lines from Sophocles and Virgil. He makes the West's legends and heroes his own and draws on this imagery to embellish the original cloth of his own writing.

But the tenacity with which he pursues this work, and the breath that animates and sustains it, come from his Biblical roots and his marginal position in a society whose prejudices he does not share because he is too recent a guest. When Max Graf, the father of the future Little Hans, asks him whether he should not protect his son from antisemitic hatred by raising him in the Christian faith, Freud replies without hesitation: "If you do not let your son grow up as a Jew, you will deprive him of those sources of energy which cannot be replaced by anything else. He will have to struggle as a Jew, and you ought to develop in him all the energy he will need for that struggle. Do not deprive him of that advantage."[90]

Although some scholars disagree,[91] Freud's attachment to the Greek chapter in his memory is not the sign of a Jewish repression that we are to see as the basis of what would become psychoanalysis. This man who did not speak Hebrew would certainly not have understood why sheaves of *shibbolim* are harvested in the Freudian fields.[92]

Freud is the heir to a Greek tradition, and this legacy is not accidental. It is with this vocabulary and these categories of thought that he forged his intellectual tools.[93] These treasures of Greek mythology, the soil in which European intelligence was rooted, had been hidden by nineteen centuries of Christianity and Enlightenment, but Freud found here the rich iconography of his psychoanalytic concepts. Greek myths inevitably echoed and nourished Freud's investigations, since they convey with such great expressive power the fantasies and metaphors of the unconscious. They reveal an astonishing tolerance for the varieties of human desire and allow for a harmonious compromise between a broad instinctual freedom and the limitations imposed by the reality principle.[94] The mythology of the Greeks understood man's irreducible duality, putting humanity onstage in its endless oscillation between the bestial and the divine.

In the eternal recurrence of mythical figures, Freud was able to read the repetition compulsion and the vicissitudes of instincts. The Biblical period, on the other hand, showed him a historical unfolding, the possibility of a transformation of fate, a potential cure.

The psychoanalytic drama, then, is enacted with Greek plots and personages, but in the linear evolution of the Jewish era.

Freud is always elsewhere. His identity cannot be confined to an enclosed space; he is never where we think we can locate him. We believe he is on the road to Rome, but he is walking alongside his father on a street in Freiberg. When he looks at Athens, Jerusalem disturbs his vision. As he speaks of a journey to an "unholy land,"[95] he slips into the skin of the aging Oedipus. A marble Moses holds his attention in Rome, but, studying the origins of the children of Israel, he makes the Jewish lawgiver a highborn Egyptian. He was born on the first day of the month of Iyar 5616 and joined to the Jewish Covenant a week later, but his ashes lie in his favorite Greek urn in Golders Green Cemetery, London.

When Austria, his adopted country, is invaded by the Nazis in March 1938, the steering committee of the Vienna Psychoanalytic Society decides that everyone should flee Austria, and that the headquarters of the Society will be relocated to wherever Freud takes up residence. Freud's comment on this decision is as follows: "After the destruction of the Temple in Jerusalem by Titus, Rabbi Yochanan ben Zachai asked for permission to open a school at Jabneh for the study of the Torah. We are going to do the same."[96]

Like all the Jews wandering from Jerusalem into exile, Freud recognizes only one country, that of the book: his works remain his one and only fatherland.

NOTES

1. Freud 1900, p. 197. For the translation of the dreams, see Anzieu 1959. This chapter is a revised version of Flem 1983a, dedicated to Jean Trebitsch and Jacqueline Godfrind.

2. On the issue of Freud's given name, see Anzieu 1959 and the pioneering work of Marthe Robert (1974).

3. See his letter to Wilhelm Fliess of April 27, 1895 (Freud 1954, p. 118) and the dream "Uncle with the yellow beard" (Freud 1900, pp. 136–145, 192–193).

4. Letter to Martha of February 2, 1886 (Freud 1960, p. 202).

5. Freud 1900, p. 193.

6. See Goux 1978, p. 13.

7. Letter of October 8, 1907 (Freud and Abraham 1965, p. 9).

8. See the letter to A. A. Roback of February 20, 1930 (Freud 1960, p. 395).

9. Freud 1900, p. 193.

10. In Jewish mysticism the Shekhina, the divine presence of God, is said to be God's feminine side; it is also the bride of God or the community of Israel.

11. Letter to Martha of July 23, 1882 (Freud 1960, p. 19).

12. Freud 1900, p. 318.

13. Letter to Emil Fluss of June 16, 1873 (Freud 1960, pp. 4, 6).

14. Letter to Karl Abraham of July 23, 1908 (Freud and Abraham 1965, p. 46).

15. Freud 1924, p. 8.

16. Freud 1900, pp. 194–195. See also Anzieu 1959, p. 257.

17. Letter of July 23, 1882 (Freud 1960, p. 22).

18. Letter of May 6, 1926 (Freud 1960, p. 367).

19. Letter to Barbara Low of April 19, 1936 (Freud 1960, p. 428).

20. Laplanche and Pontalis 1985.

21. Freud 1911b, p. 341.

22. Anna and Sophie are named in honor of the daughter and niece of his Hebrew professor and friend Samuel Hammerschlag, Mathilde in honor of Mrs. Breuer. Oliver is named after Cromwell. Jean-Martin owes his name to Charcot and Ernst to Freud's teacher Brücke.

23. Letter of July 7, 1898 (Freud 1954, p. 258).

24. Goethe 1789, p. 116.

25. Freud 1900, pp. 196–198.

26. Letter to Fliess of March 11, 1902 (Freud 1954, p. 342).

27. Letter to Fliess of March 2, 1899 (Freud 1954, p. 280).

28. Letter to Fliess of March 2, 1899 (Freud 1954, p. 280).

29. Letter to Fliess of December 3, 1897 (Freud 1954, p. 236).

30. Freud 1900, p. 194. See also Anzieu 1959, p. 252.

31. Translator's note: "that" is ça, the French translation of Freud's das Es, the id.

32. Letter to Fliess of October 3, 1897 (Freud 1954, p. 219).

33. Freud 1900, pp. 194–195. See also Anzieu 1959, pp. 257–258.

34. Letter to Fliess of August 27, 1899 (Freud 1954, p. 294).
35. Freud 1900, p. 195. See also Anzieu 1959, p. 266.
36. Freud 1900, p. 196.
37. Letter to Fliess of December 3, 1897 (Freud 1954, p. 237).
38. Letter to Fliess of February 12, 1900 (Freud 1954, p. 310).
39. Translator's note: In German, *Zucker* means "sugar."
40. Freud 1900, p. 95.
41. Scholem 1978, p. 93.
42. Letter to the members of B'nai B'rith of May 6, 1926 (Freud 1960, p. 366).
43. Letter of April 16, 1900 (Freud 1954, p. 31).
44. Letter to Martha of July 23, 1882 (Freud 1960, p. 19).
45. Freud 1900, pp. 141–144 and 269. See also Chapter 5, this volume.
46. Letter to Fliess of February 15, 1901 (Freud 1954, p. 328).
47. Letter to Fliess of August 7, 1901 (Freud 1954, p. 334).
48. Letter to Fliess of September 19, 1901 (Freud 1954, p. 335).
49. Letter to Fliess of September 19, 1901 (Freud 1954, p. 335).
50. Postcard to Fliess of October 9, 1902 (Freud 1954, p. 345).
51. Detienne 1981.
52. Letter to Fliess of January 30, 1899 (Freud 1954, p. 275).
53. Freud 1936b, pp. 241–243.
54. Jones 1953, p. 31.
55. Letter to A. Drujanow of March 3, 1910. Cited in Gay 1987, pp. 32–33.
56. Jones 1955, p. 24.
57. Freud 1936b, p. 246.
58. Rosolato (1978) connects Freud's oceanic feeling as he contemplates the ruins of the Parthenon, temple of the warrior virgin Athena, with the problematics of absence, the religious, and the feminine.
59. Freud 1919a, p. 244.
60. Freud 1936b, pp. 247–248.
61. Freud 1919a, p. 231.
62. Vernant and Vidal-Naquet 1972, p. 123.
63. Vernant and Vidal-Naquet 1972, p. 119.
64. Vernant and Vidal-Naquet 1972, p. 120.
65. Loraux 1989.
66. Sophocles, *Oedipus at Colonus*, p. 83.
67. Freud 1905c, p. 129.
68. Letter to Arnold Zweig, May 2, 1935 (Freud 1960, p. 424).
69. Letter to Fliess, March 11, 1902 (Freud 1954, p. 344).
70. Letter to Oskar Pfister, October 9, 1918 (Freud and Pfister 1963a, p. 118).
71. Letter to Enrico Morselli, February 18, 1926 (Freud 1960, p. 365).
72. Freud 1939, p. 63.
73. Freud 1914b, p. 225.
74. Freud's interest in this tomb may be connected with the fact that Julius was the name of his brother, the second son of Jacob and Amalia, who died in very early childhood.

75. Freud 1914b, p. 211.

76. Freud 1900, p. 317 and letter to Fliess, November 2, 1896 (Freud 1954, p. 171).

77. See Anzieu 1959, pp. 233–240; Certeau 1975, p. 65; and Robert 1974, p. 100.

78. Letter to Arnold Zweig, June 17, 1936 (Freud and Zweig 1970, p. 223).

79. Freud 1939, p. 55.

80. Freud 1939, p. 7.

81. Freud 1939, p. 103.

82. Freud and Zweig 1970, p. 133.

83. Cf. Freud 1900, p. 207. Translator's note: *Freud* means "joy" in German.

84. Letter to Arnold Zweig, September 30, 1934 (Freud 1960, p. 276).

85. Freud 1939, p. 125.

86. Freud 1939, p. 101.

87. Freud 1939, p. 104.

88. Letter of May 12, 1938 (Freud 1960, p. 442).

89. *Moses and Monotheism* first appeared without its author's name.

90. Graf 1942, p. 473.

91. See, for example, Bakan 1964, Haddad 1981, Lacoue-Labarthe and Nancy 1981, and Lévy-Valensi 1971.

92. *Shibboleth* is a Hebrew word meaning ear of grain, branch. The Bible (Judges 12) relates that, in the course of a fratricidal war, this noun was a password to distinguish allies from enemies, the latter pronouncing it *sibboleth*. Freud uses this Biblical word in connection with the Oedipus complex, which divides the partisans from the foes of psychoanalysis (1905a). The shibboleth metaphor also occurs in *The Ego and the Id* (1923) with regard to those who do or do not acknowledge the importance of the unconscious, as well as in the *New Introductory Lectures on Psycho-Analysis* (1933), this time distinguishing between those who can and those who cannot become skilled at psychoanalysis.

93. Levinas (1981, pp. 114–128) has clearly shown that there is no evidence of talmudic sources for the notion of the unconscious.

94. See Green 1980 and Anzieu 1970.

95. Letter to Arnold Zweig, February 20, 1939 (Freud and Zweig 1970, p. 175).

96. Jones 1957, p. 221.

5

The Man without a Country

Once upon a time, long, long ago, in the brilliant capital of an empire in Eastern Europe, there lived two Jews. One, born in Budapest, had a childhood dream of building the Panama Canal; the other, from the Moravian countryside, saw himself as a minister of state or the conqueror of an empire. Both had been brought up in the enlightened circles of a Judaism that encouraged its members to take part in Western culture. Seen in a mirror, the liberal society of their early years seems to hold out a true welcome to them. Theodor became the elegant columnist of the greatest liberal paper in the city. He was a man full of wit and good taste, with exquisite manners, one of the *Jung-Wien* poets, a friend of Arthur Schnitzler and Hugo von Hofmannsthal. As for Sigmund, he threw himself with the passion of his ancestors defending their temple into a career as a scientist, hoping to distinguish himself through some glorious discovery.

Sent to Paris as a correspondent by the *Neue Freie Presse*, the first man discovered in no uncertain terms that even the homeland of the rights of man and the citizen could harbor antisemitism. He returned, henceforth convinced that assimilation, despite its most flattering appearances, was doomed to failure. As for the second man, Paris introduced him to Charcot and his grand hysterics. Behind the *belle indifférence* of these women, he thought he could see that there was a whole world of hidden meanings to be brought to light. When he returned to Vienna, he wanted to share his new enthusiasm with his colleagues, but he met with a cool reception. The young scholar had no doubt that an element of antisemitism was involved.

Theodor and Sigmund, who, during their university years in the 1880s, had belonged to a national group of German students and had surely encountered anti-Jewish reactions there, could nevertheless believe that these would disappear. In the 1890s such blindness is no longer possible, and they have to face facts: with the decline of liberalism and the rise of pan-Germanic nationalism and the accompanying antisemitism, as well as with the election of Karl Lueger as mayor of Vienna, the Jews are now caught in a trap. They had made German culture, and especially the German language, their own, but assimilation to the surrounding world is no longer possible. To bandage their wounded, conflictual identity Viennese Jews will have to start looking for new answers.

> The repressed is foreign territory to the ego—internal foreign territory—just as reality (if you will forgive the unusual expression) is external foreign territory.
> —*New Introductory Lectures on Psycho-Analysis*[1]

Theodor Herzl and Sigmund Freud, each in his own way, imagine an answer to this crisis of Jewish identity. And, for each of them, this answer takes a geographical form.

The Zionism set forth by Herzl in *The Jewish State*[2] offers an essentially spatial suggestion, the geographical concentration of the Jewish people in a single territory and an autonomous entity, whether it be called Uganda, Argentina, or Palestine. And Freud's psychoanalytic hypothesis, too, is formulated as a spatial theory: in each one of us there is an "elsewhere," another kingdom, the unconscious. The psychic apparatus is a space, a topography.

Freud and Herzl offer their contemporaries a dream of space and conquest. Herzl proposes the creation of a Jewish state. For him, the Jewish people must be granted "sovereignty . . . over a portion of the globe."[3] Freud advances the hypothesis of an interior Promised Land, the existence of a land of refuge that each of us carries inside. Two different—if not contradictory—spatial solutions, but in a way they are symmetrical. Where Herzl encourages emigration from the outset, Freud chooses an even deeper immigration. For an external and distant elsewhere, he substitutes an internal journey, a return to the self and its origins. Where Herzl wants a collective political response, Freud is concerned with individual psychic reality. To escape suffering, Herzl enlists the Jews to leave the countries in which they are being persecuted, whereas Freud seeks to understand and analyze this suffering. The former can already envision a white flag with seven golden stars planted in the earth that has been won back; the latter is convinced that, like the horizon, fulfillment of unconscious desire is never reached. The lost country is never found again.

Despite all their differences, returning a country to the Jews or returning man to the fertile soil of his unconscious, Theodor Herzl and Sigmund Freud both appeal to the power of the dream. For Freud, "The interpretation of dreams is the royal road to a knowledge of the unconscious activities of the mind"[4]; for Herzl the royal dream leads to Zion: the time has come to leave the diaspora and finally realize the promised millennium. For Freud, in contrast, only an invisible Jerusalem remains fertile. Yes, he is suffering in Vienna, but he is not in search of a host country other than the one he is exploring on the basis of intimate knowledge of himself. It is the space of the unconscious that he wishes to conquer. Still, he formally indicates his membership in the Jewish community, joining the liberal lodge of B'nai B'rith on September 29, 1897.[5] There he gives frequent lectures on his works in progress, often before their publication. Shortly after joining, on December 7 and 14, 1897, he speaks to his "brothers" on the interpretation of dreams. Each year or so he gives another talk; thus on February 3, 1899, he speaks on the psychology of forgetting, a year later on the psychic life of the child. On April 24, 1900, he talks on Zola's *Fécondité*, followed by evenings devoted to the physiology of the unconscious, the joke, Hamlet, death, art, *La Révolte des Anges* by Anatole France, and many more.

On the occasion of his seventieth birthday he addresses his lodge brothers of B'nai B'rith, explaining what he sought from them:

It happened that in the years after 1895 two strong impressions coincided to produce the same effect on me. On the one hand I had gained the first insight into the depths of human instinct, had seen many things which were sobering, at first even frightening; on the other hand the disclosure of my unpopular discoveries led to my losing most of my personal relationships at that time; I felt as though outlawed, shunned by all. This isolation aroused in me the longing for a circle of excellent men with high ideals who would accept me in friendship despite my temerity. Your Lodge was described to me as the place where I could find such men.

That you are Jews could only be welcome to me, for I was myself a Jew, and it has always appeared to me not only undignified but outright foolish to deny it. What tied me to Jewry was—I have to admit it—not the faith, not even the national pride, for I was always an unbeliever, have been brought up without religion, but not without respect for the so-called "ethical" demands of human civilization. Whenever I have experienced feelings of national exaltation, I have tried to suppress them as disastrous and unfair, frightened by the warning example of those nations among which we Jews live.[6]

When Freud sends Theodor Herzl a copy of *The Interpretation of Dreams* on September 28, 1902, he mentions the esteem in which he holds Herzl as a poet, political leader, and fighter for the rights of their people.[7]

A little Jewish story relates that Herzl came to see Freud one day and said, "Doctor, I've had a dream. . . ." To which Freud might have replied with the final words of his dream book: "[T]he ancient belief that dreams foretell the future is not wholly devoid of truth. By picturing our wishes as fulfilled, dreams are after all leading us into the future. But this future, which the dreamer pictures as present, has been moulded by his indestructible wish into a perfect likeness of the past."[8] One can't say, "Next year in Jerusalem!" for two thousand years with impunity.

> "So you are going back to—I can't recall the name of the city."
> —Freud, to a traveler leaving London for Vienna, May 1939[9]

The same spatial preoccupation underlies the Zionist approach and psychoanalytic research at the time of its discovery. The geographical metaphor also reveals Freud's personal journeys. To understand the ties that bind him in fantasy to the Promised Land, we must place that land in the triangular landscape formed, with a single line, by Athens, Rome, and Jerusalem. Freud is a real diasporic Jew. When it comes to a choice between the visible and the invisible, he does not hesitate. Although throughout his life he is tempted by visual seductions, Freud, like Moses, condemns images and always privileges the latent over the manifest, idea over form, the word over the thing, and hence an invisible land to the incarnation of a promise.

To be sure, the fate of his people in Palestine is not a matter of indifference to him, and in the years 1920–1930 he shows his "sympathy" toward Zionism. Nonetheless he tries to see whether this movement is accompanied by a Jewish nationalism and a religious revival that he strongly opposes. On June 20, 1925, he sends a letter to Keren Hajazoth, the financial arm of the Zionist Congress: "It is a sign of our invincible will to live which for two thousand years has survived the worst persecutions. Our youth will carry on the fight."[10]

But the Promised Land has still other echoes for him, ones that are much more laden with feeling. Writing to his most intimate disciple, almost his son, Sándor Ferenczi, in 1922 he exclaims:

> Strange secret yearnings rise in me—perhaps from my ancestral heritage—for the East and the Mediterranean and for a life of quite another kind: wishes from late childhood never to be fulfilled, which do not conform to reality as if to hint at a loosening of one's relationship to it. Instead of which—we shall meet on the soil of sober Berlin.[11]

These childhood wishes that cannot be fulfilled on the shores of the Mediterranean do not, as one might expect, refer to nostalgia for a lost fatherland. Palestine is a "strip of our mother earth," one that is "tragically mad" and that "has never produced anything but religions, sacred frenzies, presumptuous attempts to overcome the outer world of appearance by means of the inner world of wishful thinking."[12] In saying this, is Freud aware that psychoanalysis, too, proceeds this way, constantly tracking unconscious desire beyond what appears to consciousness? This Palestine: Freud also says that his ancestors lived there for half a millennium, perhaps even a whole one, and that it is hard for him to say exactly what its legacy has been for him. He speaks of the land of his ancestors, now being reborn, not as a fatherland (*Vaterland*) but as a mother earth (*Muttererde*), an earth-mother.

If the land flowing with milk and honey is maternal for Freud, what about the soil of Vienna, where he has lived, against his will, ever since his father took him there at the age of 4, snatching him away from the sweet paradise of his early childhood in the countryside? Viennese soil that he cannot leave despite his hatred for it, that he can escape only for brief, idyllic journeys to the sun of Italy—this prosaic soil is associated with the paternal figure for him. He writes to Fliess: "I hate Vienna with a positively personal hatred, and, just the contrary of the giant Antaeus, I draw fresh strength whenever I remove my feet from the soil of the city which is my home."[13]

Thus on one side there is the city of reality, Vienna, the father's city, a place where he was not born but to which his father took him, the symbol of renunciations, and on the other side—elsewhere, far away—the maternal land, the Promised Land, promised like a fiancée but forbidden like a mother.

This oedipal geography also sheds light on his enormous identification with Moses, who was not entitled to take possession of the lost country and could only view it from afar without reaching it. We can also better understand why, in the series of his biblical heroes, it is always "Egyptian" figures, heroes in exile, whom he chooses: Joseph, for example, the interpreter of Pharaoh's dreams. Yet we must not forget—even if he himself seems to have ignored it—that Freud bore an eminent biblical name: the name of a king of Israel, said to be the author of one of the most beautiful erotic poems ever written, the Song of Songs. Thus Freud could have found in Solomon the precursor of psychoanalysis. For the famous judgment scene is a masterful illustration of the power of words, their ability to reveal underlying intentions. But Sigmund/Schlomo Freud could not identify with his renowned namesake, could not project himself ideally except as a hero in exile.

By the rivers of Babylon, there we sat down, yea, we wept, when we remembered Zion.

—Psalm 137.1[14]

The theme of exile haunts this dream of Freud's, inspired by Herzl's Zionist play *Das neue Ghetto*. Freud had seen it at the Karl Theater in January 1988 with his family and some friends. In it Herzl argues that, although the walls of the ghetto fell with the emancipation of the Jews, antisemitism is once again shutting them in, but this time in a dreadful moral ghetto.

In *The Interpretation of Dreams* Freud presents the account of this dream under the heading "Absurd Dreams." Here is the text:

On account of certain events which had occurred in the city of Rome, it had become necessary to remove the children to safety, and this was done. The scene was then in front of a gateway, double doors in the ancient style (the "Porta Romana" at Siena, as I was aware during the dream itself). I was sitting on the edge of a fountain and was greatly depressed and almost in tears. A female figure—an attendant or nun—brought two boys out and handed them over to their father, who was not myself. The elder of the two was clearly my eldest son; I did not see the other one's face. The woman who brought out the boy asked him to kiss her goodbye. She was noticeable for having a red nose. The boy refused to kiss her, but, holding out his hand in farewell, said "AUF GESERES" to her, and then "AUF UNGESERES" to the two of us (or to one of us). I had a notion that this last phrase denoted a preference.[15]

As he goes on to say, from the beginning of his analysis Freud himself recognizes, in his dream-thoughts, "the Jewish problem, concern about the future of one's children, to whom one cannot give a country of their own, concern about educating them in such a way that they can move freely across frontiers." His association to his intense feeling beside the well is the lamentation of the Jews in exile: "By the waters of Babylon we sat down and wept." He also associates the image with a co-religionist who had to give up his position as a doctor in a state asylum. He therefore fears, on behalf of his sons and himself, the antisemitism that could drive them from Vienna.

As Freud interprets it, the absurd neologism "*Auf Geseres/Auf Ungeseres*" and the marked preference for "*Ungeseres*" refer to the Jewish Easter, with its unleavened bread in contrast to the leavened bread usually eaten, and recalls the flight out of Egypt and the exile in the desert, in that intermediate region preceding the return to the land of Canaan.

For once Rome is not the city of fascination that Freud wants to conquer and that he assimilates to his intellectual ambition. Rome here represents the city, hostile to the Jews, from which he is driven, the reverse of Jerusalem.

The mention of the woman with the red nose, a female attendant or nun, refers to a childhood memory of his nursemaid, who was dismissed because she drank and stole, but this image also hides another scene of exile. For after the separation from his nursemaid came the departure from Freiberg to Vienna with his father and mother, while the other branch of the family went into exile in England.

If this dream, quasi-Biblical as it is, shows that Freud has a preference for the Jewish tradition, it also conveys a barely concealed plea with regard to his father, Jacob, who ineptly took him to Vienna instead of to England. For Freud, England always represents a haven from antisemitism. As is often the case, he reveals the most emotionally compelling aspect of the dream: "I was envying some relatives who, many years earlier, had had an opportunity of removing their children to another country."

At the age of 19 he had gone to Manchester for a stay of nearly two months with his half-brothers. He described his enthusiasm to his friend Silberstein:

> As for England, I . . . can say straight out that I would sooner live there than here [Vienna], rain, fog, drunkenness, and conservatism notwithstanding. Many peculiarities of the English character and country that other Continentals might find intolerable agree very well with my own makeup. Who knows, dear friend, but that after I have completed my studies a favorable wind might not blow me across to England.[16]

Seven years later he has not given up this idea, as is shown in a letter to his fiancée in which he explains that he has "got to branch out and go through the medical curriculum as fast as possible in order to set myself up in practice, probably in England, where I have relations."[17] He entertains these thoughts of emigration for some time thereafter but never acts on them. Later it is Rome, the Eternal City, that takes the place of a "dream-elsewhere." In 1907, after attending a performance of *Carmen*, he returns to his hotel and writes to his family: "With the sureness of a Roman I took the shortest way home. What a pity one can't live here always! These brief visits leave me with an unappeased longing and a feeling of insufficiency all the way round."[18]

When the hour of forced exile arrives, the Nazi invasion of Austria having compelled the sick old man to leave Vienna for London, he sets out with a twofold heroic identification. The first image he sees in his mind's eye is that of Rabbi Yochanan ben Zachai; after the destruction of the temple of Jerusalem by Titus it was he who asked permission to open in Yabneh the first school devoted to the study of the Torah. Likewise, Freud chooses to save his books and his "child," psychoanalysis. Then, crossing the English Channel, he has a dream. Now that he is finally going to set foot in England, as in his old childhood wish, he sees himself as William the Conqueror who, nine centuries earlier, had made England an asylum for the Jews of the diaspora. And when he arrives in London, one of the first visitors he receives is Chaim Weizmann, the great Zionist leader and future president of the State of Israel, whom he holds in high esteem. His son Martin, who is present as they speak, observes that, far from being tired, Freud is happy and excited.[19]

> If I forget thee, O Jerusalem, let my right hand forget her cunning. If I do not remember thee, let my tongue cleave to the roof of my mouth; if I prefer not Jerusalem above my chief joy.
> —Psalm 137, 5–6

Freud's first mention of the word *Zionist* occurs in a letter to Sabina Spielrein, the context being his deep disappointment in Jung. This woman had played a very special role between the two friends, especially at the time when their friendship ended. Sabina was Jung's patient and also his mistress. It had taken her a long time to recover from the breakup of their romantic relationship, which Jung had instigated. A short time later she married a Jewish doctor, to the great relief of Freud, who sends her an unambiguous letter on the occasion of her announcement that she is pregnant: "I am, as you know, cured of the last shred of predilection for the Aryan cause, and would like to take it that if the child turns out to be a boy he will develop into a stalward Zionist." This is surely a vivid way of distancing himself from the man he had called Joshua and charged with reaching the Promised Land that, as he thought, he himself could view only from afar. In this same letter, he adds: "We are and remain Jews. The others will only exploit us and will never understand or appreciate us."[20] And on the occasion of the Balfour Declaration in December 1917, Freud rejoices at the experiment being tried in Palestine with "the chosen people."[21]

Charmed by the writer Albert Cohen, Freud agrees to take part in a Jewish magazine associated with the Zionist struggle, as he tells Ferenczi on August 6, 1924:

> In recent days I have received an urgent request from Alb. Cohen of Geneva, who is going to publish a Jewish review and wants me to send a contribution. I had previously given my name for the editorial board, and now he has very skillfully seduced me with his statement that Einstein and I are the two most eminent living Jews. What could I do but admit that I was very flattered and promise him something innocuous? I chose "The resistances to psychoanalysis."[22]

It was in the second issue, which appeared on March 15, 1925, that Freud first published this paper, in French. He ended it by wondering whether "the fact that he is a Jew [which he never sought to conceal] may not have had a share in provoking the antipathy of his environment to psychoanalysis."[23]

In 1925, on the occasion of the opening of the Hebrew University in Jerusalem, Freud indicated his interest but expressed his sincere regrets that his state of health made it impossible for him to be present at the celebration. "A University is a place in which knowledge is taught above all differences of religions and of nations, where investigation is carried on, which is to show mankind how far they understand the world around them and how far they can control it. Such an undertaking is a noble witness to the development to which our people has forced its way in two thousand years of unhappy fortune."[24] He agrees to take part in an honorary capacity, since this university is dear to him; he had, in addition, hoped that a chair of psychoanalysis would be created there and offered to his disciple, Max Eitingon.

Freud's clearest statement about Zionism is found in a letter to Professor Thieberger, dated April 25, 1926: "Towards Zionism I have only sympathy, but I make no judgment on it, on its chances of success and on the possible dangers facing it.[25] He thus indicates both a certain reserve and a certain political realism. He also agreed to become an honorary member of Kadimah, a Zionist association of Viennese Jewish students that his son Martin had joined enthusiastically.

His son Ernst, an architect, went to Palestine in 1927 to direct the construction of a house for Chaim Weizmann.[26] According to Ernest Jones, who had spoken with Weizmann in the 1920s and reported it to Freud, Weizmann told him that immigrants arrived in Palestine from Galicia without clothing but with Marx's *Capital* and Freud's *The Interpretation of Dreams* under their arms.[27]

As for the psychoanalysts in Freud's circle, at least three of them proved more than sympathetic to Zionism. Max Eitingon, one of the first foreigners to come to Freud, spent time in Palestine in 1910 before emigrating there in 1933 and founding the Psychoanalytic Society of Palestine. Siegfried Bernfeld campaigned for Jewish Zionist youth in Austria, was secretary to Martin Buber, and (in addition to analytic texts, including some on Freud) published a number of Zionist works and the review *Jerubaal*.[28] David Eder, an English psychoanalyst, was recruited by Weizmann to be the first diplomatic representative of the Zionist executive in Jerusalem and formulated a policy of rapprochement with regard to the Arabs.

A patient, Joseph Wortis, made notes on his psychoanalysis in 1934–1935 that include various conversations he had with Freud on the subject of antisemitism and Zionism. Freud, he says, explained to him that Jews were led to strengthen their bonds with other Jews on account of the external pressures to which they were subject. "As long as Jews are not admitted into Gentile circles, they have no choice but to band together."[29] And, Wortis relates, in connection with the renewal of Palestine Freud said, "I am not much of a Zionist—at least not the way Einstein is, even though I am one of the curators of the Hebrew University in Palestine. I recognize the great emotional force, though, of a Jewish center in the world, and thought it would be a rallying point for Jewish ideals." And he added a subtle comment:

> If it had been in Uganda, it would not have been anything near so good. The sentimental value of Palestine was very great. Jews pictured their old compatriots wailing and praying as in the olden days at the old wall—which by the way was built by Herod, not by Solomon—and felt a revival of their old spirit. I was afraid for awhile, though, that Zionism would become the occasion of a revival of the old religion, but I have been assured by people who have been there that all the young Jews are irreligious, which is a good thing.[30]

During the same period Freud carries on a correspondence with the writer Arnold Zweig, who had just moved to Palestine. Zweig had emigrated out of Zionist conviction but finds himself disappointed as soon as he arrives. He does not adapt to the conditions of life; he lacks material comfort, and Hebrew seems impossible for him to master: he considers himself a German writer, a German European. Freud emphasizes this difference between them: "We hail from there [ancient Palestine]; though one of us considers himself a German as well, the other does not," adding: "When you tell me about your thoughts, I can relieve you of the illusion that one has to be a German. Should we not leave this God-forsaken nation to themselves?"[31]

Yet, though Freud does not identify with German nationalism, he is equally opposed to the Jewish variety and is glad to see Zweig disillusioned with Zionism. By return mail Freud writes: "I know you are cured of your unhappy love of your so-called Fatherland. Such a passion is not for the likes of us."[32] What is understood is: leave nationalism to the Christians.

As the months pass, Zweig complains more and more to Freud, even considering returning to Germany several times, and he asks the advice of his friend back in Vienna. Freud keeps him from "the folly of returning to Eichkamp, . . . that is, to the concentration camp and death," adding: "My passport runs out in April. I do not want to ask the Third Reich for an extension. But I do not want to sever the connection with the German people of my own accord."[33] A week later Freud sends him a long letter of support in which he encourages him to remain where he is—more, no doubt, for reasons of safety than because of Zionist idealism:

> Dear Meister Arnold,
>
> Your letter moved me very much. It is not the first time that I have heard of the difficulties the cultured man finds in adapting himself to Palestine. History has never given the Jewish people cause to develop their faculty for creating a state or a society. And of course they take with them all the shortcomings and vices in the culture of the country they leave behind them into their new abode. You feel ill at ease, but I did not know you found isolation so hard to bear. Firmly based in your profession as artist as you are, you ought to be able to be alone for awhile.
>
> In Palestine at any rate you have your personal safety and your human rights. And where would you think of going? You would find America, I would say from all my impressions, far more unbearable. Everywhere else you would be a scarcely tolerated alien. . . . I really think that for the moment you should remain where you are.[34]

And the following year, on December 20, 1937, Freud writes:

> In your interest I can scarcely regret that you have not chosen Vienna as your new home. The government here is different, but the people in their worship of antisemitism are entirely at one with their brothers in the Reich. The noose around our necks is being

tightened all the time even if we are not actually being throttled. Palestine is still British Empire at any rate; that is not to be underestimated.[35]

Omce again Freud shows his confidence in England. When he is forced to live there himself, however, he speaks quite differently and advises Zweig to choose the United States instead: "In most respects England is better, but it is very difficult to adapt oneself here and in any case you would not have my presence near you for much longer. America seems an Anti-Paradise to me, but it has so much space and so many possibilities and ultimately one does come to belong there."[36]

Space and movement play a special role in Jewish history (exile, diaspora, confinement in the ghetto, wandering, deportation, immigration, return); for psychoanalysis, too, there are always topographies and displacements, transferences, repression, forward movements and resistances, alienness. And for Freud, it is as though the essential point were not to see a Promised Land except from afar. What matters is the freedom to imagine the voyage to another land, a desirable elswhere. We need such an ability, but there is no question of actually departing. Thus, in 1927, when the psychoanalytic community is in crisis over the issue of whether non-physicians should practice analysis, Freud emphasizes the importance of having the different societies arrive at a common decision; otherwise, he writes, "it would destroy the right we have hitherto enjoyed of freedom to emigrate wherever we wish."[37]

Emigration is a privilege, and it is also an inner necessity. What is at issue is not so much leaving one land for another as moving into the interior of one's own psyche with more freedom, traveling toward another world inside, migrating from one culture to another, one language to another, one domain of knowledge to another, from science to poetry, from theory to fiction.

To realize the promise of a visible country is to court disappointment. It is better to sublimate a desire like this or to fulfill it at a distance, through the mediation of friendship, for example. Thus, when his friend Marie Bonaparte, who had such a soothing influence on the last years of his life, goes to Egypt and the Middle East in December 1938, Freud guides her itinerary and identifies with her gaze: "The Sinai isn't worth your interest. You know, the mountain of Yahweh wasn't on the peninsula but in Western Arabia, and a giving of the law on Sinai simply didn't occur. See my Moses, which I alternately find impressive and highly displeasing. It would be a shame to miss Jerusalem." And he confides: "You know, on this trip you'll also be seeing for me, impaired as I am for traveling."[38]

It was not given to him to see Jerusalem with his own eyes. His fidelity to the Jewish tradition did not lead him to embody the invisible temple of his fathers but to inhabit it with words. The man without a country is a man of the book.

NOTES

1. Freud 1933, p. 57.
2. Herzl 1896.
3. Herzl 1896, p. 28.
4. Freud 1900, p. 608.
5. Klein 1985, especially Chapter 3.
6. Letter of May 6, 1926 (Freud 1960, pp. 366–367).
7. Simon 1957, p. 274.
8. Freud 1900, p. 621.
9. Jones 1957, p. 230.
10. Reik 1940, p. 30.
11. Letter of March 30, 1922 in Jones 1957, p. 84.
12. Letter of May 8, 1932, in Freud and Zweig 1970, p. 40.
13. *Vom vaterstädtischen Boden*, literally, "from the soil of the paternal city." Letter of March 11, 1900 (Freud 1954, p. 311).
14. Freud cites the beginning of this verse in his analysis of the dream "My son the Myops" (1900, p. 442).
15. Freud 1900, pp. 441–442. Subsequent citations are from pp. 442–444. See also Anzieu 1959, p. 344.
16. Freud 1992, p. 127.
17. Letter of October 5, 1882 (Freud 1960, pp. 32–33).
18. Letter of September 24, 1907 (Freud 1960, p. 266).
19. M. Freud, 1967, p. 211.
20. Letter of August 28, 1913 (Carotenuto 1984, pp. 120–121).

21. Freud and Abraham 1965, p. 264.

22. Unpublished letter communicated by Judith Dupont, quoted in Chemouni 1988, p. 113 (trans. S. F.).

23. Freud 1925a, p. 222.

24. Freud 1925b, p. 292.

25. Cited in Simon 1957, p. 275.

26. Chemouni 1988, p. 150. A niece joined with Gershom Scholem and others in 1919–1920 to form a small Zionist colony in Munich; see Scholem 1977.

27. Jones 1957, p. 30.

28. See the chapter on Bernfeld in Chemouni 1988.

29. January 17, 1935 (Wortis 1954, p. 144).

30. Wortis 1954, p. 146.

31. Letter to Zweig of August 18, 1932 (Freud and Zweig 1970, p. 40).

32. Letter to Zweig of January 28, 1934 (Freud and Zweig 1970, p. 45).

33. Letter to Freud of February 15, 1936 (Freud and Zweig 1970, p. 121).

34. Letter to Zweig of February 21, 1936 (Freud and Zweig 1970, p. 122).

35. Letter to Zweig (Freud and Zweig 1970, p. 154).

36. Letter to Zweig of March 5, 1939 (Freud and Zweig 1970, p. 178).

37. Letter to Max Eitingon of March 22, 1927, quoted in Jones 1957, p. 294. See also Pontalis 1990, pp. 86–87.

38. Letter of December 27, 1938 in Schur 1972, p. 115 (trans. S. F.).

6

The Man of the Book

Two dates for the death of a father and the birth of a son: Friday, at four in the afternoon, the sixth of Adar 5616 (February 21, 1856) and Tuesday, the first day of the month of Iyar 5616 (May 6, 1856) at 6:30 in the evening. On the commemorative page of his bible—the bilingual Bible illustrated and annotated by the liberal Rabbi Ludwig Philippson—Jacob Freud chose to inscribe in Hebrew, with the German in the margin, these two events of his life: "My father, the late Rabbi Schlomo, son of Rabbi Ephraim Freud, entered into his heavenly abode" and, several weeks later, "My son, Schlomo Sigismund [Sigmund in the German text] was born."

Three marriages; twelve children; a double bilingual inscription; the same name for the rabbi grandfather, learned and cultivated; and a grandson called upon to become so. In giving his newborn son the name of his recently deceased father, as tradition required, Jacob marks this first son of a third marriage (the fourth son after Emmanuel, Philipp, and no doubt a boy who died at a young age) with the wish to see him bring new renown on the family patronym after Rabbi Schlomo and Rabbi Ephraim Freud.[1]

Thus Jacob initiates his son into the study of the Book of Books from his seventh year on. Before it was his first reading primer, the Philippson Bible fascinates the curious child with its sumptuous engravings: scenes of Egypt, Israel, Rome, Persia, and Greece with armed warriors, pagan idols and temples, musical instruments, ancient jewelry and marbles, funerary rites, animals and plants, ruins, coins, and various inscriptions: an entire world of dream and travel.

Jacob, who as a young man had suffered from being merely a wandering Galician Jew, as the records designate him, subject to a number of humiliations and restrictions on his freedom, was very relieved when, in 1848, civil rights were granted to Jews. In this context, he was receptive to the messages of the Philippson Bible, which sought to reconcile traditional orthodoxy with the reformist movement promoting assimilation. If the Rabbi had decided, despite the Mosaic prohibition, to show engravings of gods and illustrate the customs and practices of foreigners, he had done so with a pedagogical intent. He suggested that the reader know and understand the world around him so as to be integrated into it more easily. Jacob chose to bring up his son in a Judaism of the Enlightenment and the movement toward emancipation.

At the same time that it offers an introduction to Jerusalem, the family Torah points the way to Athens and Rome: from now on, the boundary between outside and inside, the visible and the invisible, is blurred. In revealing forbidden images, a desire—ambivalent—is awakened.

At around the age of 6, little Sigmund was also invited by his father to have another troubling experience. For Jacob thought it would be fun, one day, to let the boy and his sister Anna destroy a beautiful book illustrated with color plates, the account of a journey to Persia, probably the work published in 1862 by Dr. Heinrich Brugsch, professor and curator at the Egyptian Museum of Berlin.[2] The young Freud tore it up "leaf by leaf, like an artichoke."[3] Deflowering this volume, with the complicity of his little sister, filled him with the utmost joy.

The happiness of transgression, touching what must not be touched: the book and the other sex. Page and flower. Paper and knowledge become imbued with the delicious and disturbing perfume of these first plastic, visual, tactile, and sexual excitations, forbidden and strangely encouraged. The adult Freud, recording the memory of this first "passion" of his as a bibliophile in association to his dream of the botanical monograph, notes briefly that it was "not easy to justify from the educational point of view!" Indeed, since the inconsistency of his father's attitude, his possible ambivalence with regard to the written word, or the radical distinction he seems to make between biblical texts and profane works, invite the young Freud, from the outset, to take pleasure in the book and to play with it. With the same ludic intensity he discovers the sacredness of the text and the joy of sacrilege. On the one hand, a bible of the Jewish Enlightenment, with anthropological commentaries by Rabbi Philippson and a great many archeological illustrations of all the countries of the Middle East and the Mediterranean basin, including Persia with its art, its idols, its jewels, and its literature[4]: a book to read, study, and respect, an apprenticeship in mastery, knowledge, and fidelity. On the other hand, the Persian journeys described by German scholars of the period. Authorized images, impious images. The first commandment: "Thou shalt not make unto thee any graven image, or the likeness of anything that is in heaven above, or that is in the earth beneath, or that is in the water under the earth."[5] An apprenticeship in the law and in the pleasure of transgression.

The feeling of crumpled pages under his fingers, the bright color of torn pictures, the exaltation of an equivocal shredding: his father's invitation authorizes and erotizes the games of coming to know. What is written is sexual.

The bidding to adhere to the learned tradition of his forefathers is conjoined with permission to betray it. Decipher with the gaze, tear up with the hands: texts are profaned, texts are venerated. Freud belongs to the book, and the book belongs to him: a twofold marriage sealed by his father from childhood on and explicitly confirmed on the day of his thirty-fifth birthday in the dedication in Hebrew, citing Judges 13:25: "Go forth and read my book."

For his thirty-sixth year, which Hebraic tradition considers the symbolic entry into the age of manhood, Jacob invokes his Bible, Numbers 21:17, like a muse charged with inspiring his son: "Spring up, O well; sing ye unto it"—unto him.

In this month of May 1891, Freud finishes writing his thesis on aphasia. His father's wish to see him become a scholar is being fulfilled, but in a secular way. Whether by chance or by personal resolve, to show that new acquisitions of the function of language are localized in the same place as the first language learned, he chooses, as an example of subsequent acquisition, training in foreign languages and learning the Greek and Hebrew alphabets.[6] Athens and Jerusalem are always joined in Freud's thought and desire.

Nine years later, in 1900, the son in turn gives a book to his father: his own book. A posthumous gift, since Jacob Freud passes away in October 1896, a silent offering until the summer of 1908. It is only then that Freud, who has just turned 52, Jacob having been dead almost twelve years, admits the bond of writing that links him to his father. In the preface to the second edition of *The Interpretation of Dreams*, he writes: "This book has a further subjective significance for me personally—a significance which I only grasped after I had completed it. It was, I found, a portion of my own self-analysis, my reaction to my father's death—that is to say, to the most important event, the most poignant loss, of a man's life."[7]

From the Book of Books to the book of dreams (and the dream of writing), from father to son, there were three connections: the reading of the Philippson Bible, ripping the pages from the Persian journey of Heinrich Brugsch, and, probably, the work of the writer Ludwig Börne.

Freud mentions the illustrated bible of his childhood only once in his oeuvre, in association to the last personal dream, the sole dream of childhood anxiety, offered in *The Interpretation of Dreams*: "my beloved mother, with . . . people with birds' beaks." He explains: "The strangely draped and unnaturally tall figures with birds' beaks were derived from the illustrations in Philippson's Bible. I fancy they must have been gods with falcons' heads from an ancient Egyptian funerary relief."[8]

His father's bible, now his own, is at once a book of images and of writing, to be read from left to right in German and right to left in Hebrew, the sacred alphabet and Gothic letters side by side: at the top of each page is the bible story and, below it, the commentaries. Above, the sentences; below, the engravings. See in order to know. Look in order to reflect and interpret. Freud was steeped in this book that showed him the infinite riches of the levels of meaning in a story.

This influence, early and deep, was enlarged by the sexual meaning joined with it.

The happy and disturbing experience of the torn book, deflowered in the company of his little sister, is also mentioned only once by Freud, in association to his dream of the botanical monograph. Like the childhood dream of his mother and the figures with birds' beaks, this dream is interpreted in March 1898, which suggests that, behind the account of the Persian journey, there also lies the Philippson Bible, rich in botanical iconography. Indeed, the first engraving, corresponding to the story of Genesis, is a *Ficus carica*, the third the *Cupressus sempervirens*, the cypress being a sign of immortality. The sixth engraving, chosen to illustrate the story of the Flood, is the *Olea europaica*, of which it is said that, the moment evening falls, the woodpigeon returns to it, an olive branch in its mouth. And, further on, the *Atropa mandagora* and the *Platanus orientalis* or *Pistacia vera*, corresponding to the story of Abraham, Isaac, and Jacob. The many pictures of plants, often accompanied in the commentaries by monographs, have a distinctive feature that must have attracted the gaze of the young Freud: standing out against the Gothic and Hebrew letters, they are all written in Roman characters.

Hidden even further is the influence of the work of Ludwig Börne, and in particular a text, four and a half pages long, entitled "The Art of Becoming an Original Writer in Three Days." Written in 1823, it remained unknown for fifty years, to be revealed in a letter of Freud's to Sandor Ferenczi of April 9, 1919, as he was turning 63:

> I received Börne very early as a present, perhaps for my thirteenth birthday, read him with great enthusiasm, and always had a strong recollection of some of these little essays. Naturally not the one on cryptomnesia. When I reread it, I was astonished at how much some things that are in there correspond almost word for word with some things I have always represented and thought. So he could really be the source of my originality.[9]

This private communication will be discreetly confirmed in Freud's (1920b) paper, "A Note on the Prehistory of the Technique of Analysis," first signed anonymously "F." Speaking of himself in the third person, Freud relates that

> when he was fourteen he had been given Börne's work as a present, that he still possessed the book now, fifty years later, and that it was the only one that had survived from his boyhood. Börne, he said, had been the first author into whose writings he had penetrated deeply. He could not remember the essay in question, but some of the others that were contained in the same volume—such as "A Tribute to the Memory of Jean Paul," "The Artist in Eating," and "The Fool at the White Swan Inn"—kept on recurring to his mind for no obvious reason over a period of years.[10]

Freud is aware that the "apparent originality" of his psychoanalytic technique of free association may well be seen in the light of the "cryptomnesia" Börne mentions at the end of his paper, as cited by Freud:

> And here follows the practical application that was promised. Take a few sheets of paper and for three days on end write down without fabrication or hypocrisy, everything that comes into your head. Write down what you think of yourself, of your wife, of the Turkish War, of Goethe, of Fonk's trial, of the Last Judgment, of your superiors—and when three days have passed you will be quite out of your senses with astonishment at the new and unheard-of thoughts you have had. This is the art of becoming an original writer in three days.

Freud neglects to mention that this advice applies not only to his patients, with the fundamental rule of analytic treatment, but to his own work of putting thoughts into words. And what if, in one of the first exercises in the analysis of spontaneous association to which Freud subjects himself, the famous forgetting of the name of Luca Signorelli, behind the series of the names *Botticelli, Boltraffio, Bosnia, Trafoi,* and *Herzegovina* (*Herr*=Lord), there were also hidden Ludwig Börne, born Loeb Baruch?[11]

In telling about his discovery of these works, Freud gives two different dates: to Ferenczi he writes that it perhaps occurred on his thirteenth birthday, to the public he says he was 14. This hesitation attached to the number thirteen might well disguise the trace of an event traditionally celebrated at that age, the bar mitzvah, the entry for every adolescent boy into the community of men. We have no evidence one way or the other for Freud's having gone through this religious ceremony. But it would be very surprising if his father—who had him circumcised, initiated him into the Torah, and observed the major holidays of the Jewish calendar even when Freud was 18 years old[12]—had not invited his son to this rite of passage.

The complete works of Ludwig Börne, defender of the Enlightenment and champion of Jewish emancipation, could seem to Jacob to be on a continuum with the teachings of Rabbi Philippson and thus the ideal present to mark this symbolic date, all the more so because the writer was, like Jacob's son, born on May 6, though seventy years earlier.

What distress was Freud seeking to escape in burying this memory? The mark of paternal authority? Guilt over wanting to escape his father's Jewish culture? But Börne encouraged him to it, surely beyond what Jacob Freud could have hoped—as was true of Börne's own father, who, it is said, liked to read what his son wrote but would have preferred that it not be written by his son.

Loeb Baruch was born in the Frankfurt ghetto in 1786, to a family of bankers and court Jews. He began by studying medicine, then political science. In Berlin he attended the salon of Henriette Herz, took courses with Schleiermacher, and met Fichte, Schlegel, and Rahel Varnhagen. In 1818, he converted and changed his name in order to found a journal called *Die Wage* (*The Scale*) that dealt with art, theater, and literature but ran into difficulties because it allowed political allusions to slip in. He had to give up the journal and went as an exile to Paris. A brilliant pamphleteer, he wrote in a humorous and satiric vein, as with the texts mentioned by Freud, but also published political writings. He died on February 12, 1837; a monument, made by David, was erected in his memory in the Père-Lachaise cemetery.[13]

Börne was pleased to find how quickly the Jews adopted Western ways, Judaism for him being nothing but "an Egyptian mummy whch looks as if it is alive, but whose corpse refuses to decay."[14] He considered himself a citizen of the world, yet he knew that others did not see him this way: "Some people criticize me for being a Jew, others praise me for so being, still others forgive me for it, but all of them are conscious of it."[15] In an ironic summary, he observed: "As soon as my enemies felt that they were sinking before Börne, they found an anchor in Baruch."[16]

Freud, who had no doubt that one of the resistances encountered by psychoanalysis had to do with his Jewishness, always refused to convert or change his name. Perhaps Börne's experience confirmed him in this resolution: one must draw strength from the status of an excluded minority instead of seeking to escape one's condition. But Freud also hoped to be inscribed in Greco-Roman culture, to assimilate the Western library without losing his affiliation with the people of the Book, adding his culture of reference to his culture of membership instead of subtracting it.

Commenting in 1920 on his rereading of "The Art of Becoming an Original Writer in Three Days," Freud explains that he "was particularly astonished to find expressed in the advice to the original writer" some opinions which he himself had always cherished and vindicated. He goes on to quote the final words of the piece, but the first ones must have resonated just as much for him, especially with regard to his textual and archeological concept of repression:

> The way to become a good original writer in three days has not yet been shown. And yet it's so easy! You don't have to learn anything, but only to unlearn a lot; nothing to come to, but much to forget. The way the world is today, the heads of learned men, and hence also their works, are like the old manuscripts from which you first have to scratch away the boring squabbles of a stepfather of the Church or the twaddle of a monk to get to a classical Roman.[17]

In the books of his childhood, Freud encounters at one and the same time the holy text and its interpretations, words and images, Gothic script, Hebrew letters, and the Greek alphabet. His culture is polymorphous. The Book and the books initiate him into the diversity of feelings, the infinitely complex machinery of the human heart.

Accompanying the Bible, Bruschg, and Börne is the entire Western library.

Freud loves the giants of literature: Homer, Shakespeare, Cervantes, Goethe, the great classics that convey the totality of human experience and the entire palette of emotions. His powerful need to write has its origin in this early passion for books. He is quite ready to admit that he is a bookworm, a library rat.

> *The Three Witches*: Show his eyes and grieve his heart;
>   Come like shadows, so depart.
> (A show of eight kings, the last with a glass in his hand, Banquo's ghost following.)
> *Macbeth*: Thou art too like the spirit of Banquo; down!
>   Thy crown does sear mine eye-balls. And thy hair,
>   Thou other gold-bound brow, is like the first.
>   A third is like the former. Filthy hags!
>   Why do you show me this? A fourth! Start, eyes!
>   What, will the line stretch out to the crack of doom?
>   Another yet! A seventh! I'll see no more:
>   And yet the eighth appears, who bears a glass
>   Which shows me many more; and some I see
>   That two-fold balls and treble scepter carry:
>   Horrible sight! Now, I see, 'tis true;
>   For the blood-bolter'd Banquo smiles on me,
>   And points at them for his.
>   —Shakespeare, *Macbeth* IV.i.110–124.

Freud has a premonition that his works will spring forth from him into infinity, like the fertile line of the kings of Scotland. At age 22, when his preliminary papers on neurology are published, Shakespeare appears beneath his pen to speak of the sense of oddness that comes over him as his first texts come one right after the other. He writes to his friend Wilhelm Knöpfmacher:

> I am also sending you herewith my collected works, not my complete ones as I have reason to suspect, for I am awaiting the correction of a third, and a fourth and fifth keep appearing in my

prescient mind, which is startled by them like Macbeth by the English kings: "What! Will the line stretch out to the crack of doom?"[18]

Macbeth, murderer of Banquo, is terrified to discover the numberless heirs of his rival, killed but victorious after death. Freud identifies with the murderer, even though he is comparing his future writings to the lineage of the victim, offshoots caught between fear and dazzlement, fascination and hate. He finds himself decentered, master and murderer of his books to come. Something always escapes the wish to write.

From the outset, he is aiming at the Collected Works, but, since one text keeps on following the other, will they ever be complete? Terminable work, interminable work, stretching out to the crack of doom—and even beyond, perhaps, as he likes to imagine at the end of his trajectory, in London, 1939: "I am only waiting for *Moses*, which is due to appear in March, and then I need not be interested in any book of mine again until my next reincarnation."[19] An oeuvre without end and without beginning: Freud chooses not to include his pre-analytic texts. *Exeunt* eels, petromyzon, crayfish, aphasia, and cocaine.

In 1887 he tells Fliess: "I am busy writing three papers at the same time,"[20] and, a month later, he writes: "The two papers on brain anatomy and the general characteristics of hysterical affections are going ahead as a relaxation in my spare time to the extent that changes in mood and work permit."[21] In 1888: "Such time and opportunity as there has been for work has gone on a few articles for Villaret, part of the translation of Bernheim's *Suggestion*, and other similar matters not worthy of note."[22] *The Psychopathology of Everyday Life* and the Dora case are being written at the same time: he passes indifferently from one manuscript to the other.

Freud thought that his best work occurred every seven years.[23] During World War I, alone as at the time of the "splendid isolation" of his beginnings, in the course of six feverish, urgent weeks Freud writes twelve papers on metapsychology: "They are war-time atrocities, like a lot of other things," he announces ironically to Karl

Abraham.[24] He continues the following year with *Introductory Lectures on Psycho-Analysis*, writing in his free time: five of the lectures are finished on August 10 in Salzburg, seven on the twenty-seventh in Bad Gastein, nine in Vienna by the end of September: "Two Chinese porcelain dogs are on my desk, laughing at me, I think, when I write."[25]

In the winter of 1917, the mood is somber and the office unheated. His frozen fingers refuse to wield the pen, but, on sunny days, he finishes his introductory lectures and, on the train taking him from Csorbato to Vienna, writes his paper on a childhood memory of Goethe's and then begins work on "The Taboo of Virginity."[26] "I think I have finished with sowing and shall not get to the reaping," he confesses at the end of 1919.[27] But his discouragement is followed by a new effervescence: after "'A Child Is Being Beaten'" he writes the first draft of *Beyond the Pleasure Principle* in two months,[28] rewrites on the eve of his vacation an earlier article found in a drawer, "The 'Uncanny'" and, while he is at it, conceives *Group Psychology and the Analysis of the Ego*, which soon takes on the proportions of a book.[29] In 1927, he "all at once" writes a paper on fetishism, then, in only five days, a work on humor, followed by *The Future of an Illusion*.[30] One summer month in 1929 is enough for him to conceive *Civilization and Its Discontents*. Up to the very last moments of his life, he takes up the pen and writes still more important technical papers: *An Outline of Psycho-Analysis*, which remains unfinished, and, of course, *Moses and Monotheism*,[31] which he lives to see in English translation and finds to be "not an unworthy leavetaking."[32]

Thus, as he intuited at age 26, the line of his work was a very long one, ceaselessly fertile. More than 150 papers and books were born from his pen, not to mention approximately 20,000 letters. This abundance did not impress him; on the contrary, he felt that he had always carefully limited his production: "Self-criticism is not a pleasant gift, but next to my courage it is the best thing I have, and it has exercised a strict selection in what I have published. Without it I could have given three times as much to the world. I treasure it all the more since hardly anyone credits me with it."[33]

But I, that am not shap'd for sportive tricks,
Nor made to court an amorous looking-glass:
I that am rudely stamp'd, and want love's majesty
To strut before a wanton ambling nymph;
I that am curtail'd of this fair proportion,
Cheated of feature by dissembling Nature,
Deform'd, unfinish'd, sent before my time
Into this breathing world, scarce half made up,
And that so lamely and unfashionable,
That dogs bark at me as I halt by them.[34]

Freud's writings extend across literary genres and bend them to his own style: case histories; "the key to dreams"; a collection of jokes; dialogue with an impartial interlocutor; biographies and fragments of autobiography; lessons and lectures; prefaces; translations; theoretical essays; historical, anthropological, literary, and aesthetic pieces; cultural meditations; . . . but not a single novel! And yet (noisy protest and secret pleasure?) Freud confesses that he is a novelist despite himself at the time of the first hysterics in 1893–1895, then strongly denies in 1905 that he is the author of a *roman à clef* with Dora and is "psychoanalytic" for Leonardo in 1910 and "historical" with regard to Moses in 1934—yet at the same time offers each neurotic a novel about his family.[35]

Did Freud ever sense within himself the stirrings of a novelistic fiction? Didn't he dream of writing stories born from his imagination? According to Stekel, Freud spoke to him about this in the course of a walk in the woods at Berchtesgaden: "In my mind, I always construct novels, using my experience as a psychoanalyst; my wish is to become a novelist."[36] And he admitted to the Italian writer Giovanni Papini, who visited him in 1934, that in truth he was "a scientist by necessity and not by vocation," that his nature led him more toward becoming an artist, but that poverty had prevented him from choosing literature: "Ever since childhood, my secret hero has been Goethe. . . . I have been able to win my destiny in an indirect way and have attained my dream: to remain a man of letters, though still in appearance a doctor."[37]

Though these reminiscences may be unreliable, at least the correspondence with Martha shows that Freud was not insensitive to the attractions of literature, as he admits, with a certain coquetry, on the eve of turning 28:

> Here's a surprise for you. Over and again—I don't know how many stories have come into my mind, and one of them, a tale in an oriental guise, has recently taken a pretty definite shape. You will be astonished to hear that I am becoming aware of literary stirrings, when previously I could not have imagined anything further from my mind. Shall I write the thing down, or would it embarrass you to read it? If I do so it will be only for you, but it will not be very beautiful. Also I have very little time just now. Still I believe that if the train of thought comes back it will really get done by itself. In that event I will write it, and you will chuckle to yourself without saying a word about it to anyone.[38]

Did Freud ever put into words his "tale in an oriental guise"? Did he destroy it, along with all his papers, in April 1885, sacrificing to the Sphinx his first dreams of writing?

> I have destroyed all my notes of the past fourteen years, as well as letters, scientific excerpts, and the manuscripts of my papers. . . . They will now have to be thought all over again, and I certainly had accumulated some scribbling. But that stuff settles round me as sand drifts round the Sphinx; soon nothing but my nostrils would have been visible above the paper.[39]

Is this the Egyptian Sphinx of the desert or already the Sphinx of Oedipus, an enigmatic figure echoing the endless line of the kings of Scotland before the eyes of Macbeth?

His desire to write wavers between certainty and hesitation. He is filled with doubt. At one moment he exclaims, "Why didn't I become a gardener instead of a doctor or writer?"[40] But then he confesses how insecure he is with regard to his talent: "I have often felt as though I had inherited all the defiance and all the passions with which our ancestors defended their Temple and could gladly sacrifice my life for one great moment in history. At the same time I always felt so helpless and *incapable of espressing these ardent passions even by a word or a poem.*"[41]

A dejected mood, a brief disappointment—or is he afraid that he cannot find a satisfactory outlet for the ferment roiling inside him? Is he seeking a literary expression for it? He was proud when, after passing his university entrance examinations at 17, he became aware that he had a personal style:

> Finally, my German paper was stamped with an *exc[ellent]*. . . . [M]y professor told me—and he is the first person who has dared to tell me this—that I possess what Herder so nicely calls an *idiotic* style—i.e., a style at once correct and characteristic. I was suitably impressed by this amazing fact and do not hesitate to disseminate the happy event, the first of its kind, as widely as possible—to you, for instance, who until now have probably remained unaware that you have been exchanging letters with a German stylist. And now I advise you as a friend, not as an interested party, to preserve them—have them bound—take good care of them—one never knows.[42]

To our pleasure, his friend Emil Fluss listened to him.

> I am one of those human beings who can be found most of the day between two pieces of furniture, one formed vertically, the armchair, and one extending horizontally, the table, and from these . . . sprang all civilizations. . . . Since this position does not involve all parts of the body in equal measure, and the nobler parts protrude above the table, I am compelled, for the due occupation of both, to engage in two activities: reading and writing.[43]

The appreciation of euphony;[44] the pleasure taken in deflecting words from their usual context or forging new words; the search for clarity, order, and transparency; and the concern for a style appropriate to his aim never leave him, accompanying Freud as far as the darkest reaches of the death instinct: for him, words are always the bearers of enlightenment. The question of how to put his investigations and concepts into form, how to set them forth, preoccupies him and extends over all his pages.

Thus, as early as the *Studies on Hysteria*,[45] Freud announces to Breuer that the primary question before them in presenting their research "is whether we should describe it historically and lead off with all (or two) of the best case histories, or whether, on the other hand, we should start by dogmatically stating the theories we have devised as an explanation."[46] Freud will always have a preference for genetic exposition. This is the pedagogical procedure he had especially admired in Charcot. Charcot was able to improvise his lessons almost entirely, which gave them a "distinctive charm."[47] He thought aloud and had his listeners take part in "the unfolding of his suppositions and investigations." Freud acknowledges that he was "captivated by the storyteller's art as much as by the perspicacity of the observer." He listened to "his little stories that show how a given medical experiment led to a new discovery." The man standing before him was no longer a doctor or an instructor but a "sage." With a touch of nostalgia, Freud recalls his stay in Paris: "Whoever sat one day among his audience will bring back memories of the voice and appearance of the Master and of the fine hours during which the magic of a great personality drew him irrevocably to the interests and problems of neuropathology."

In June 1892 the magic is still at work, and Charcot inspires Freud's way of writing *Studies on Hysteria*: it is in the historic mode, not the dogmatic mode, that he chooses to set forth his ideas. He seeks to reduce the gap between author and reader, explains his approach as faithfully as possible, and is open about his doubts and impasses. He has his readers undertake the journey with him and tries to gain their confidence. He hopes, of course, to prove the accuracy of his observations, but, like his Parisian master, he is not above captivating with the storyteller's art.[48]

The Interpretation of Dreams, too, shows us how Freud's thought developed, as if he were writing before our eyes. His book is nothing but a progressive, and very skillfully conducted, revelation of his principal thesis. His reader is invited to follow him in his progression from shadow to clarity, from the unknown toward a new knowledge. He proceeds step by step up to the full theoretical conclusion.

Freud writes part of his dreambook while on vacation at Berchtesgaden, working in a large, quiet room "with a view of the mountains,"[49] using as a paperweight several archeological figurines. Every day he gathers mushrooms with his children and intends to go to Salzburg as soon as the rain starts in order to track down some ancient Egyptian objects that put him in a good mood and speak to him of faraway times and places: "I have got on so well with my work here, in peace and with nothing to disturb me, and in almost complete health, and in between times I have gone for walks and enjoyed the mountains and woods. . . . After five hours work to-day I have a trace of writer's cramp."

Freud tells Fliess about the plan for his book,

> on the model of an imaginary walk. First comes the dark wood of the authorities (who cannot see the trees), where there is no clear view and it is very easy to go astray. Then there is a cavernous defile through which I lead my readers—my specimens with its [sic] peculiarities, its details, its indiscretions, and its bad jokes—and then, all at once, the high ground and the prospect, and the question: "Which way do you want to go?"[50]

We see here how Freud uses his daily life to foster his scientific creativity. He transforms his most physical experiences and sensations into verbal comparisons and expressions. His abstract formulations are rooted in the metaphors of his intimate life. From the outset Freud does not take them in a figurative sense: archeology, writing, optical observations, or journeys, before becoming bearers of his vision of the unconscious, are literal parts of his personal universe. His metaphors are first his passions.

It is easy to imagine Freud pursuing his theoretical path as he walks through forests and mountains, then, back at his desk, continuing his walk on an abstract level but with the same energy, the same curiosity, the same enthusiasm. From his interest in mushrooms he draws the comparison of the navel of the dream, the point at which it is attached to the Unknown, from his passion for archeology the conviction that the past remains alive and holds a hidden truth that can be brought to light, from his love of literature the most profound knowledge of the human soul. *The Interpretation of Dreams* is conceived as a voyage, a dream walk into the midst of the archaic and oedipal wishes of childhood; it is a return to the maternal landscape. Freud is at once in his mother's womb, in the womb of his pregnant wife, and himself the bearer of a child about to be born: his dreamchild.

The writing of his oeuvre, the originality of its composition, has to do with his very personal way of moving constantly from one conceptual space to another, from the pleasure of childhood to the seriousness of the adult. And it has to do with his ability to travel from the visual to the virtual, the everyday to the speculative, to mingle science and autobiography, to occupy in a fertile back-and-forth two positions that his research training taught him to keep clearly separate: the position of the scientist and the position of the artist. In a letter to Ferenczi he admirably sums up his process of creation: "The sequence of a bold stroke of imagination and an implacable critique in the name of reality."[51] This ability to play is one he shares with children and writers.[52]

In *The Psychopathology of Everyday Life* Freud compares style to the mechanism of the slip of the tongue—both reveal the author's unconscious:

> A clear and unambiguous manner of writing shows us that here the author is at one with himself; when we find a forced and involved expression which (to use an apt phrase) is aimed at more than one target, we may recognize the intervention of an insufficiently worked-out, complicating thought, or we may hear the stifled voice of the author's self-criticism.[53]

Freud is quite prepared to be critical of himself and is rarely satisfied with his own style. He has within him a hidden sense of form, an appreciation for beauty, a seeking after "perfection."[54]

The question of case histories, in particular, preoccupies him greatly. He considers that he has not found an irreproachable and exemplary way of reconstructing them, but it seems important to him not to give up the attempt.[55] During the Wednesday evening meetings, Freud sometimes gives advice to his disciples. Impelled by pedagogic duty, he suggests, for example, that Sadger present his work a bit more attractively.[56] On another occasion, Freud emphasizes that unformulated case histories have not been fully thought through, concluding that a careful and yet artistic exposition, as in his presentation of the Dora case, is the only acceptable procedure.[57]

Freud constantly faces the problems inherent in writing about a knowledge of the invisible, accessible only through the zigzags, quantum leaps, oblique pathways, and winding passages of unconscious associations. He has to admit that linear exposition is not very appropriate for the descriptions of psychic processes, which are intertwined and unfold simultaneously in different psychic strata.[58] Freud is not intimidated by doubts or obstacles: he describes himself as an explorer braving wild oceans or a chemist handling explosive materials. Attracted by novelty and uncertainty, he is not one of those "believers" who require scientific discourse to serve as a "catechism" for them.[59] It is clear to him that "[i]n developing a new science, one has to make its theories vague. You cannot make things clear-cut. But when you write, the public demands that you make things definite, else they think that you do not know what you are saying."[60] Attentive to this adventurous aspect of his intellectual approach, Freud, like a mountain guide, warns his reader about pitfalls, preparing him to leap into the unknown, the uncertain: "If we have the courage to proceed in the same way, we shall be setting forth on a path which will lead us first to something unexpected and incomprehensible, but which will perhaps, by a devious route, bring us to a goal."[61]

Since he likes to speak directly to his readers, Freud imagines that they fall into three temperamental categories: "the sceptical, the optimistic, and the ambitious."[62] He seeks to win the reader's trust and win his conviction; guessing the problems that will arise in his mind and the nature of his criticism, he tries to reply point by point. He takes his resistances into account, as though he were one of his patients in analysis, and no doubt hopes to be read in turn with a certain associative freedom. Here, for example, are some of his remarks to the reader in his *Introductory Lectures on Psycho-Analysis*: "You will protest with some annoyance . . . . I should reply: Patience,

Ladies and Gentlemen! I think your criticism has gone astray. . . . That is what I should say in order to retain your interest. . . ."[63] "I should like to invite you to follow me along another track."[64] "You will break off at that, but only to take up your resistance at another point."[65] And finally he makes clear what his didactic aim is: "I could not pretend to make you into experts; I have only tried to stimulate and enlighten you."[66]

At several points along the way, Freud discusses his manner of presenting things and agrees that it is not always easy to realize his initial goals, since in the very material he is treating there is "something . . . which takes charge of one and diverts one from one's first intentions."[67] Poets speak of inspiration, grace, or the Muse, Freud of this "something," the unconscious.

In *Beyond the Pleasure Principle*, he puts his cards on the table and gives warning that what is about to follow is "speculation, which the reader will consider or dismiss according to his individual predilection." He reveals what moves his pen and perhaps solicits the reader's interest: "It is further an attempt to follow out an idea consistently, out of curiosity to see where it will lead."[68] He is not afraid to call his theorization of individual or collective psychic processes a theoretical fiction, vision, or "scientific myth."[69] "'So muss denn doch die Hexe dran!'—the Witch Metapsychology. Without metapsychological speculation and theorizing—I had almost said 'phantasying'—we shall not get another step forward."[70]

When he is walking into unknown territory, hell and literature are never very far away. Goethe, with his Faust and Mephistopheles, often lends support to Freud's boldness. At the end of *Beyond the Pleasure Principle*, Freud sketches a little dialogue with his reader, imagining that the latter is questioning him about his own conviction regarding the hypotheses he has set forth. He replies that he does not know the extent to which he believes in them, but that it seems to him that scientific curiosity allows one to "throw oneself into a line of thought and to follow it wherever it leads, . . . or, if the reader prefers, as an *advocatus diaboli*, who is not on that account himself sold to the devil."[71] And again he turns to a poet, Rückert, and to the Bible, to console himself for the slowness with which scientific knowledge is advancing: "'What we cannot reach flying we must reach limping. . . . The Book tells us it is no sin to limp.'"[72]

> Again ye come, ye hovering forms! I find ye,
> As early to my clouded sight ye shone!
> Shall I attempt this once to seize and bind ye?
>
> —Goethe, *Faust*[73]

In 1930, the Goethe Prize awarded by the city of Frankfurt-am-Main was given to "the scholar, writer, and warrior, Sigmund Freud." At the same time Walter Muschg's study *Freud écrivain* appeared, saluting Freud's "spontaneous tendency to narration, an innate sensual love of the word, a feeling for metaphor, auditory and rhythmic sensitivity, the union of poetry and the daily life of language."[74] This historian of literature finds in Freud a need to write that is stronger than his need to speak, perhaps even to act, and sees him above all as a powerful creator of language, one who reveals a rare unity of substance and form. Freud's writings are inhabited by a multitude of compelling figures: Dora and Little Hans, obviously, but also a young married couple, Freud's friend Otto, a Viennese professor—as well as Faust, Oedipus, Hamlet, Lady Macbeth, and all the literary characters Freud loves to bring onstage in his own works, along with his intelligent grandson (the child with the spool) and of course the protagonist, the modest and omnipresent hero, the author himself.

"That Freud forged his own destiny is already sufficiently proved by the work of art he created in the element of language," declares Binswanger in honor of his friend's eightieth birthday,[75] and, ten years earlier, Alfred Döblin had declared, "Here someone is speaking who has something to say."[76] Thus, in the last years of his life, Freud was praised as an artist, a master writer; he accepted this, although earlier he had several times understood such praise as a form of resistance to psychoanalysis.[77]

A speech given by Thomas Mann[78] (who was avidly read by Freud) on May 8, 1936 in Vienna, then on June 14 in his vacation home, made a strong impression on him: the novelist describes the scientist as a knight between death and the devil and speaks of his highly evocative prose style. For Mann, Freud was an artist and, like Schopenhauer, a European writer.

Einstein also paid homage to the stylist: "I quite specially admire your achievement [*Moses and Monotheism*], as I do with all your writings, from a literary point of view."[79] As for his biographer, Ernest Jones, he finds that Freud's Viennese grace and suppleness add a great deal to the charm of his style. Jones sums up Freud's twofold talent as follows: "If William James wrote textbooks of psychology as if they were novels and his brother Henry wrote novels as if they were textbooks of psychology, Freud may be said to have combined the two aims in an enchanting degree."[80]

> "My own immortal works have not yet been written."
> —Sentence uttered by Freud in a dream[81]

Why does Freud write? This question would make no sense if Freud himself had not tried to answer it from time to time in the context of the bonds of friendship and writing that accompany his life. To Silberstein, the friend of his youth, he had revealed the crucial stakes of writing. When he was over 50 he was still full of enthusiasm and an almost Romantic impetuosity: "I admire you for being able to write this way," he confides to Pfister, "so gently, humanely, full of consideration, so objectively, so much more for the reader than against the enemy. . . . But I couldn't write like that, I'd rather write nothing, that is; in fact I write nothing. I could only write in order to free *my* soul, to put forward emotion."[82]

Like all artists and writers, Freud likes to think of himself as the father of his works; like inventors and discoverers, "he would recall the myth of Adam, who, when God brought the creatures of Paradise before him to be distinguished and named, may have experienced to the fullest degree . . . intellectual enjoyment."[83]

To write is to invent the world, to give one's name to a new territory, an island, a star, an area of the brain, a plant. To write is to conquer death and win for oneself a life after life. But Freud is no fool.

Stronger than this feast of immortality is an immediate need, an inner necessity, that guides his hand on the paper:

> No one writes to achieve fame, which anyhow is a very transitory matter, or the illusion of immortality. Surely we write first of all to satisfy something within ourselves, not for other people. Of course when others recognize one's efforts it increases the inner gratification, but nevertheless we write in the first place for ourselves, following an inner impulse.[84]

One summer day in 1929, when he has just finished *Civilization and Its Discontents*, Freud explains to his friend Lou, with a touch of coquetry and lightheartedness, the basic obviousness of his experience of writing: "But what else can I do? One can't smoke and play cards all day, I am no longer much good at walking, and most of what there is to read doesn't interest me anymore. So I wrote, and in that way the time passed quite pleasantly."[85]

> My only consolation, when I went upstairs to sleep, was that Mama would come to kiss me when I was in bed. But this goodnight was so brief, and she went back down so quickly, that the moment I heard her coming up, then when in the corridor with the double door there passed the light sound of her blue muslin garden dress, on which hung little strings of braided straw, was a painful moment for me. It announced what was to follow, when she would have left me, when she would have gone back downstairs.
>
> —Proust[86]

A tireless walker, Freud travels through the pages of his books and letters with the same intensity, the same effervescence, the same haste that take hold of him when he crosses forests and mountains or goes back and forth to his beautiful Italy. But he has not reflected very much on these ardent and intimate pleasures; he has lived them, journeys and writings often intermingled, without especially wanting to single out the unconscious part. Some notes scattered here and there speak of a connection between the acts of writing and urinating. Freud, who did not much care for America, went as far as to claim that, because he suffered from prostate trouble there, what he wrote at that time had also deteriorated.[87] In *Inhibitions, Symptoms, and Anxiety*, the first examples he gives are those that he can feel most distant from and that at the same time cause the most suffering: no longer being able to write with the fingers nor walk with the feet. The two functions, the two pleasures, are as one for him: "As soon as writing, which entails making a liquid flow out of a tube onto a piece of white paper, assumes the significance of copulation, or as soon as walking becomes a symbolic substitute for treading upon the body of mother earth, both writing and walking are stopped because they represent the performance of a forbidden sexual act."[88]

If writing is associated with filiation and murder, it also arises from a dream of incest and from the wish to nestle into words as one once did into the warmth—now lost—of the first bonds.

> Writing was in its origin the voice of an absent person; and the dwelling-house was a substitute for the mother's womb, the first lodging, for which in all likelihood man still longs, and in which he was safe and felt at ease. [*Civilization and its Discontents*][89]

NOTES

1. Mijolla 1981.
2. See Fourton 1981.
3. This and the following two citations are from Freud 1900, p. 172.
4. Pfrimmer 1982, pp. 372–373.
5. Exodus 20:4.
6. Freud 1891.
7. Freud 1900, p. xxvi.
8. Freud 1900, p. 583.
9. In Jones 1955, p. 344.
10. Like the following three citations regarding Börne, this is from Freud 1929, p. 265.
11. Freud 1896b, pp. 291–295. Baruch means "blessed" in Hebrew and is the first word of prayers: "*Baruch ata Adonai* ("Blessed art thou, Lord).
12. Freud 1992, p. 63.
13. My information on Börne comes from Poliakov 1968, and from the *Encyclopaedia Judaica* and *Brockhaus* of 1901. Hannah Arendt (1938) cites him in

her book on Rahel Varnhagen, and Jones (1953, p. 272) notes that Freud went to visit Börne's grave in Paris. In a letter to Silberstein of March 7, 1875, Freud indicates that he knows the work of Karl Grün on Börne (Freud 1992, p. 96).

14. Poliakov 1968, p. 398. In *Moses and Monotheism* (1939) Freud speaks of the Jewish religion as a sort of fossil.

15. Poliakov 1968, p. 356.

16. Poliakov 1968, p. 400.

17. Börne 1823, p. 124 (trans. S. F.).

18. Letter of August 6, 1878 (Freud 1960, p. 6). His very first published works are *"Über den Ursprung der hinteren Nervenwurzeln im Rückenmark von Ammocoetes (Petromyzon Planeri)"* ("On the Origin of the Posterior Nerve Roots in the Spinal Cord of Ammocoetes"), *"Beobachtungen über Gestaltung und feineren Bau der als Hoden beschriebenen Lappenorgane des Aals"* ("Observations on the Formation and Fine Structure of the Lobed Organs of the Eel, Described as Testicles"), and *"Über Spinalganglien und Rückenmark des Petromyzon"* ("On the Spinal Ganglia and Spinal Cord of Petromyzon") (1877a, b, 1878).

19. Letter of March 5, 1939, in Freud and Zweig 1970, p. 178.

20. Letter of November 24, 1887, in Freud 1954, p. 52.

21. Letter of December 28, 1887, in Freud 1954, p. 53.

22. Letter of May 28, 1887, in Freud 1954, p. 56.

23. Jones 1955, p. 396.

24. Letter of August 1, 1915, in Freud and Abraham 1965, p. 239.

25. Letter of August 19, 1915, in Freud and Abraham 1965, p. 241.

26. 1917a,b.

27. Letter of December 15, 1919, in Freud and Abraham 1965, p. 289.

28. 1919b, 1920c.

29. 1919a, 1921. See Jones 1957, pp. 38–43.

30. 1927a,b,c.

31. 1938a, 1939.

32. Jones 1957, p. 276.

33. Letter to Ferenczi of October 17, 1910, in Jones 1955, p. 455.

34. This monologue, spoken by Gloucester in Shakespeare's *Richard III*, is cited in Freud 1916b, p. 314.

35. "Family Romances," 1908a.

36. Stekel 1950, p. 66.

37. Cited in Ruitenbeek 1973, pp. 99, 101.

38. Letter to Martha of April 1, 1884, in Jones 1957, p. 418.

39. Letter to Martha of April 28, 1885, in Freud 1960, pp. 140–141.

40. Letter to Martha of July 13, 1883, in Freud 1960, p. 40.

41. Letter to Martha of February 2, 1886, in Freud 1960, pp. 202–203, emphasis added.

42. Letter to Emil Fluss of June 16, 1873, in Freud 1960, p. 4.

43. Letter to Eduard Silberstein of August 13, 1874, in Freud 1992, pp. 48–49.

44. Jones related that he asked Freud one day why he used the word *Narzismus* instead of *Narzissismus*, which would have been more correct. Freud's "aesthetic

sense was stronger than his philological conscience, and he replied simply, 'I don't like the sound of it.'" (Jones 1955, p. 402).

45. Breuer and Freud 1893–1895.

46. Freud 1892, p. 147. Freud sets forth very clearly the advantages and disadvantages of these two modes of exposition in one of his very last papers, "Some Elementary Lessons in Psycho-Analysis":

> An author who sets out to introduce some branch of knowledge—or, to put it more modestly, some branch of research—to an uninstructed public must clearly make his choice between two methods or techniques.
>
> It is possible to start out from what every reader knows (or thinks he knows) and regards as self-evident, without in the first instance contradicting him. An opportunity will soon occur for drawing his attention to facts in the same field which, though they are known to him, he has so far neglected or insufficiently appreciated. Beginning from these, one can introduce further facts to him of which he has no knowledge and so prepare him for the necessity of going beyond his earlier judgments, of seeking new points of view and of taking new hypotheses into consideration. In this way one can get him to take a part in building up a new theory about the subject and one can deal with his objections to it during the actual course of the joint work. A method of this kind might well be called *genetic*. It follows the path along which the investigator himself has travelled earlier. In spite of all its advantages, it has the defect of not making a sufficiently striking effort upon the learner. He will not be nearly so much impressed by something which he has watched coming into existence and passing through a slow and difficult period of growth as he would be by something that is presented to him ready-made as an apparently self-contained whole.
>
> It is precisely this last effect which is produced by the alternative method of presentation. This other method, the dogmatic one, begins straight away by stating its conclusions. Its premises make demands upon the audience's attention and belief and very little is adduced in support of them. And there is then a danger that a critical listener may shake his head and say, "All this sounds most peculiar: where does the fellow get it from?" [Freud 1938b, p. 281, emphasis in original]

47. This and the following citations in this paragraph are from Freud 1984, p. 56 (trans. S. F.).

48. See also his homage to Charcot (Freud 1893).

49. This account of the stay at Berchtesgaden are from letters to Fliess of August 1, 6, and 20, 1899, in Freud 1954, pp. 288–292.

50. Letter to Fliess of August 6, 1899, in Freud 1954, p. 290.

51. Letter of April 8, 1915, cited in Grubrich-Simitis 1986, p. 113 (trans. S. F.).

52. See Freud 1907b on literary creation and daydreams as continuations of child's play and 1920c, Chapter 2, on child's play as one of the first normal activities of the psychic apparatus.

53. Freud 1901, p. 101.

54. Letter to Fliess of September 21, 1899, in Freud 1954, p. 298.

55. See for example, Freud 1905b, pp. 7–8 (Dora); 1909, pp. 155–156 (Rat Man); 1914c, p. 13 (Wolf Man).

56. Meeting of December 21, 1910 (Nunberg and Federn 1974, p. 104).

57. Meeting of April 21, 1909 (Nunberg and Federn 1967, p. 210).

58. Freud 1920a, p. 160.

59. Freud 1920c, p. 64.

60. Blanton 1971, pp. 47–48.

61. Freud 1913b, pp. 293–294.

62. Freud 1937b, p. 223.

63. Freud 1916–1917, pp. 26–27.

64. Freud 1916–1917, p. 36.

65. Freud 1916–1917, p. 49.

66. Freud 1916–1917, p. 463.

67. The passage continues: "Even such a trivial achievement as the arrangement of a familiar piece of material is not entirely subject to an author's own choice; it takes what line it likes, and all one can do is to ask oneself after the event why it has happened in this way and no other" (Freud 1916–1917, p. 379).

68. Freud 1920c, p. 24.

69. Freud 1921, p.135.

70. Freud 1937b, p. 225.

71. Freud 1920c, p. 59.

72. Freud 1920c, p. 64.

73. This passage was quoted by Freud in his address at Goethe House, Frankfurt (Freud 1930, p. 209), read there by Anna Freud on August 28, 1930, on the occasion of his receiving the Goethe Prize.

74. Like the previous citation, this is from Muschg 1930, p. 159 (trans. S. F.). Muschg's paper originally appeared in French, along with a paper by Schotte (1930). Relatively little has been written on Freud's style. See Baudry 1984, Goldschmidt 1988, Holt 1965, Lacoste 1981, Mahoney 1987, 1989, Roustang 1977, Schönau 1968.

75. Binswanger 1970, p. 200 (trans. S. F.).

76. Cited by Muschg 1930, p. 205, trans. S. F.

77. This is the case with Havelock Ellis, to whom Freud replies in "A Note on the Prehistory of the Technique of Analysis" (1920b). When his thesis of aphasia was published, Freud confided to his sister-in-law Minna his disappointment that Breuer had said nothing to him about it, except to soothe him by praising his style. (Letter of July 13, 1891, in Freud 1960, p. 229.)

78. Mann 1936.

79. Cited in Jones 1957, p. 243.

80. Jones 1955, p. 210.

81. Freud 1900, p. 453.

82. Letter of January 24, 1910, in Freud and Pfister 1963, p. 30, emphasis in original.

83. Freud 1893, p. 13.

84. Said to Marie Bonaparte, as cited in Jones 1955, p. 397.

85. Freud and Andréas-Salomé 1985, p. 181.

86. Proust 1913, p. 154 (trans. S. F.).

87. See the letters to Ernest Jones of January 27, 1910, in Jones 1955, p. 60 and to Marie Bonaparte of August 20, 1938, in Jones 1957. In the second of these, he notes:

> Perhaps it will interest you to learn (and to see) that my handwriting has come back to what it used to be. For weeks it has been disturbed as the result of my last attack of urinary trouble which is now subsiding. There is an inner connection between urinating and writing, and assuredly not only with me. When I noticed the first signs of prostatic hypertrophy in the functioning of the bladder, in 1909 in New York, I suffered at the same time from writer's cramp, a condition foreign to me until then. [p. 236]

88. Freud 1926b, p. 90.

89. Freud 1929, p. 91.

7

In the Witch's Kitchen

Late at night, Freud sits down at his desk, seized with an urgent desire to write. He scribbles with a single stroke, decisive, quick, broad, without erasures. His hand glides over the page, carried along by the pen. Curious to see what will spring forth, he lets the words flow, the ideas arrange themselves, the detail of his thoughts take final form. He invents, "abashed and miserable." So many things are "stirring" inside him.[1] In the exaltation of autumn 1895, he fills two notebooks in a few days. As if in "child's play,"[2] he overcomes the accumulated problems he has not been able to resolve before. He seems to have "found the secret."[3]

On September 15, in the train taking him back from Berlin, where he visited his friend Wilhelm Fliess, Freud opens his suitcase, takes out some paper—it is already too dark for reading, and not yet dark enough to go to sleep—and, bumping along in the dim light of the railway compartment, begins to write the first draft of *Project for a Scientific Psychology*.[4] Back in Vienna, he uses each moment of free time to give form to the whirlwind of ideas that rushes in on him. In the letter to Fliess of October 20, he describes, in his metaphorical fashion, the inspiration that took hold of him, the mechanism of his creativity:

> One strenuous night last week, when I was in the stage of painful discomfort in which my brain works best, the barriers suddenly

lifted, the veil dropped, and it was possible to see from the details of neurosis all the way to the very conditioning of consciousness. Everything fell into place, the cogs meshed, the thing really seemed to be a machine which in a moment would run of itself.[5]

Entry on an equal footing into "the witch's kitchen,"[6] the chance to stand alongside the pot as the work in progress is cooking: this is what we are offered in Freud's voluminous correspondence with Fliess from 1887 to 1904 and with Emil Fluss, Eduard Silberstein, and Martha Bernays from 1871 to 1886. After 1904, it is with Jung, Pfister, Ferenczi, Andréas-Salomé, Abraham, Zweig, and Marie Bonaparte that the epistolary dialogue continues, a correspondence in which not only his work is rooted but also his running commentary on it. Written during the gestation and birth of his books, these thousands of letters,[7] of which only a part have been published, reveal the heart of his approach. The letters give us intimate access to Freud's intellectual workshop.

The oeuvre itself, from *Studies on Hysteria* to *Moses and Monotheism*, describes its own composition. The genealogy of Freud's texts takes us onto the construction site of work that is always in progress, never complete, and likewise the task of writing that accompanies it. Freud does not remove his basting threads. He invites the reader to come behind the wings, right into the artist's dressing room. Investigating the unconscious, Freud in turn sees himself as called upon to investigate the way he accounts for it and describes it to his readers. From the first volume to the last, like the red thread in the rigging of the English Navy, runs the question of style. The involuntary appearance of novelistic style in the serious exposition of science, the constant dialogue with poets who know that there is more in heaven and earth than academic wisdom can dream of, the fear of encountering his double in the guise of a writer, the art of embroidering images and comparisons ad infinitum so as to penetrate behind the mask of the psyche: this is what appears throughout Freud's writings. The experience of writing and Freud's relation to it forms part of his analyses, is interwoven in the fabric of his texts, gives shape to his thought, and embodies what he hopes to demonstrate. Scholarship or poetry, science or fiction, psychoanalysis transcends contradiction and carves out a third path, the path of "a theoretical fiction."[8]

Freud's work is the work of writing, the work of a writer. He lives on intimate terms with words, with their magic, their images. For him, language—the German language—is not "an article of clothing" but his "own skin."[9] Five months before his death, he recognizes that "not even my pen is the same; it has left me like the doctor and other external organs."[10] From language to skin, pen to hand, there is no gap, no distance, but an essential, organic continuity. For Freud, to write is to draw sustenance from this bodily contact.

> The potent core
> Of nature lore
> From all that seek it shrinking!
> Who's never thought
> Finds it unsought,
> Possesses it unthinking.
>
> —Goethe[11]

Unsettled and amazed, Freud discovers that he is being led along by the very object of his investigation: he is tracking the unconscious, but it is the unconscious that holds him at its mercy and dictates what he writes. On June 20, 1898, he confides to his friend Fliess that his dream-book "is going curiously; it is nearly finished; written as if in a dream."[12] On July 7, he explains: "At the beginning of a paragraph I never knew where I would end up."[13] Some time earlier, he had remarked: "It is only in writing that I can fill in all the details."[14] In 1911, despite his reluctance to get embroiled in matters of religion, Freud dives into it: It is the order [that is, the command] of unconscious connections"[15]; two days later, he confesses: "I am entirely *Totem and Taboo*."[16]

The writing of his works is not the last phase of research carried out elsewhere, the final version, necessary for conveying his results to the public. What gives rise to the work is the process of writing, with its meanders, its obstacles, its sudden surges, its multiple tributaries, and its deltas. A great letter writer from adolescence on, Freud has gotten into the habit of thinking as he writes and of writing to work out his thoughts. No impression, no emotion, no idea, no experience has really become his own before being set down on paper. Thus Freud lets himself be carried away by words and eagerly welcomes their outpouring: "When I sit down to work and take my pen in hand, I am always curious about what will come forth, and that drives me irresistibly to work."[17]

Like a dream, his writing comes forth from the wellspring of the unknown in his unconscious. He dives into it and draws inspiration there. When he receives the young Bruno Goetz, after having read poems of his that he found beautiful but obscure, he tells him: "You are hiding behind your words instead of letting yourself be carried by them. Head high! You have no reason to be afraid of yourself."[18]

When he gets involved in writing, Freud takes indirect routes. He likes to cite a passage he attributes to Oliver Cromwell: "You never get so high as when you don't know where you are going."[19] These zigzag paths, like those of the knight in chess, turn out to be the surest means of inviting his patients to find their repressed truths and to draw the most fruitful theoretical conclusions from them. And yet this discovery never ceases to surprise him. As he tells Jung, "I see that you go about working in the same way as I do; rather than take the obvious path that leads straight ahead, you keep your eye peeled for one that strikes your fancy. This is the best way, I think; afterwards one is amazed at the logical sequence in all these digressions."[20]

In the fever of his self-analysis and his first discoveries, Freud tells Fliess how the unconscious seizes hold of him, inspires him in waves: "Inside me there is a seething ferment, and I am only waiting for the next surge forward."[21] And, fifteen days later: "Herewith a few fragments thrown up on the beach by the last surge. . . . Thus the whole thing grows in my anticipation and gives me the greatest pleasure."[22]

The Interpretation of Dreams, an oneiric self-portrait and the first psychoanalytic manifesto, links the man Freud and his creation in a single movement: "None of my works has been so completely my own as this; it is my own dung-heap, my own seedling."[23] Freud has carried it in his body, suffering from headaches, stomachaches, cardiac problems, and moments of depression throughout the writing process. He has protected the fruit of his gestation and is afraid lest he be too quick to reveal certain theoretical innovations: to do so "would be like sending a six-months female embryo to a ball."[24] A bit later, he tells Fliess that "after the terrible pangs of the last few weeks, a new piece of knowledge was born to me."[25] *The Interpretation of Dreams* is his "dream-child."[26]

Freud oscillates between metaphors of childbirth and those of romantic conquest. Sending Fliess his bibliography, he asks him to consider *il catologo delle belle*, the catalog of beautiful women, an allusion to the aria in which Leporello lists all of Don Juan's seductions.[27] Working on *Totem and Taboo*, Freud describes himself as being in labor: "There are a great many things boiling in my head, but they are very slow to come out." The task is greater than he had imagined: "I feel as if I had intended only to start a little liaison and then discovered that at my time of life I have to marry a new wife."[28] And a little while later another book-child sees the light of day: "The Moses of Michelangelo," published anonymously at first and only later "legitimized," feels to him like "a love-child."[29]

This writing along with the unconscious engages Freud in a battle between light and darkness: "I have never yet imagined anything like my present spell of intellectual paralysis. Every line I write is torture. . . . I open all the doors of my senses and take nothing in. . . . I have been through . . . odd states of mind not legible to consciousness—cloudy thoughts and veiled doubts, with barely here and there a ray of light."[30] And at the beginning of 1899: "After the fall of the meteor gleams a light that brightens the gloomy sky for a long while thereafter. For me it is not yet extinguished. In this brightness, then, I suddenly glimpsed several things."[31]

He has to learn to trust these alternate moods of dark clouds and bright flashes that pass through him. Sometimes interesting thoughts buzz in his head and then flee again without his making any effort to hold onto them, because he knows that their appearance in consciousness, followed by their disappearance, means nothing with regard to their ultimate destiny. He cannot force himself to work: "I have to wait until things move inside me and I experience them."[32]

At other times, however, he is devastated by moments of blockage, stagnation, and resistance that make him doubt his talent, as though these hindrances reminded him all too clearly that, although his way of writing is that of a poet, he himself is not one. In a letter to Fliess dated April 19, 1894, he writes: "As I was so completely unable to work, it was painful to realize that in case of chronic illness I could not count on being able to do scientific work. . . . 'The present state of knowledge of the neuroses' was abandoned in the middle of a sentence, and everything is as it was in the Sleeping Beauty's castle when the catalepsy overtook it."[33]

Sixteen years later, despite his publications and successes, he still has the same feeling. As he explains to Pastor Pfister:

> I really can't imagine that a life without work would be comfortable for me; fantasizing and work are one and the same for me and nothing else is fun for me. That would be a recipe for happiness, if it were not for the horrible thought that productivity is entirely dependent on one's being in the right mood. What can one begin on a day, or during a period of time, in which thoughts fail one or words don't come? It's impossible to stop trembling at this possibility. And so I have . . . a secret request: just no illness, no impairment of my capacity for achievement by physical suffering, Let us die in harness, as King Macbeth says.[34]

And he confides to his friend Lou Andréas-Salomé:

> I should have been sure of myself throughout my life if I could have been sure of my productive capacity at all times and in all moods. Unfortunately, this has never been the case. There have always been days in between when nothing would come and when I have been in danger of losing all ability to work and to struggle, owing to certain minor fluctuations in mood and physical health. A most unsuitable condition for one who is no artist and doesn't aim at being one.[35]

It is not, of course, enough for the unconscious to encourage the irruption of major ideas, since a dazzling moment may be followed by disillusionment, as Freud tells Ferenczi in connection with his papers on metapsychology: "The thing resisted any depiction and presented such frightful gaps and difficulties that I broke off."[36]

On several occasions he tries to force himself, to "go out to meet" ideas[37] instead of waiting for them to come to him, but his temperament is against this. Freud describes himself as an "impulsive"[38] and "intuitive"[39] researcher, not a systematic and inductive one; he ascribes this to the "fragmentary" nature of his experiences and the "sporadic" nature of his inspiration.[40]

To express how hard it is to give form to the intuitions that his unconscious presents to him, Freud uses metaphors of warfare, especially in 1914. He describes his work to Ferenczi in these terms: "I have fared in this matter as the Germans have in the war. The first successes were surprisingly easy and great, and they thus tempted me to continue, but now I have arrived at such hard and impenetrable things that I am not sure of getting through."[41] Two weeks later he uses the same imagery: "I am living, as my brother says, in my private trench; I speculate and write, and after hard battles have got safely through to the first line of riddles and difficulties. Anxiety, hysteria, and paranoia have capitulated. We shall see how far the successes can be carried forward."[42]

But, whatever the obstacles, whether flying or limping Freud pursues his course and puts his whole soul into it. A man like him "cannot live without a hobby-horse, a consuming passion—in Schiller's words, a tyrant." And, he adds, "I have found my tyrant, and in his service I know no limits."[43]

Freud tries to know the psyche with an almost sensual passion. His exploration of a new domain of knowledge passes through the deepest intimacy with his object: "There is something in the very material that pushes me forward, deeper into sexual symbolism, into the utter dedication, the boldness, of being on familiar terms with the unconscious."[44]

Right up to the end, beyond difficulties and disappointments and despite the hypothesis of the death instinct, he maintains an intact

curiosity and an intense wish to penetrate and conquer the object of
his investigation.

> Why do I o'er my papers once more bend?
> Ask not too closely, dearest one, I pray:
> For, to speak truth, I've nothing now to say;
> Yet to thy hands at length 'twill come, dear friend.
> Since I can come not with it, what I send
> My undivided heart shall now convey,
> With all its joys, hopes, pleasures, pains, today:
> All this hath no beginning, hath no end.
>
> —Goethe, Sonnet IX[45]

Freud lives pen in hand; he writes everywhere, all the time, and
has always done so. Already at age 15 he is carrying on a voluminous
correspondence with his fellow student Eduard Silberstein, accompanied by other writings: a biblical sketch, a "masterpiece"[46] that goes
astray to the young author's great distress ("I have not suffered a similar loss for years"),[47] a dialogue between two stars, written during "an
Egyptian darkness,"[48] a small "travel diary,"[49] an "awful nocturne"
in which he competes with Poe, "playbills . . . for a children's theater," "a scientific essay on Goethe's mouthparts," and a treatise with
the Latin title "de mediis, quibus in amoribus efficiendis utuntur
poetae [on the means poets are accustomed to use in matters of love],
which alone sufficed to immortalize me as Aristotle's fortunate successor."[50] What a wide range of literary models for an ambitious young
man! Later he will say that he wanted to emulate Lessing, the author
of *Nathan the Wise*.[51]

From adolescence on, Freud reveals the double motive behind
the writing of a letter: the wish to address the other and the pleasure
of writing as such: "I am keeping a travel diary just for you, from which
you will gather more than you really ought to know."[52] He has so much
to say that he announces to his friend Silberstein that he will send
reams of letters—letters sent under a seal of secrecy, because he wants
to write in complete frankness about anything that occurs to him.
Sometimes he even uses Spanish to make his confessions, this being

the official language of the Academia Castellana, founded by the two friends as a way of communicating their shared mythology.

What he proposes to do is send, each Sunday, "a letter that is nothing short of an entire encyclopedia of the past week, and that with total veracity reports all our doings, commissions and omissions, and those of all strangers we encounter, in addition to all outstanding thoughts and observations and at least an adumbration, as it were, of the unavoidable emotions."[53]

The joys of friendship are combined with the attachment to writing. In the letters to his friend, Freud's pleasure in writing unfolds, without reservation, in abundance and haste. Yet his impatience to get an answer by return mail and the profusion of the letters he sends trouble more than one correspondent. When Jung delays twenty-five days before responding (Freud counted them, suspecting a Fliessian twenty-three-day period), he is reproached, though not without an effort at understanding, "as though the promptness and length of my last letter had frightened you away." "I don't wish to importune you," he continues, "in the event that you yourself don't feel the need of corresponding at shorter intervals. But I can't help responding to my own rhythm, and the only compromise-action I am capable of is not to post the letter I am now writing until Sunday."[54]

This disparity in the rhythms of writing letters is a concern of Freud's from the beginning. He never really tames the exuberance of his pen and calls on each of his partners in letter-writing to respond in kind. With Silberstein, the demand takes on a biblical tone: "If you reply on the wings of an eagle, or like a flash of lightning, you will not have done too much,"[55] with Fliess a Greek one: "Daimonie [demon], why don't you write?"[56]

The space of letter-writing is also the space in which Freud's style expands. His passion for putting thoughts and feelings into words shines forth as he explains what writing means for him: "In our letters we shall transmute the six prosaic and unrelenting working days of the week into the pure gold of poetry."[57] With Silberstein, Freud is always interested in the form a letter can take. Thus the letter of August 13, 1874 is constructed like a three-story building. Freud entitles the first floor "Of literary and friendly correspondence in general and of our own in particular." To begin with, he explains, it is important not to imitate the *misera plebs contribuens* (the wretched taxpayers): "What a mess! The mere fulfillment of the meanest need! No trace of artistry! With all the signs of a difficult birth but quite without its accomplishment! The whole letter might be a postscript, a brief appendage to the salutation of Dear Friend, My Dearest, or Dear Sir." This radical critique suddenly leads him to the thought that, if God took six days to create the world, his aim was "to show mankind that in any task it is essential to observe a rational order and a logical sequence of steps." And the young man concludes: "The selfsame order must also be reflected in our letters, but it must not be artificial or lifeless, rather that of a work of art."[58]

To write is to reinvent the world, to sketch one's dreams there and, through the power of the word, to give birth to living creatures and to things: a demiurge sleeps in the heart of every writer. At age 18, in connection with a student newspaper he and three fellow students had founded and he was also instrumental in suppressing, Freud speaks of this omnipotence straight out, though with a wink: "I gave it life and I have taken its life away, so blessed be my name for ever and ever, Amen."[59]

From early on, Freud is caught up in the urgent and vital hand-to-hand combat of putting his life into words, and, later, creating an oeuvre of words. Writing is inevitable, an impulse he cannot escape under penalty of death: "If I cannot read and write letters, I am afraid I shall catch . . . cholera . . . out of deadly boredom."[60]

At every stage of his life, Freud finds a correspondent—Silberstein in Vienna and Leipzig, Fluss in Freiberg, Martha in Hamburg, Fliess in Berlin, Jung in Zurich, Lou in Göttingen, Ferenczi in Budapest, and so forth—to whom to send the fragments of a self-portrait that is never finished. In order to write, Freud must have an Other, an *alter*, a public, with whom to undertake a unique dialogue. As he explains to Wilhelm Fliess in the midst of their epistolary friendship: "I cannot write entirely without an audience, but do not at all mind writing only for you."[61] And, at the end of their relationship, he unashamedly admits: "I was sorry to lose my 'only audience,' as Nestroy called it. For whom shall I write now?"[62]

The pen never leaves his hand. One correspondence ends, and another immediately takes up the relay. After his brotherly exchange of letters with Silberstein, Freud the lover writes to Martha Bernays. During their four-year engagement, Freud writes to her every day, sometimes even more than once a day. Thus we see him furtively tearing several sheets of paper from his laboratory notebook, taking a pen lying on Professor Brücke's desk, and composing a love letter while his experiment is in progress: "I have to write to Martha."[63]

A scrap of paper, an old envelope rummaged from his belongings, will do in a pinch, but he offers his fiancée stationery engraved with their monogram, an M and S intertwined, that is "useless" to anyone but themselves.[64] On the way to visit her in Hamburg, he can't help scribbling down his impressions of the trip, though his letter will arrive at its destination on the same train as he. If he can't find a moment during the day, he tells her his thoughts at night. Returning from an evening at Charcot's house, he intends to take up his pen, but, since he has no light, he must wait until the next day: "I had meant to write to you at night but couldn't find the matches, and so had to take off my elegant clothes and go to bed by the light of the moon."[65]

Against his will, he must learn moderation and rein in the irresistible wish to write every minute in anticipation of the future: "I am only too willing to write to you more often; best of all I would like to write to you all day long, but what I still prefer is to work all day so as to be able to hold you in my arms for years and years."[66]

Freud also tells his fiancée about how he is writing his first scientific papers, quickly and feverishly, sometimes stimulated by cocaine. On June 2, 1882, he announces to her that he is collecting everything that has been written on this "magical drug."[67] Three years later, on May 17, 1885, he writes: "I took some cocaine, watched the migraine vanish at once, went on writing my paper as well as a letter to Prof. Mendel, but I was so wound up that I had to go on working and writing and couldn't get to sleep until four in the morning."[68]

Freud left traces of his experience with cocaine not only in his correspondence but also in his published work, especially in the report of his presentation to the Vienna Psychoanalytic Society on March 5, 1885, in which he describes the drug's efficacy in his own case.[69] Thus, long before he looks into himself and finds there the source of a new theory and a new career, Freud does not hesitate to use an isolated fact of self-experience as the basis for a scientific demonstration. He explains this in the "Contribution to the Knowledge of the Effect of Cocaine" in 1885. These papers announce, twelve years in advance, Freud's approach to a psychopathology of everyday life in which the observer is located within the observation itself, affect and objectivity standing side by side to say something new about the human soul.

Freud uses the drug to launch his quest for the traces of the unconscious and to sustain his patient research. The letters to Fliess, restored to their original, uncensored version, show that he used it longer than had been believed, since, as late as June 12, 1895, he writes: "I need a lot of cocaine. Also, I have started smoking again. . . . I must treat this psychic fellow well or he won't work for me. I demand a great deal of him. The torment, most of the time, is superhuman."[70]

Freud will always have recourse to artificial stimulants—mainly nicotine, once he gives up cocaine—to sustain his intellectual efforts. "Since I can no longer smoke freely, I no longer want to write," he tells Arnold Zweig on May 2, 1935, "or perhaps I am just using this pretext to veil the unproductiveness of old age." But his interest in writing remains intense, since he immediately adds: "Moses won't let go of my imagination. I visualize myself reading it out to you when you come to Vienna, despite my defective speech."[71]

> The Witch with strange gestures draws a circle and places peculiar objects in it; meanwhile the glassware begins to ring, the cauldrons to drone, making music. Finally she brings a great tome and within the circle arranges the marmosets, who must serve her for a pulpit and hold the torch. She beckons Faust to join her.
>
> —Goethe, Faust[72]

The magic of Venice, the heat of summer: every moment of well-being or vacation takes Freud away from his desk. In order to get to work he needs a certain amount of physical distress, a feeling of discomfort, and above all an absence of leisure. "Such cutbacks in work do not, in my case, lead to production, just as I'm going to paste together the third edition of *The Interpretation of Dreams*," he writes to Pfister.[73] During World War I his analytic practice has of course been greatly reduced, but it was hard for him to take advantage of this enforced freedom: "I have been used to extensive work for the past twenty years, and I cannot possibly use more than a fraction of my spare time for my writing."[74] To Karl Abraham, who asks him how he finds the time to write after his long days in the consulting room, he replies that, on the contrary, writing gives him a much-needed rest from analysis.[75] Throughout the day he hears and takes in so much that he feels "the need to give out something, to change from a passive recipient attitude to an active creating one.[76]

Freud likes to let his impulses carry him along; he can endure no constraint when he is writing his texts, nor can he conform to any regular schedule or force himself to work. He is proud of this, seeing in it the mark of the true writer and not of a mere scientific workman. If he finds himself obliged to accept a delay, he is highly critical of the fruit of his labor: "I produced, or rather aborted, something about psychogenic disturbances of vision—poor, like everything I do to order."[77]

Writing is a pleasure for Freud. He wants only love children, "Sunday children," as he said of his daughter Sophie. "I can't in any way endure work with a deadline, because then it stops being a pleasure and becomes a chore like everything else one does day after day."[78]

There is a time to write and then a time to stop writing. During his over-long engagement to Martha, Freud compared the need to decide on the date of the wedding to the need to decide when, finally, to submit a paper for publication. "Preparation for marriage is like the writing of a paper: one never finishes it; one just has to set oneself a deadline and break off somewhere."[79] Sending Fliess the page proofs to mark his decision to publish *The Interpretation of Dreams*, despite the shame he feels at revealing intimate details of his dream life, he notes, in French, that one can't make an omelet without breaking eggs.[80] In connection with his paper "'A Child Is Being Beaten,'" he uses the image of a craftsman: "I produce the goods as they come from the workshop, including the shavings."[81] Is this a memory of the happy little boy in Freiberg who, on the ground floor of the house where he was born, played with scraps of tinplate in the locksmith's shop?

To play with ink, words, and paper, Freud chooses large sheets and lets his pen run freely over them, just as he walks with long strides through the streets of Vienna or on the mountain roads of Italy. Setting his pen-holder between his thumb and his index and third fingers, he traces such thick lines, in his vigorous and regular, slightly slanted Gothic script, that at first glance they seem to be interlaced with one another. Yet they form a loose and legible fabric in which generous downstrokes nearly touch the letters above and below without interfering with them. No punctuation mark is missing: hyphens, dashes, and periods appear in their right places. There are few or no erasures. In the silence of his office, amid the blue smoke of his cigars, hours pass as though in an instant. In a semicircle around him, the figurines of the ancient gods of the Mediterranean and the Orient are present as he cooks his works. But his true protectors, the kindly guides who accompany him right to the edge of the witch's boiling cauldron and encourage him to drink a full draught from it, are the poets. They are called Virgil, Sophocles, Cervantes, Shakespeare, Lessing, Schiller, Heine, and Goethe.

This is how Sigmund Freud writes.

NOTES

1. Letter to Fliess of October 8, 1895, in Freud 1954, p. 126.
2. Letter to Fliess of September 23, 1895, in Freud 1954, p. 124.
3. Letter to Fliess of October 15, 1895, in Freud 1954, p. 127.

4. 1895a.

5. Freud 1954, p. 129.

6. This is a scene in Goethe's *Faust* (1808–1832, pp. 56–63).

7. Estimated at around 20,000. See Mijolla 1981.

8. Freud 1900, p. 603.

9. Letter to Zweig of February 21, 1936, in Freud and Zweig 1970, p. 122.

10. Letter to Marie Bonaparte of April 28, 1939, cited in Schur 1972, p. 220.

11. From the scene "The Witch's Kitchen," Goethe 1808–1832, p. 62.

12. Freud 1954, p. 257.

13. Freud 1954, p. 258.

14. Freud 1954, p. 249.

15. Jones 1955, pp. 350, 351.

16. Letter to Ferenczi of August 11, 1911, cited in Jones 1955, p. 356.

17. Cited in Knoepfmacher 1979, p. 447.

18. Goetz 1976, p. 219 (trans. S. F.).

19. Blanton 1971, p. 32.

20. Letter of October 1, 1910, in Freud and Jung 1970, p. 358.

21. Letter of May 16, 1897, in Freud 1954, p. 200.

22. Letter of May 31, 1897, in Freud 1954, p. 206.

23. Letter to Fliess of May 28, 1899, in Freud 1954, p. 281. In a letter of August 20, 1873 to his childhood friend Eduard Silberstein, Freud makes the same observation with regard to an imaginary dialogue he had written: "My 'celestial conversation' does not deserve the praises you have so profusely bestowed upon it, and I hope that you have not been dazzled by the scientific data, which are not correct, the whole thing having been a brainchild of mine, as Caballero would say, or having sprung from the dregs of my brain, as Schiller would put it" (Freud 1992, p. 41).

24. Letter to Fliess of June 12, 1895, in Freud 1954, p. 121. At this time Freud's wife was pregnant with their sixth child; a girl, Anna, would be born six months later. Had she been a boy, her name would have been Wilhelm.

25. Letter to Fliess of November 14, 1897, in Freud 1954, p. 230. Freud would write to Abraham on March 16, 1914: "Tomorrow I am sending you the 'Narcissism,' which was a difficult birth and bears all the marks of it." And, on March 25: "Since finishing the 'Narcissism' I have not been having a good time. A great deal of headache, intestinal trouble, and already a new idea for work" (Freud and Abraham 1965, pp. 167–168).

26. Letter to Fliess of March 23, 1900, in Freud 1954, p. 313.

27. Letter of May 25, 1897, in Freud 1954, p. 202.

28. Jones 1955, pp. 352–353.

29. Letter to Ferenczi of November 30, 1911, in Jones 1955, p. 367.

30. Letter to Fliess of June 22, 1897, in Freud 1954, pp. 210–211 (the letter is mistakenly dated June 12).

31. Freud 1985, p. 338.

32. Letter to Fliess of December 3, 1897, in Freud 1954, p. 236.

33. Freud 1954, p. 83.

34. Letter of March 6, 1910, in Freud and Pfister 1963b, pp. 32–33 (trans. S. F.).

35. Letter of July 27, 1916, in Freud and Andréas-Salomé 1966, p. 51.

36. Freud and Ferenczi 1996, p. 43.

37. Letter to Abraham of December 11, 1914, in Freud and Abraham 1965, pp. 204–205.

38. Letter to Jones of May 22, 1910, in Jones 1955, p. 68.

39. Letter to Jung of December 17, 1911: "I can see from the difficulties I encounter in this work [*Totem and Taboo*] that I was not cut out for inductive investigation, that my whole make-up is intuitive, and that in setting out to establish the purely empirical science of ΨA I subjected myself to an extraordinary discipline" (Freud and Jung 1974, p. 472).

40. Letter to Lou Andréas-Salomé of April 2, 1919, in Freud and Andréas-Salomé 1985, p. 95.

41. Letter of December 2, in Freud and Ferenczi 1996, pp. 33–34.

42. Letter of December 15, in Freud and Ferenczi 1996, pp. 36–37.

43. Letter to Fliess of May 25, 1895, in Freud 1954, p. 119.

44. Letter to Pfister of January 24, 1910, in Freud and Pfister 1963b, p. 31 (trans. S. F.).

45. Freud cites this sonnet in a letter to Martha, written at night on August 18, 1882, in Freud 1960, pp. 25–26.

46. Letter of July 30, 1873, in Freud 1992, p. 27.

47. Letter of August 2, 1873, in Freud 1992, p. 28.

48. Letter of August 16, 1873, in Freud 1992, p. 37.

49. Letter of August 9, 1872, in Freud 1992, p. 9.

50. Letter of February 21, 1875, in Freud 1992, pp. 89–90.

51. Wortis 1954, p. 122.

52. Letter to Silberstein of August 17, 1872, in Freud 1992, p. 11.

53. Letter of September 4, 1874, in Freud 1992, pp. 57–58.

54. Letter of November 11, 1909, in Freud and Jung 1974, p. 259.

55. Letter of July 24, 1873, in Freud 1992, p. 26.

56. Letter of July 23, 1895, in Freud 1985, p. 134.

57. Letter to Silberstein of September 4, 1874, in Freud 1992, p. 58.

58. Freud 1992, p. 48.

59. Letter to Silberstein of January 30, 1875, in Freud 1992, p. 86.

60. Letter to Silberstein of July 30, 1873, in Freud 1992, pp. 27–28.

61. Letter of May 18, 1898 in Freud 1985, p. 313.

62. Letter of September 19, 1901, in Freud 1954, p. 337.

63. Letter of June 27, 1882, in Freud 1960, pp. 10–11.

64. Letter of July 23, 1882, in Freud 1960, p. 18.

65. Letter of January 20, 1886, in Freud 1960, p. 194.

66. Letter of February 14, 1884, in Freud 1960, p. 98.

67. Cited in Jones 1953, p. 81.

68. Freud 1960, p. 145.

69. Freud 1974.

70. Freud 1985, p. 132.

71. Freud 1960, p. 424.

72. Goethe 1808–1832, pp. 61–62.

73. Freud and Pfister 1963b, p. 48 (trans. S. F.).

74. Letter to Jones of December 25, 1914, in Freud and Jones 1993, p. 309.

75. Letter of July 3, 1912, in Freud and Abraham 1965, p. 120.

76. Letter to Jones of April 15, 1910, in Jones 1955, p. 396.

77. Letter to Jung of April 12, 1910, in Freud and Jung 1974, p. 306.

78. Letter to Pfister of December 14, 1911, in Freud and Pfister 1963a, p. 54 (trans. S. F.).

79. Letter to Martha of May 7, 1885, in Freud 1960, p. 143.

80. Letter of August 6, 1899, in Freud 1954, p. 290.

81. Letter to Andréas-Salomé of August 2, 1920, in Freud and Andréas-Salomé 1985, p. 105.

8

The Shade of the Poet

I was struck several times—please permit me to remark upon it—
with inexpressible admiration for the lovely, lovely shadow you cast,
that shadow you fling to the ground with a certain noble disdain and
without the least notice, that lovely shadow lying even now at your
feet. Forgive the admitted audacity of such a bold presumption. I
wonder if you might possibly consider parting with it—I mean, sell-
ing it to me.

—Adalbert von Chamisso, *Peter Schlemihl*[1]

Freud's words are always mingled with the words of poets, bound
up with them, as though he had formed a pact with them: he will walk
in their shadow right through to the heart of the unconscious in order
to bring back the secrets of how the human soul is made. But in exchange he will give up the possibility of being admired as a literary
creator: the only creativity he can claim is scientific.

Writers teach him the magic words that open the doors of the
Mothers.[2] Poetry enriches analytic theory; it is its metaphorical foundation and guarantees its authenticity. As the intuition of science and
the knowledge of fiction are allied and combined, there emerges a
novelistic science, a theoretical fiction.

Face to face, throughout his career, stand Freud and the figure
of the writer, Freud and his double. This is an encounter that is de-

sired, sought, deferred, avoided, denied, omnipresent, with bonds of fascination and envy that are troubled, ambivalent. Poets and novelists are precious allies, but the grace and elegance with which they handle words, and the breadth of their observations of the soul's hidden movements, also give rise to discouragement: "We may well heave a sigh of relief at the thought that it is nevertheless vouchsafed to a few to salvage without effort from the whirlpool of their own feelings the deepest truths, toward which the rest of us have to find our way through tormenting uncertainty and with restless groping."[3]

To define his own task of setting thoughts to words, Freud calls on novelists and poets. Again and again in his texts, he questions his literary double so as to draw the contours of his own identity as a writer. As early as the *Studies in Hysteria*, published in 1895, Freud admits that he is unusually concerned with the fact that his accounts of patients (and not of illnesses) "read like short stories." He wanted to mark his works with "the serious stamp of science," and here he is led by the nature of his subject, and not his personal preference, to behave like a poet. And he adds: "The fact is that local diagnosis and electrical reactions lead nowhere in the study of hysteria, whereas a detailed description of mental processes such as we are accustomed to find in the works of imaginative writers enables me, with the use of a few psychological formulas, to obtain at least some kind of insight into the course of that affection."[4]

There is a disturbing familiarity to poetic writing, arising as it does like a ghost amid the seriousness of science, and Freud makes a pretense of justifying himself by pleading innocent. The slippage into novelistic style simply imposes itself on him, almost against his will, the way a young woman, dragged by a stranger into a fast waltz, might find herself falling in love with her cavalier before she can help it.

In the *Studies*, Emmy, Lucy, Katharina, and Elisabeth are the inspiration for vivid, penetrating portraits, rich with personal impressions and with comparisons, sometimes bold and unexpected, that bring onstage the devil, hieroglyphs, opera, the Bible, chess, and literary pamphlets. Freud listens to his heroines with the refined ear of a lover of words, surprised and fascinated to discover that hysterics have the gift of symbolizing with their bodies the literal meaning of verbal expressions and perhaps of going back to the very source of language. In return, despite the *belle indifférence* he claims to have, he must acknowledge that he is writing much more in the manner of an author of fiction than as a professor of medicine. And at the end of the especially novelistic story of Elisabeth von R., who was in love with a forbidden man, Freud admits that, during the spring of 1894, two years after their analytic encounter, he heard that his patient was going to attend a ball to which he could get himself invited. He explains: "I did not allow the opportunity to escape me of seeing my former patient whirl past in a lively dance. Since then, by her own inclination, she has married someone unknown to me."[5]

In the aftermath of this dancing memory, perhaps surprised in retrospect to have found himself at this very ball, Freud wonders about the metamorphosis that is taking place in him: he has become a poet, a novelist. This happened unbeknownst to him, he says, but the associations to his confession suggest that inclination was involved as well.

Though the figure of Mephistopheles runs through the *Studies on Hysteria*, and though the words of the poet are discreetly called upon to encourage Freud at a moment when he experiences his task as especially arduous—"'Her mask reveals a hidden sense,'"[6]—the name of Goethe is not mentioned explicitly. Anonymous in Freud, it is only under the pen of Josef Breuer, in his chapter on theoretical considerations, that the author of *Faust* appears in broad daylight to emphasize the continuity between the ordinary man's reactions and the highest spheres of human fulfillment.

Freud does not yet feel ready to name the man who offers him the precious alchemy of a poetic language to represent the unrepresentable, a man who is one of his first masters on the path toward knowledge of the unconscious,[7] and who is his model "*si parva licet,* etc."[8]

To suppress the name of his initiatory guide is to blur the fact of otherness, to confuse identities, to take possession of the shadow of the poet so as to get pleasure from his words and his secret knowledge. It is through Goethe's mouth that Freud speaks, giving his journey into the past the poet's patents of nobility: "As the great poet, using his privilege to ennoble (sublimate) things, puts it, *Und manche liebe*

Schatten steigen auf; /Gleich einer alten, halbverklungnen Sage,/Kommt erste Lieb' und Freundschaft mit herauf."[9] It is also with Goethe's lips that he falls silent: "The best you can expect to learn/You cannot tell the youngsters anyhow."[10]

Between speech and silence, with writers as his spokesmen and guardrails, Freud delves into the paradoxical knowledge of the unknown. He hides behind his poetic double to introduce ideas born from a literary intuition, sparing himself the trouble of proving what is obvious to him through the evidence of art and gaining support not from the "truth" of a passage but from its beauty, the power of its form. To breathe into his own writings the enchantment banished by science, "to restore to the word some of its former magic,"[11] he turns not to the distant academic style of citations set off in quotation marks but to the sparkle of literature, joining his words to those of writers and making them his own: linked, mixed, incorporated into the very warp and weft of his theoretical development.

By seeking legitimacy from poets and novelists, psychoanalysis is conceived from the outset as a discipline that places the subjective, the intimate, at the heart of its approach. In contrast to scientific discourse, which wants to do away with every trace of the personal, psychoanalysis is based on the particular, on language and emotion. When the positivist rejects as unscientific the discourse that confesses subjectivity, psychoanalysis sees him as blind for trying to disguise it.[12] Science condemns affect; psychoanalysis finds in it another human truth. As does literature.

Yet Freud never stops trying to justify this "conversion" from the scientific to the literary, this displacement toward fiction, as though his own work were in danger of being undermined by poetry, infiltrated behind his back, denatured, leaving behind fertile dialogue and joyous intimacy for a disturbing excess, a threatening proximity. And so, in the mirror held up by his poetic double, his reflection is disturbed and annoyed; the evidence of the entente is blurred, irritation wins out over fascination. Freud must widen the distance, reaffirm that he is not an artist but a scientist. Though he lets himself be accompanied and preceded by writers, he is not one himself; he is well aware of the limitations of his talents, and, above all, his project is a different one. Moreover, to establish the legitimacy of a new discipline he cannot allow himself to forego the world of the university if he does not want to fall into discredit. He has not forgotten the slap delivered early on by Krafft-Ebing: "a scientific fairy tale."[13] Meant to be insulting, this reply nonetheless showed an understanding, however involuntary, of what Freud was trying to do: create a body of knowledge at the center of which would be the ruptures brought about by passion.

Freud himself, surprised by his discovery, at first feels exiled on the shores of the novel. His own way of writing along with the unconscious puzzles him, because it is inconsistent with his notion that a man of science should be able to master the conditions of his research and not submit to the arbitrariness of inspiration. But whether it is consistent or not, it suits both his literary sensibility and the object of his investigations.

He had thought he would conduct an exploration of the unconscious, yet it is the unconscious that explores him. The laws and mechanisms he discerns are ones he must obey: he cannot elude what he elucidates. There can no longer be a separation between the object of observation and the observer. Freud cannot discuss the unconscious without dealing with it. His knowledge of the unconscious—and the writing of this knowledge—does not stand outside the unconscious. Freud draws this knowledge from the threefold well of self-analysis, the unspoken words of his patients' suffering, and literary narratives. Writers help psychoanalysis move forward along the royal road leading to the interpretation of the unconscious: they universalize it. Freud matches his steps to theirs, allies himself with their magic power, appropriates their immemorial wisdom, and melts into their shadow until he is no longer separate from it. But it is with his own name that he wants to sign his books and triumph over human ignorance. Going beyond art and science, he offers a discipline that breaks with traditional divisions. And yet he can found and promote it only in the name of the scientificity of the Enlightenment and Reason. He remains a child of his century.

Thus his confession is marked by wavering: at one moment he sees himself as a novelist, at another he protests strongly that he is no such thing. But the question of writing still haunts him.

> "And what do you get out of it? I mean out of the particular mental function which we call consciousness, and which is nothing but the confounded activity of a damned toll-collector—excise man— deputy chief customs officer, who has set up his infamous bureau in our top story and who exclaims, whenever any goods try to get out: 'Hi! Hi! exports are prohibited . . . , they must stay here . . . here, in this country.'"
>
> —E. T. A. Hoffmann, *The Devil's Elixirs*[14]

The Interpretation of Dreams, 1900: overture in three phases: epigraph, foreword, method. If he cannot bend the gods above to his purposes, he will shake up the underworld.[15] Here Freud is speaking through the mouth of Vergil. A line of Latin verse expresses his determination to travel along all the roads of memory, like Aeneas long ago, among the dead as well as the living. Freud does not just walk in the footsteps of the ancient hero in quest of his shades; he relies on the authority of the Roman poet to make his way toward regions of the unknown and try to map them. He is Aeneas and Virgil, the hero and the narrator of the hero's story.

Freud chooses to portray himself in order to draw the portrait of the dreamer. Yet he calls his work not *Portrait of the Dreamer* but *The Interpretation of Dreams*. What he must do, therefore, is connect the singular to the universal, the subjective to the objective. He calls on literature to bridge the gap between the intimacy of the unique and experiences shared by everyone. Literature will mediate between his past and his patients, assuring a language common to all.[16]

Relying on works of language to create a work of language, Freud nevertheless continues to claim the backing of science. He inscribes the citation from the *Aeneid* on the pediment of the first book that he signs alone and, immediately below, in the foreword to the reader, he defends himself strongly against being taken for a man of letters. He is eager to explain that, to be sure, he is an author, but one who writes as a scientist and not as a poet.[17] Accordingly, he says, he should never have exposed his private life to the eyes of the world as authors of fiction do in the guise of their art. However, he had to resign himself to relating the intimate details of his own dreams in order to further the clarity of his argument. He does not mention explicitly either the names of the poets who inspire and support his speculations or the role of the poet within himself.

In the *Studies on Hysteria* he said he had been surprised to find that, in spite of himself, he was behaving like a novelist and leaving the safe shores of scientific practice; now he acknowledges that he is behaving like an author of fiction and feels it necessary to explain and justify himself to his readers, as though this were a sin—and far too secret a pleasure.

Having established this distance, Freud hastens to ally himself with a certain traditional approach to dreams,[18] that of common sense, the Bible, the ancient world, and poets, which he contrasts with the scientific theories of his time. In a footnote he explains that dreams invented by writers also conform to his interpretation, and that he believes this concordance between his research and the creation of a poet proves the accuracy of his analysis.

Freud turns to "that great poet and philosopher"[19] Schiller as he introduces his method and sets forth the rule of free association. This literary reference ennobles the analytic work that is coming into being. The writer enables Freud to compare the resistances triggered by "involuntary thoughts" emerging in the process of interpretation to the pitfalls of poetic creation. In a long citation, he uses another man's words to show that neither shame nor fear should prevent ideas from coming to mind in a rush or imagination from being seized with vertigo:

> Looked at in isolation, a thought may seem very trivial or very fantastic, but it may be made important by another thought that comes after it, and, in conjunction with other thoughts that may seem equally absurd, it may turn out to form a most effective link. Reason cannot form any opinion upon all this unless it retains the thought long enough to look at it in connection with the others.

With a bit of pride, Freud goes on to state that it is not very hard to reproduce "what Schiller describes as a relaxation of the watch upon the gates of Reason," and that most of his patients "achieve it after their first instructions." "I myself," he says, "can do so very completely, by the help of writing down my ideas as they occur to me."[20] Freud does not generalize a method from his free writing; he asks his patients to associate aloud. The writing is a personal practice used for his dream journal, manuscripts, and correspondence, though it is mentioned incidentally here and there in *The Interpretation of Dreams*. Thus, to illustrate the work of condensation performed by the dream, and to indicate how "brief, meagre, and laconic" it is "in comparison with the range and wealth of the dream-thoughts," Freud observes that "[i]f a dream is written out it may perhaps fill half a page. The analysis setting out the dream-thoughts underlying it may occupy six, eight, or a dozen times as much space. This relation varies with different dreams; but so far as my experience goes its direction never varies."[21]

Written as though in a dream, the dream-book does not escape the oneiric grammar it describes. Freud's writing is wedded to the dreamwork, miming it in its condensations, its deformations, its absurd, childlike symbolic images in which nakedness, death, and sex are veiled and then unveiled to utter a knowledge of the unutterable. Censorship infiltrates his text as it does the text of the dream. Here, too, the man of letters comes to his aid to justify his dissimulations: when he interprets his dreams for his readers, he says, he inevitably distorts the way poets do.[22]

A few months before the publication of his "Egyptian" book on dreams, in his autobiographical paper "Screen Memories," Freud is still not talking about himself directly. In a practice common at the time, he uses a fictive persona to speak of his childhood memories and youthful fantasies, "a man of university education, aged thirty-eight. Though his own profession lies in a very different field, he has taken an interest in psychological questions."[23] In *The Interpretation of Dreams* he presents himself in his own name. Like any writer, he hopes to capture the attention of the public and win its assent. "I must ask the reader to make my interests his own for quite a while," Freud writes before relating his first dream, "and to plunge along with me into the minutest details of my life; for a transference of this kind is peremptorily demanded by our interest in the hidden meaning of dreams."[24] As his master Charcot taught him, it is not enough to convince; one must also charm.

The involuntary poet of his nights, a novelist despite himself when he writes about hysterical patients, Freud is uneasy, as he unfolds the story of Dora, about Viennese doctors who might read his account as a roman à clef. For his part, he cannot confuse the shaping of a literary plot with the rules of a medical dissection. Yet, although what he wants is to stand squarely on the side of medicine and in no way to comply with novelistic procedure or to offer an extra measure of aesthetic delight, it is surely literary creativity that he has in mind as he sets forth the conflicts of his young patient. Whether as model or anti-model, fiction is his reference point:

> I must now turn to consider a further complication to which I should certainly give no space if I were a man of letters engaged upon the creation of a mental state like this for a short story, instead of being a medical man engaged upon its dissection. The element to which I must now allude can only serve to obscure and efface the outlines of the fine poetic conflict which we have been able to ascribe to Dora. This element would rightly fall a sacrifice to the censorship of a writer, for he, after all, simplifies and abstracts when he appears in the character of a psychologist. But in the world of reality, which I am trying to depict here, a complication of motives, an accumulation and conjunction of mental activities—in a word, overdetermination—is the rule.[25]

> You appeared to me in a dream; it was as if I were standing behind the glass door of your little room and caught a glimpse of you seated there at your desk between a skeleton and a sheaf of dried plants. Fat tomes by Haller, Humboldt, and Linnaeus were spread open before you, and on your sofa lay a volume of Goethe and the *Magic Ring*, I looked at you a long while, then at every object in the room,

and then at you again; but you remained perfectly still, not drawing a single breath; you were dead.

—Chamisso, *Peter Schlemihl*[26]

This is how Peter Schlemihl speaks to Adalbert von Chamisso, the creature to his creator. The man of fiction has just sold his shadow to the devil. He seized the purse offered by the Evil One and, in a kind of mad frenzy, took out gold, and more gold, endless amounts of gold. He spread it on the floor and piled it up around himself, his heart feasting on the metallic noise that rang out over and over again. He ended up rolling on this treasure, and night finds him lying on his ocean of riches when sleep finally closed his eyes. It is then that Peter Schlemihl dreams of the writer who gave him life: he sees him among his books and the insignia of his science, and he is dead.

The man without a shadow and the man of letters (likewise a botanist, which is what his character becomes) are the reflections of one another, captives of a mutual self-portrait. In his story Chamisso writes to himself indirectly, passing with his accomplice, Peter Schlemihl, through the realms of lack, rejection, deceptive appearance, fear of not being the only one of one's kind and the wish not to be, impotence, and separation, before seeing the earth open up as a wondrous garden and accepting, by dint of study and science, his fate and the inevitable role of the unknowable that his fate harbors.

Writing is connected as closely as can be to the shadow, the double, and death: we cannot look our double in the face without dying. To write is to face the play of mirrors, and even to summon it up as Don Giovanni does the statue of the Commandant. Freud is well aware of this, fearing as he does that he will encounter a Viennese writer he thinks he resembles, as though seized with the vertigo of an impossible symmetry.

It was at this time, ten years ago—ten years ago today—that there befell me the incomprehensible adventure that has cast its shadow on my life up to the present and that will find its conclusion today thanks to you, without your suspecting it or taking any part in it.

For there is a diabolical connection between us, that you are as little
able as I to explain, but you must at least know that it exists.
—Arthur Schnitzler, "The Prophecy"[27]

Freud has just turned 50 and can hardly believe that Arthur
Schnitzler has honored him by drawing on his work: "You may imagine," he writes to Schnitzler, "how pleased and elated I felt on reading that you too have derived inspiration from my writings."[28]

During the summer of 1906, Freud succumbs to the delicious
seduction of *Gradiva*, a "Pompeiian phantasy."[29] With the conscious
pretext of studying its treatment of delusions and dreams, he models
his words on those of the novelist, Wilhelm Jensen, and, throughout
his commentary, tries to demonstrate the analogy, even the identity,
between the writer and the psychoanalyst. Never has Freud been so
ready to acknowledge his dreams of writing. But he bides his time.
Sixteen years later (he is now 66), convinced that death is approaching and he has nothing to lose, he makes a most intimate confession
to Schnitzler, a confession—he uses the word twice—surrounded by
multiple rhetorical precautions:

Now you too have reached your sixtieth birthday, while I, six years
older, am approaching the limit of my life and may soon expect to
see the end of the fifth act of this rather incomprehensible and not
always amusing comedy . . . .

I will make a confession which for my sake I must ask you to
keep to yourself and share with neither friends nor strangers. I have
tormented myself with the question why in all these years I have
never attempted to make your acquaintance and to have a talk with
you (ignoring the possibility, of course, that you might not have
welcomed my overture).

The answer contains the confession which strikes me as
too intimate. I think I have avoided you from a kind of reluctance to meet my double. Not that I am easily inclined to identify myself with another, or that I mean to overlook the difference in talent that separates me from you, but whenever I get
deeply absorbed in your beautiful creations I invariably seem to
find beneath their poetic surface the very presuppositions, in-

terests, and conclusions which I know to be my own. Your determinism as well as your skepticism—what people call pessimism—your preoccupation with the truths of the unconscious and of the instinctual drives in man, your dissection of the cultural conventions of our society, the dwelling of your thoughts on the polarity of love and death: all this moves me with an uncanny feeling of familiarity. (In a small book entitled *Beyond the Pleasure Principle*, published in 1920, I tried to reveal Eros and the death instinct as the motivating powers whose interplay dominates all the riddles of life.) So I have formed the impression that you know through intuition—or rather by detailed self-observation—everything that I have discovered by laborious work on other people. . . . But forgive me for drifting into psychoanalysis; I just can't help it. And I know that psychoanalysis is not the means of gaining popularity.[30]

The question of identity and doubling suffuses German Romanticism, and Freud does not escape this preoccupation, arising from modern individualism, that leads each person to live out a destiny of election mingled with exclusion. It is this knowledge of the missing shadow that Freud, in his turn, is dealing with, pushing dispossession even further: man does not just lose his shadow, that little private domain of light dancing at his feet, but he is entirely lost, divided by the power of an invisible part of himself that eludes him and governs him.

> As I was walking, one hot summer afternoon, through the deserted streets of a provincial town in Italy which was unknown to me, I found myself in a quarter of whose character I could not long remain in doubt. Nothing but painted women were to be seen at the windows of the small houses, and I hastened to leave the narrow street at the next turning. But after having wandered about for a time without enquiring my way, I suddenly found myself back in the same street, where my presence was beginning to excite attention. I hurried away once more, only to arrive by another *détour* at the same place yet a third time.
>
> —Freud, "The 'Uncanny'"[31]

But what is Freud looking for when he writes *Delusions and Dreams in Jensen's "Gradiva"*? The pleasure of slipping into the oneiric intimacy of imaginary characters to find confirmation of his interpretation of dreams? Or finding a surge of joyful evidence for the kinship between psychoanalysis and archeology, between the psychoanalyst and the poet? All of this, no doubt, but also the powerful attraction of reliving, in a sweet, secret familiarity, his own youthful turbulence in the fears and feelings of the hero of this "Pompeiian phantasy." The final words of his essay reveal how hard it is for him to leave the two protagonists, as though he had almost forgotten that "Hanold and Gradiva are only creatures of their author's mind."[32]

What emotions, what experiences, what fantasies are evoked by the journey Freud undertakes alongside these fictional beings with a joy so vivid that he cannot help repeating Jensen's story almost word for word instead of commenting on it?[33] His early letters suggest some answers and offer us the chance to see how Freud himself reached into his own soul, as writers do, in order to know the souls of other human beings.

Here we discover a young man athirst for science and reserved with the ladies. In the summer of 1872, when he is 16, his "Gradiva" is named Gisela. He falls hopelessly in love with her, but she is unaware of this.[34] He confides this Platonic passion, in Spanish, to his friend Eduard Silberstein:

> I shall try to make my confessions easier by framing them in our official language. . . . I took a fancy to the eldest [of the Fluss children], by the name of Gisela, who leaves tomorrow, and . . . her absence will give me back a sense of security about my behavior that I have not had up to now. Knowing my character, Your Honor will rightly think that instead of approaching her I have held back and nobody, not even she, knows any more about it than His Majesty, the King of the Turks.

He surrounds his confession with rhetorical precautions, keeping a distance from his feelings by the use of a foreign language, stepping behind a biblical citation in order to hide his emotions, and exhorting his friend to keep his letters completely confidential: "I am not afraid of making myself ridiculous by telling Your Honor all this because Your Honor knows that people are altogether brutal and foolish [Jeremiah 10:8] and would to God it were the last of our foolishness! But remember your duty not to let these notes fall into anyone else's hands if you want me to speak of my feelings again."[35]

Two weeks later, the young lover is once again in a confessional mood: "Only the nonsensical Hamlet in me, my diffidence, stood in the way of my finding it a refreshing pleasure to converse with the half-naive, half-cultured young lady." Gisela has left for Breslau; Freud remains in Freiberg and pursues his reverie even as he seeks to ward it off. He even claims that what is occurring is a "transference": "It would seem that I have transferred my esteem for the mother to friendship for the daughter."[36]

Like Hanold, Jensen's hero, the adolescent Freud keeps at arm's length the romantic and sensual upheavals that agitate and trouble him. And yet, behind the defense, part of him is still concerned with accuracy. The young man admires Eleanore Fluss, a cultivated woman and great reader familiar even with the classics, a woman possessed of "sound judgment" and "knowledgeable about politics, . . . who is guiding the household into the modern mainstream." Beneath the praise we see his disappointment in not having found the same cultural stimulation in his own mother: "Other mothers—and why disguise the fact that our own are among them? We shan't love them the less for it—care only for the physical well-being of their sons; when it comes to their intellectual development the control is out of their hands."[37]

Has he forgotten, at this time, the demonstration *ad oculos* that his mother gave him, back when he was 6, to illustrate that man is made of earth and returns to earth by rubbing the palms of her hands together until small blackish fragments of epidermis came loose? This lesson impressed him so deeply that it recurred in association to his dream of The Three Fates[38] and probably influenced his irresistible attraction to figurative reasoning and the visual.

One year later he tells Silberstein that he has given up his fondness for this girl: "Not because another has taken her place; indeed, that place can remain empty."[39] At the age of puberty, detachment seems to him to be the best solution; in his mature years he will make this into a theory, arguing that the edifice of civilization rests on the principle of the renunciation of the drives. He will also note, doubtless with reference to himself, that it is much easier for a scientist to be abstinent than for an artist.[40]

On December 31, at the stroke of midnight, he does not kiss the charming Gisela, who has come to celebrate New Year's Eve at the Freuds'. He has taken refuge in his room and writes to his friend that he still feels "awkward in the company of ladies."[41] His studies are what elate him, especially his classes in zoology and philosophy. He feels "close to the source from which science springs at its purest and from which one will be taking a good long drink."[42]

In the same letter, he notes that Gisela Fluss has gone to Italy, "though only as far as Verona."[43] One year later, Freud himself embarks on his first journey on Italian soil, like Hanold prompted by scientific motives. He has received a stipend to study the reproductive organs of the eel in Trieste.[44] Though not yet 20, he is a Member of the Imperial and Royal Zoological Station of that city.[45] During the few moments of leisure that he allows himself, he walks around the town. At the beginning of his stay, it seems to him to be full of "Italian goddesses," which, he writes to his friend Eduard, he finds intimidating.[46] These beauties who appeared on the first day later disappear mysteriously. Does he forbid himself to look at them, since he had found something rather shady about them?

A few days later, when he is on an excursion to a nearby town, the women once more seem attractive to him, more beautiful than in Trieste. Walking through the streets of Muccia to see the sights, he is surprised to discover a number of large signs advertising local midwives. The "*bambini*" and "*ragazzi*" playing in the alleys, as well as his encounters with several pregnant women, seem to him to justify the proliferation of midwives: "I did not bother to check whether the local women, perhaps influenced by the marine fauna, bear fruit the whole year round, or whether they do so at certain times and all together."[47] Goddesses and prostitutes, or midwives and pregnant women: the dangers of the opposite sex shine forth in broad daylight. The Latin world will remain for Freud a bewitching domain of overwhelming drives. This first impression will be repeated in places other than Italy and Paris.[48]

Just as the amorous chatter of the honeymooning Gretas and Augusts annoys the young Norbert Hanold, the outer manifestations of sexual desire disturb the young Sigmund, who prefers to devote himself tirelessly to zoology (as does Gradiva's father): "cell detritus swimming before my eyes, which disturbs me even in my dreams."[49] But in a common irony of the unconscious, having set aside the obscure object of his temptations he spends his days, sometimes even his nights, hunting the sexual organs of eels! He tells Silberstein that his work involves proving that "certain of their characteristics are in fact sex distinctions." Only the anatomist can prove this, he continues, "(seeing that eels keep no diaries from whose orthography one can make inferences as to their sex); he dissects them and discovers either testicles or ovaries."[50] And, to protect himself definitively from the allure of the fair sex, he notes that, since dissecting human beings is not allowed, he has nothing to do with them.

> Norbert Hanold stopped . . . and said with a peculiar tone, "Please go ahead here." A merry, comprehending, laughing expression lurked around his companion's mouth, and, raising her dress slightly with her left hand, Gradiva *rediviva* Zoë Bertgang, viewed by him with dreamily observing eyes, crossed with her calmly buoyant walk, through the sunlight, over the stepping stones, to the other side of the street.
>
> Wilhelm Jensen, *Gradiva*[51]

Thirty years later, in 1906, human dissection has a name: psychoanalysis. Having proved the theoretical and practical coherence of his invention, Freud for the first time allows himself to leave his place behind the couch to undertake an analytic journey in the realm of the novel. *Gradiva* solemnizes the wedding of psychoanalysis and the poet. Never again will the appeal to the truth of fiction be so explicit, so straightforward. Poets know "a whole host of things between heaven and earth of which our philosophy has not yet let us dream"[52];

they outstrip science, drawing from sources not yet explored by it and, in some cases, possessing the most profound knowledge of the human soul. It is this poetic knowledge, the ultimate criterion of authenticity, against which Freud measures himself: while he cannot claim to reach its aesthetic heights, he can arrive at its truth by other pathways.

To ward off the suspicion that he has introduced a secret meaning into a poetic narrative, communicating his own point of view as though it were the novelist's, Freud keeps as close as possible to the original text, modeling his words on the writer's and even letting Jensen serve as commentator. In reproducing the text almost entirely in the author's own words, Freud steps into the background so that only the poet has a voice and the identity of fictional truth and analytic truth shines forth.

The procedure by which the novelist has Gradiva cure the illusion of her childhood friend is, Freud tells us, wholly consistent with the psychoanalytic method. Freud does grant a distinction, namely that he must formulate the laws governing the unconscious, whereas the writer does not need to acknowledge them and can simply embody them in his creations. Freud sums up by declaring that the poet and the scholar "probably draw from the same source and work upon the same object, each of us by another method," the writer finding within himself what the analyst learns from others. Poet and scientist are inseparable: "Either both of us, the writer and the doctor, have misunderstood the unconscious in the same way, or we have both understood it correctly."[53]

And so, alone among scientists, Freud writes that he "ventured . . . to become a partisan" of the ancients, the superstitious, and writers.[54] Is the man of letters, then, alone in the face of the whole of science? Not at all, Freud replies, if he himself "may count [his] own works as part of science,"[55] part of a science that is unafraid to walk alongside fiction and use it as a source for the knowledge of human beings—knowledge, however, that he intends to submit to the criteria of scientific truth. Freud's work, his theoretical fertility, and the radical break it entails with what came before it, arise from this back-and-forth between art and science.

Dichtung und Wahrheit (*Poetry and Truth*) is the title of Goethe's memoirs: these are the two poles of Freud's entire project of investigation, investigation into a past that is impossible to refind intact, a past that is elusive and knows many disguises. The mysteries of artistic creation, he hopes, will help him to discover some of its secrets. There is a knowledge that is enigmatic, hidden, always hand in glove with the diabolical; it is this Faustian knowledge that he wants to attain and thinks he can approach through the words of his patients and through his own inner quest, but also through penetrating into the magic of art.

The journey to Pompeii comes to an end, and so does the delicious idyll with literature. To map out the territory of a new knowledge of love, Freud again and again turns to the poets. Yet he sees them not only as allies but also as rivals: admiration and wonder are mingled with envy and a touch of irritation. They are the ones who have known best how to depict the irregularities of the heart—"up till now," Freud adds. Now psychoanalysis is able to carry on from there. Freud admits that the poet is especially sensitive to the hidden movements of the souls of others as well as having "the courage to let his own unconscious speak." But he holds against poets their obligation "to produce intellectual and aesthetic pleasure." To be sure, they have been enchanting humanity for thousands of years, but they are not able to offer scientific knowledge. And so, "though her touch may be clumsier and the yield of pleasure less," science will inevitably focus on the obscure reasons of the heart. And, concluding this bittersweet dialogue between science and fiction, Freud, who has just distanced himself from poetic speech and declared his allegiance to science, congratulates himself on having done so, as though he has thereby attained the highest degree of the life of the mind: "Science is, after all, the most complete renunciation of the pleasure principle of which our mental activity is capable."[56]

Freud has not completely resolved the ancient quarrel that set him against the two former suitors of his fiancée, two artists. Carried away by intense jealousy, he had written to Martha: "I think there is a general enmity between artists and those engaged in the details of scientific work. We know that they possess in their art a master key to open with ease all female hearts, whereas we stand helpless at the strange design of the lock and love first to torment ourselves to discover a suitable key to it."[57]

As he sees it, the artist and the scientist are fighting over a single territory, that of the soul, and in particular the female soul. Science is getting involved with love, and Freud fears that he will lose out in both areas. Here we have the beginnings of his fascination with the exceptional people who, mingling art and science, have won immortality.

> Is this the seat of the gods here?
> Indeed, the gates and columns show
> That intelligence and labor and the arts dwell here.
> Where activity is enthroned and sloth is in retreat,
> Vice cannot easily be master.
> I boldly dare to enter the gate.[58]

Freud never quarrels for very long with poetry; it remains a friend, a comforter, and a muse, even if he pretends to resist it. At the beginning of "Leonardo da Vinci and a Memory of His Childhood," he addresses the "profane" readers who might reproach him for leaving the domain of the pathological for that of art, thereby insulting the memory of a great man. Once again he borrows from Schiller, declaring here that psychoanalysis in no way seeks "'to blacken the radiant and drag the sublime into the dust.'"[59]

Then it is Freud's turn to succumb to the enigmatic charm of Leonardo, that "Italian Faust" who echoes his own questioning: Is it possible to convert intellectual curiosity into *joie de vivre*? And can one man combine art and science in equal measure? No, replies Freud for Leonardo: "Though he left behind him masterpieces of painting, while his scientific discoveries remained unpublished and unused, the investigator in him never in the course of his development left the artist entirely free, but often made severe encroachments on him and perhaps in the end suppressed him."[60]

In paying tribute to the biographical acuity of the novelist Dimitri Sergeievitch Merezhkovsky, who made Leonardo the hero of "a great historical novel," Freud distinguishes between two modes of writing, "the way of writers of imagination, . . . in plastic terms" and the other, "in plain language."[61] Is it because he was too free in using a poetic style—or took too much pleasure in writing this lively, sparkling essay[62]—that he is afraid he lapsed into a kind of historical novel, a fear that will be repeated, more than twenty years later, in connection with his *Moses?*

He anticipates the criticism to which his inferences might give rise, "the criticism, even from friends of psycho-analysis and from those who are expert in it, that I have merely written a psychoanalytic novel,"[63] a work that is "partly fiction."[64] Given the inadequate information at his disposal, he does not exaggerate the accuracy of his conclusions and is not sure that he can account for the great Leonardo's "vacillation between art and science."[65] Freud acknowledges that psychoanalysis is unable to explain "how inevitable it was that the person concerned should have turned out the way he did and in no other way."[66] Perhaps he is also wondering about his own destiny: Why did he become this strange ferryman of the soul, this conquistador of dark continents, instead of an enchanter, an artist with words, colors, or sounds?

> In anticipation of such high happiness,
> I now enjoy the highest moment.
>
> —Goethe, *Faust*[67]

The last act: "like a dancer balancing on the tip of one toe,"[68] Freud leaves the scene of writing. He signs *Moses and Monotheism* three times. A mosaic book: three essays—as on the theory of sexuality—of which the first two first appeared in the journal *Imago* in 1937, two contradictory prefaces (one written in Vienna, in March, before the exile, the other in London, in June), and a summary in the middle of the third essay. Freud does not erase the marks of this unusual approach; he brings together the scattered fragments of former publications without eliminating the seams or the prefaces that "contradict each other and indeed cancel each other out."[69] He does not try to disguise the gaps, the logical inconsistencies, the unevenness of his progress, the scars of the final book. The division remains obvious. This is Freud's final lesson: always remain at the heart of separation and the unknown. Acknowledge its lacunae. Now, that is boldness.

To read *Moses and Monotheism* is to read Freud writing *Moses and Monotheism*. Never before has he left so many traces of the process of composition. Like the traditions and legends relating to the heroic figure of Moses, he reveals "the construction and transformation" of his own ways of writing: "confusions and contradictions and their unmistakable signs . . . of continuous and contentious revisions and superimpositions."[70] Further on, with regard to the biblical accounts, he writes: "The text as we possess it today will tell us enough about its own vicissitudes."[71]

Moses never let go of Freud's imagination, following him throughout his life "like an unlaid ghost,"[72] offering him a strong figure of identification in all the important moments of his existence: the self-analysis, the dissention within the psychoanalytic movement.[73] In 1914, he tries to approach the biblical hero through Michelangelo's statue in Rome:

> How often have I mounted the steep steps from the unlovely Corso Cavour to the lonely piazza where the deserted church stands, and have essayed to support the angry scorn of the hero's glance! Sometimes I have crept cautiously out of the half-gloom of the interior as though I myself belonged to the mob on whom his eye is turned—the mob which can hold fast no conviction, which has neither faith nor patience, and which rejoices when it has regained its illusory idols.[74]

Twenty years later, Moses is still a statue. Not a marble sculpted by Michelangelo but "a bronze statue with feet of clay,"[75] overturned by Freud, the sculptor of doubt and intellectual boldness, the iconoclast fascinated by images. In 1914, Freud had imputed to the man of the Renaissance a daring, sacrilegious interpretation of the biblical figure, but his essay had remained anonymous. His disciple, Karl Abraham, had wondered at this: "I am looking forward to 'Moses,' but I do not quite understand [the decision to publish anonymously]. Do you not think that the lion's paw will be recognized in any case?"[76]

At the end of his life, exiled in the promised land of England, the old lion has "little or nothing to lose."[77] He tells us that he speaks, thinks, and writes "as I wish or as I must."[78] He takes the risk of pub lishing his "construction," his "edifice," expecting major objections and critical attacks but not concealing the gaps or incoherences in the piece. Uncertainty is even set at the center of his approach: "I have already laid stress on the factor of doubt in my introductory remarks; I have, as it were, placed that factor outside the brackets."[79] Doubt and method are not mutually exclusive; one is a part of the other. Freud is not afraid to conclude that his work is ultimately a riddle without an answer.[80] What matters is not to answer or to know what the point is of asking the question, but to investigate.

On fifty-seven large pages, Freud writes the first manuscript of *Moses and Monotheism*. On the first page, he notes the date, August 9, 1934, and, as a subtitle, "A Historical Novel." In the following intro- duction, he compares the marriage of history and fiction to the issue of the coupling of a horse and a donkey: sometimes the historical novel presents itself as history, other times as a novel. Certain authors set out from history but do not try to respect it; what they hope to do is arouse emotions. Others do not hesitate to invent characters and events, but they nonetheless aspire to historical truth by way of fic- tion. When Freud himself, who, as he says, is neither a historian nor an artist, uses this term to introduce one of his works, he does so because it corresponds to another definition. He explains that he was trained to observe phenomena closely, and that as a result he tends to associate fiction and invention with blame and error. His aim is to gain some knowledge of the figure of Moses, but there is no histori- cal basis for this character study. What one must do, therefore, is treat each element of the text as a sign and fill in the gaps between frag- ments by favoring the hypothesis that seems most plausible, even though it does not necessarily coincide with the truth. And truth is often implausible.

Freud chose to delete the term "A Historical Novel," and so the introduction he spelled out was not published.[81] To form the portrait of his *Moses* he needed "poetic license"[82] (as well as the reconstructive skill of the archeologist)[83] and thus once again had to rely on the power of the novel, that power of the artist who "is free to fill in the gaps in memory according to the desires of his imagination" and "to picture the period which he wishes to reproduce according to his intentions."[84] Yet he was still a doctor, a scientist, and not a historian or an artist. He had at first thought he could justify the ballerina's lightness, but then confidence, mingled with modesty, won out and he delivered his "theoretical fiction" as a "portion of forgotten truth."[85] He is quick to characterize his account as lacking artistic merit, announcing with the transparency of a man who is no longer afraid to reveal himself: "I found myself unable to wipe out the traces of the history of the work's origin, which was in any case unusual."[86]

Clinical explorations, theoretical propositions, meditations on civilization, literary constructions: Freud weaves the thread of his self-analysis throughout all his texts. In this last "novel" it is also the man Freud whose portrait he draws, the unvarnished inscription of an elderly man who is well aware that writing, like the body, is marked by life. In the preface, written in London in June 1938, Freud discreetly notes his age as he mentions "the city which, from my early childhood, had been my home for seventy-eight years."[87] Before leaving Vienna, he had wondered whether he was strong enough to finish his project: "I meant, of course, the weakening of creative powers which goes along with old age."[88] And, in a rare confrontation with his own career as a writer, he adds: "As regards *internal* difficulties, a political revolution and a change of domicile could alter nothing. No less than before, I feel uncertain in the face of my own work; I lack the consciousness of unity and of belonging together which should exist between an author and his work."[89] And, in his very last words to the reader, he simply admits that what he has written "is all I can offer."[90]

Freud's writing began with *The Interpretation of Dreams*, carried along by his own dreams and his mourning for his dead father. Forty years later, the curtain falls with *Moses and Monotheism*, about the death of the father and his own death. And on the sacrilege of sacrileges—the murder of the text: "In its implications the distortion of a text resembles a murder: the difficulty is not in perpetrating the deed but in getting rid of its traces."[91] Making the man Moses no longer a father but a son, no longer a Jew but an Egyptian, taking it upon himself to deal with the biblical tradition in a personal manner—but "this is the only way in which one can treat material"[92]—amounts to the murder of the sacred father: "To deprive a people of a man whom they take pride in as the greatest of their sons is not a thing to be gladly or carelessly undertaken, least of all by someone who is himself one of them."[93]

Belonging and challenging, obeying and depriving, tradition and treason. To end his work, Freud closes the Book, that Bible in which his father had inscribed his birth date and his name along with the wish that he might become a scholar. It is from filiation and its murder that writing emerges.

"'What is to live immortal in song must perish in life.'"[94]

NOTES

1. Chamisso, pp. 6–7. This novel was written in 1813 and published in Germany, then in all of Europe the following year.

2. Translator's note: the allusion is to *Faust* Part II, Act 1, lines 6215–6302 (Goethe 1808–1832, pp. 157–159).

3. Freud 1929, p. 133.

4. Breuer and Freud 1893–1895, pp. 160–161.

5. Breuer and Freud 1893–1895, p. 160.

6. Breuer and Freud 1893–1895, p. 139, n. 1.

7. See Prokhoris 1988 and Urtubey 1983.

8. "If I may compare small things to great," a quotation from Virgil's *Georgics* 4.176 in the letter to Fliess of October 4, 1892 (Freud 1954, p. 63). The reference is to the second part of *Faust*, in connection with the second part of Freud's own text on paralysis in children.

9. "And the shades of loved ones appear, and with them, like an old, half-forgotten myth, first love and friendship," lines from the Dedication to *Faust* quoted in the letter to Fliess of October 27, 1897 (Freud 1954, p. 225).

10. These words of Mephistopheles (translator's note: *Faust* I: 1841–1842, translation in Goethe 1808–1823, p. 44) are often alluded to by Freud, from *The Interpretation of Dreams* to the final words of his speech upon accepting the Goethe Prize in 1930.

11. Freud 1905d, p. 283.

12. See Certeau 1987.

13. Cited in letter to Fliess of April 26, 1896 (Freud 1985, p. 184).

14. Quoted in Freud 1919a, p. 234.

15. *Flectere si nequeo superos, Acheronta movebo,*Vergil, Aeneid 6:312, quoted in Freud 1900, p. 608.

16. See Starobinski 1954.

17. Freud 1900, pp. 2–3.

18. Freud 1900, p. 3.

19. Like the two following citations, this is in Freud 1900, pp. 102–103.

20. Freud 1900, p. 103.

21. Freud 1900, p. 279.

22. Freud 1900, p. 142.

23. Freud 1899, p. 309.

24. Freud 1900, pp. 105–106.

25. Freud 1905b, pp. 105–106.

26. Chamisso 1813, pp. 12–13. Freud cites Chamisso in *Moses and Monotheism* (1939, p. 9).

27. Schnitzler 1927, p. 99. Freud mentions this story in "The 'Uncanny'" (1919a, p. 251).

28. Letter of May 8, 1906 (Freud 1960, p. 123).

29. Freud 1907a, p. 10.

30. Letter of May 14, 1922 (Freud 1960, pp. 197–198).

31. Freud 1919a, p. 237.

32. Freud 1907a, p. 93.

33. Though his conscious wish is to offer a brief summary so as to remind the reader of the content of the story, he reproduces it almost in its entirety, either quoting the novelist's actual words or following him with extreme fidelity, to the point where the first of the essay's four chapters uses forty-one pages to "sum up" the hundred and three pages of the original account.

34. Unless she read, twenty-seven years later, the few lines he devoted to her under cover of anonymity in his paper on screen memories: "I was seventeen, and in the family where I was staying there was a daughter of fifteen, with whom I immediately fell in love. It was my first calf-love and sufficiently intense, but I kept it completely secret" (1899, p. 313).

35. Letter of August 17, 1872 (Freud 1992, p. 12).

36. Letter of September 4, 1872 (Freud 1992, pp. 16–17).

37. Letter of September 4, 1872 (Freud 1992, p. 17).

38. Freud 1900, p. 205.

39. Letter of August 20, 1873 (Freud 1992, p. 41).

40. Freud 1908b.

41. Letter to Silberstein of January 17, 1875 (Freud 1992, p. 83). In his commentary on *Gradiva*, Freud cites this passage from Jensen: "'Hitherto, the female sex had been to him [Hanold] no more than the concept of something made of marble or bronze, and he had never paid the slightest attention to its contemporary representatives'" (1907a, p. 12).

42. Letter to Silberstein of April 11, 1875 (Freud 1992, p. 109). Freud describes Hanold in these terms: "He was wholly absorbed in his studies and had turned completely away from life and its pleasures" (1907a, p. 14).

43. Letter to Silberstein of January 17, 1875 (Freud 1992, p. 112).

44. On this occasion he publishes one of his first scientific works (Freud 1877).

45. Letter to Silberstein of March 28, 1876 (Freud 1992, p. 141).

46. Letter to Silberstein of April 23, 1876 (Freud 1992, p. 153).

47. Letter to Silberstein of April 23, 1876 (Freud 1992, pp. 152–153).

48. In his letters to Martha he describes Paris as a "magically attractive and repulsive city" (letter of November 24, 1885) and says that he could compare it "to a vast overdressed Sphinx who gobbles up every foreigner unable to solve her riddle," adding: "Paris is simply one long confused dream, and I shall be very glad to wake up" (letter of December 3, 1885, Freud 1960, pp. 185–188).

49. Letter to Silberstein of April 5, 1876 (Freud 1990, p. 142).

50. Letter to Silberstein of April 5, 1876 (Freud 1990, p. 149).

51. Jensen 1903, pp. 181–182.

52. Freud 1907a, p. 8.

53. Freud 1907a, p. 92.

54. Freud 1907a, p. 7.

55. Freud 1907a, p. 53.

56. Freud 1910c, p. 165.

57. Cited in Jones 1953, p. 111.

58. *The Magic Flute*, Act 1, Scene 15 (trans. S. F.). Freud was a great admirer of Mozart's operas. In a letter to Emil Fluss of March 6, 1874 (Freud 1990, p. 33), he announces to his friend that he is going to see *The Magic Flute*. In Manuscript J, sent to Wilhelm Fliess in 1895, he tells the story of a woman patient who has a sexual association while singing the *seguidilla* from the first act of *Carmen*; by way of interpretation, Freud replies with the page's aria from Act 2 of *The Marriage of Figaro* (Freud 1954, pp. 138–139). On August 7, 1901, he writes, again to Fliess, that he is going to Salzburg the following day to see a performance of *Don Giovanni* (Freud 1954, p. 333). *The Magic Flute* has a further connection to psychoanalysis, since it was staged by Freud's most famous little patient, Herbert Graf, who was "Little Hans." Graf offered a version of it in Salzburg in 1937, under the direction of Toscanini, in 1955 with Georg Solti, and in New York in 1972 and 1973, with scenery by Chagall.

59. Freud 1910b, p. 63.

60. Freud 1910b, pp. 63–64.

61. Freud 1910b, p. 73.

62. He himself will tell Lou Andréas-Salomé that his *Leonardo* is "the only truly beautiful thing I have ever written" (letter of February 9, 1919, Freud and Andréas-Salomé 1985, p. 90).

63. Freud 1910b, p. 134.

64. Letter to Hermann Struck of November 7, 1914 (Freud 1960, p. 306).

65. Freud 1910b, p. 134.

66. Freud 1910b, p. 135.

67. Faust's last words in Part II, Act V, 11585–11586 (trans. S. F.). In a letter to Fliess of November 2, 1895 Freud writes of his "confidence in the correctness of [his] psychological assumptions," adding, "I am enjoying a moment of real satisfaction. Meanwhile the time has not yet come to enjoy the climax and then sit back and relax. The later acts of the tragedy will still demand a lot of work" (1954, p. 132).

68. Freud 1939, p. 58.

69. Freud 1939, p. 57.

70. Freud 1939, p. 16.

71. Freud 1939, p. 43.

72. Freud 1939, p. 103.

73. See Chapter 4. An early, though indirect, reference to his identification with Moses can be found in a letter to Fluss of September 18, 1872, in connection with the Jews he met during his travels: "I'm fed up with this rabble" (1990, p. 228, trans. S. F.).

74. 1914b, p. 213. Freud first published this essay in the journal *Imago*. As in the letter to Fluss, he uses the word *Gesindel*, "rabble, mob."

75. Freud 1939, p. 17.

76. Freud and Abraham 1965, p. 169.

77. Freud 1939, p, 54.

78. Freud 1939, p. 57.

79. Freud 1939, p. 31.

80. Freud 1939, p. 137.

81. See Yerushalmi 1989.

82. "We touch here on the problem of poetic license versus historical truth" (Freud and Zweig 1970, p. 77).

83. The archeological metaphor, too, appears between the lines here. It is taken up and theorized in a text written at about the same time, "Constructions in Analysis" (1937a).

84. Freud 1939, p. 71.

85. Freud 1939, p. 73.

86. Freud 1939, p. 103.

87. Freud 1939, p. 57. To know Freud's age, all we have to do is add to these seventy-eight years the four spent outside Vienna.

88. Freud 1939, p. 54.

89. Freud 1939, p. 58 (emphasis in original).

90. Freud 1939, p. 137.

91. Freud 1939, p. 43.

92. Freud 1939, p. 27, n. 2.

93. Freud 1939, p. 7.

94. Freud cites this line from Schiller on p. 101, n. 2.

9

The Metaphor Man

His lynx eye immediately perceives the paper, recognizes the handwriting of the address, observes the confusion of the personage addressed, and fathoms her secret.

—Poe, "The Purloined Letter"[1]

What was Freud's gaze like? With what eye did he stare at the world?

The Wolf Man remembers his black eyes looking at him penetratingly, yet not in such a way as to make him at all uneasy.[2] Bruno Goetz, the young poet, felt comforted by the wonderfully benevolent, warm eyes that showed his deep knowledge of men: "When the time came for us to part, he held out his hand to me and looked into my eyes, and once again I experienced the kindness, so affectionate and melancholy, of his gaze. In all my life I have never forgotten that look."[3] "Curious and penetrating, . . . lively and kindly": these are also the words of his disciple, Theodor Reik, who stayed close to him for thirty years.[4] For Hanns Sachs, Freud's eyes, like his mind, were able to see what others could not; he tells how, in the forest of the Tatras, where the tastiest of mushrooms, the *Herrenpilz* or boletus, grew, the inventor of psychoanalysis organized contests to unearth the best specimens—but no one, relative or disciple, ever found them before he did.[5]

In the dramatic circumstances of March 1938, after the invasion of Austria, when the Nazis broke into Freud's apartment to ransack it, Freud's gaze made the intruders withdraw. "A frail and gaunt figure" appeared on the threshold of the dining room, Jones reports: "It was Freud, aroused by the disturbance. He had a way of frowning with blazing eyes that any Old Testament prophet might have envied, and the effect produced by his lowering mien completed the visitors' discomfiture. Saying they would call another day, they hastily took their departure."[6]

Herman Nunberg, an attentive observer, describes Freud's gaze in both the literal and the figurative sense:

> [Freud] saw what was happening in the human mind. For many years I had the opportunity to watch [him] during discussions in the meeting of the Society. When a speaker's remarks aroused his particular interest or when he was trying to make his own point especially clear, he would lift his head and look intensely, with extreme concentration, at a point in space, as if he were seeing something there. This tendency to *see* what he was thinking was reflected in his writings. They contain many pictorial elements, even when dealing with highly theoretical concepts. . . . [W]e may say that he first looked and then believed. . . . Only a man with such a vision could discover and see the laws governing the intricate labyrinth of the human mind.[7]

Freud himself declares one day, "See, always see, always keep your eyes open, be aware of everything, hold back from nothing, always be ambitious—however, don't be blinded or let yourself get swallowed up."[8] Look without succumbing to the attraction of images, represent the world through your senses, and transform it through the work of thought: this is the way he goes about things.

> I was afraid I might be completely blinded in my mind if I looked at things with my eyes and attempted to apprehend them with one or the other of my senses; so I decided I must take refuge in propositions, and study the truth of things in them.
>
> —Plato, *Phaedo*[9]

Freud is a visual person, a "seer." For him, seeing and thinking go together, but he also knows that the visible dazzles and paralyzes. The image haunts and obsesses him; throughout his life, it combines prohibition and fascination, attraction and mistrust. "You are requested to close an eye/the eyes"[10]: this is the command written on a railway poster in the dream accompanying the death of his father. In it we read his wish to open the eye: the good one, the inner one, the eye that enables him to see without perceiving, to know beyond the visible and the invisible. If the light of the eyes must be extinguished, this is because appearances are deceptive and illusory: Thou shalt not make idols or any images, he read in his father's strange and extraordinary illustrated Bible. Thus Freud stubbornly tries to look with the eyes of the mind, to transform his sense perceptions into psychic elaborations. The humanity of man, for him, stems from this never-finished transformation, this ceaseless labor of thought and culture.

His entire oeuvre is bent on the search for establishing words and meanings. How to reveal the nature of the psychic apparatus, how to describe its mechanisms, its interlocking structures, its circuits? Freud is aware that there can only be approximations, attempts, preliminary scaffolding. The titles of his papers convey this: sketch, essay, notes, contribution, introduction, as does the frequent use of the present tense. He never offers the reader a conclusive, dogmatic text but instead an always open construction site, research in progress, thinking as it is being thought, and he invites his reader to accompany him step by step, *in vivo*.

He wants to give form to the formless, a shape to the unshapable, and an image to the unimaginable—but a literary image. To get beyond the contrast of the perceptual and the psychic, image and word, the path of metaphor opens out in front of him as a royal road. Through intellectual creativity and associative freedom, literary talent and literary pleasure, through psychic compromise but above all out of theoretical necessity, Freud deploys an infinite kaleidoscope of figurative expressions, comparisons, and analogies throughout his psychoanalytic work.

In the migrations it sets in motion, the disguises in which it cloaks thought, and the scenarios it stages, metaphor gives access to something of the truth of the unconscious. The unconscious itself is inaccessible (invisible and inaudible, like the vowels of the divine tetragrammaton[11]) and is manifest only in the endless and countless succession of its offshoots; it is the site of thing-representations and not word-representations. Thus what Freud is passionately interested in doing is discovering the ruses and detours through with the unconscious presents itself in ever-renewing figurations. What fascinates him in the image is not so much the visible or visual as it is the quality of figurability. It is not theoretically indifferent that Freud first approached the description of the psychic apparatus through the dream: from the outset the dream provides the field of observation in which the visual and the figurative intersect.[12] Like dream-thoughts, metaphor displaces, condenses, and represents; its role in Freud's text is to sustain conceptual exploration and embody the very processes it describes.

> Our words will not be blind.
> —Sophocles, *Oedipus at Colonus*[13]

From the other side of the visible, where the unknown can no longer be tracked by the microscope nor unearthed with the pickaxe, Freud discovers and describes the infinite figures of the unconscious with words that cut through, carve out, unveil, words that become microscope and telescope, pickaxe and shovel, scalpel and lancet, words that are uttered and written to speak forth the black knowledge of the soul. Freud had but a single instrument: words, words, words, magical and yet paltry, powerful and always limited.[14] If there is one Freudian passion, one belief that was never given up, it is words: it is important to him to do everything he can so that others will be able to understand him.[15]

His writing navigates the border between the already-known and the unknown. What matters is not to oberve and then describe, to demonstrate and draw a conclusion, but to risk being carried along by the freedom of words and metaphors, to take shortcuts and detours led by the unconscious, to confront ambiguity and uncertainty, to proceed with his eyes covered as if in a game of blind man's bluff, without being afraid of losing his footing in the whirlwinds of the unknown. "I maintain that one should not make theories—they must fall into one's house as uninvited guests while one is occupied with the investigation of details."[16]

Between what the unconscious knows and the writing of this knowledge, there is no gap, no distance. Writing about psychoanalysis and inventing it go hand in hand, born of the same movement, the same inspiration. Under Freud's pen, traditional categories are erased: they no longer contradict one another but are mutually supportive. Foundation and form are united. Science and aesthetics, theory and autobiography merge in a conquering advance, simultaneously impulsive and reflective, rational and at the level of the unconscious. The writer's art and the inventiveness of his metaphors are the surest way to reach the unknown forces of the soul. Aesthetics are a method. The royal road leading to the unconscious passes through the play of the associations and words that weave its narration.

Freud begins the account of the unconscious by writing that

> words are the essential tool of mental treatment. A layman will no doubt find it hard to understand how pathological disorders of the body and mind can be eliminated by "mere" words. He will feel that he is being asked to believe in magic. And he will not be so very wrong, for the words which we use in our everyday speech are nothing other than watered-down magic.[17]

Going against the entire scientific tradition and his own medical training (in which seeing is perceiving), Freud continues to defend the knowledge of words. At the beginning of his *Introductory Lectures on Psycho-Analysis* he warns his readers that their prior culture and habits of thought predispose them against the ideas of psychoanalysis. For here seeing has disappeared; one can no longer look at an anatomical preparation, a chemical precipitate, or the contraction of a muscle. The psychoanalyst is not, like the professor of medicine, a guide and interpreter who, as it were, leads one through a museum: "Nothing takes place in a psycho-analysis but an interchange of words." Those people "who are only impressed by visible and tangible things—preferably by actions of the sort that are to be witnessed at the cinema—never fail to express their doubts whether 'anything can be done about the illness by mere talking.'" With the uncultivated temptations of the visible, Freud contrasts the charms, so constantly overinvested by him, of the word:

> Words were originally magic and to this day words have retained much of their ancient magical power. By words one person can make another blissfully happy or drive him to despair, by words the teacher conveys his knowledge to his pupils, by words the orator carries his audience with him and determines their judgments and decisions. Words provoke affects and are in general the means of mutual influence among men.[18]

He pleads his cause, certain that challengers will cast doubt on the scientific nature of his enterprise, that he will be classed among "laymen, poets, natural philosophers, and mystics."[19]

If words, through their magic power, are the sole medium of the talking cure, they are also the sole instrument of Freud's theoretical laboratory. In some passages, he asks himself the question of the use and limitations of language. Thus, in *Beyond the Pleasure Principle*, he admits that science uses a language that is unavoidably figurative, but he seems to dream of a lexicon that would be more appropriate to the aim of his investigation:

> [We are] obliged to operate with the scientific terms, that is to say with the figurative language, peculiar to psychology (or, more precisely, to depth psychology). We could not otherwise describe the processes in question at all, and indeed we could not have become aware of them. The deficiencies in our description would probably vanish if we were already in a position to replace the psychological terms by physiological or chemical ones. It is true that they too are only part of a figurative language, but it is one with which we have long been familiar and which is perhaps a simpler one as well.[20]

At the end of his career, in the *Outline of Psycho-Analysis* of 1938, he acknowledges once again that the real cannot be reached because we are clearly obliged to translate all our inferences into the very language of our perceptions: reality will always be unknowable. There is something in the very nature of the unconscious that remains veiled. No word, no image will ever fully capture it. It is not certain that Freud resigned himself to this.

> "Where, Messer Ludovico, have you found all this stupidity?"
> —Question asked of Ariosto by his patron,
> Cardinal Hyppolytus d'Este[21]

From his first writings to his final notes dashed off in London,[22] Freud played with metaphor in order to penetrate the human enigma. At the same time, he also questioned this way of proceeding, one that had come to him spontaneously and that he felt he had to justify, as though metaphor belonged to writers alone and not to scientists.

In the *Studies on Hysteria* Freud uses a series of evocations announcing the principal metaphors that will occur throughout his work: the devil[23]; the Bible[24]; the reference to the medical disciplines, surgery, and dentistry; games (chess, patience); and opera; but especially, and emphatically, archeology (the strata and the unearthing of a buried city) and the metaphor of writing and the text: the productions of the unconscious appear in the form of hieroglyphics, archives, illustrated volumes, or literary pamphlets. Freud allows himself all these many different analogies. Drawn from his own preoccupations, they seem necessary to him, even indispensible, but he believes he must justify a practice that is highly unusual for the serious man of science:

> I am making use here of a number of similes, all of which have only a very limited resemblance to my subject and which, moreover, are incompatible with one another. I am aware that this is so, and I am in no danger of over-estimating their value. But my purpose in using them is to throw light from different directions on a highly complicated topic which has never yet been represented. I shall therefore venture to continue . . . to introduce similes in the same manner, though I know this is not free from objection.[25]

Whereas writers permit themselves poetic license, Freud, for his part, discovers the fecundity of sequences entangling and intersecting to the point of unknowability. Free association is not only a technique that accompanies and facilitates the revelation of the unconscious; metaphorical freedom is the hallmark of Freud's writing. To delineate the map of dark continents, to theorize highly abstract notions, Freud, the scholar and poet of the unconscious, employs a profusion of images that simultaneously ravish, surprise, and precisely describe the always elusive unconscious. Right up to the end, he makes use of the metaphorical scenario that is never synonymous with illustration. Although he adores the theater (and the theatrical metaphor is present throughout his work, from Draft L in 1897, with its psychic "scenes,"[26] and later the primal scene), Freud is strongly mistrustful of the cinema. In connection with Pabst's film *The Mysteries of a Soul*, he writes to Karl Abraham on June 9, 1925: "My chief objection is still that I do not believe that satisfactory plastic representation of our abstractions is at all possible. We do not want to give our consent to anything insipid."[27] Did he want to be the only one to make use of images? Or, caught between the fascination and the taboo of representation, could he acknowledge the value only of literary images?

In *The Interpretation of Dreams*, making an analogy that he perhaps thinks too bold or less acceptable to his readers, he writes:

> I see no necessity to apologize for the imperfections of this or of any similar imagery. Analogies of this kind are only intended to assist us in our attempt to make the complications of mental functioning intelligible by dissecting the function and assigning its different constituents to different component parts of the apparatus. So far as I know, the experiment has not hitherto been made of using this method of dissection in order to investigate the way in which the mental instrument is put together, and I can see no harm in it. We are justified, in my view, in giving free rein to our speculations so long as we retain the coolness of our judgment and do not mistake the scaffolding for the building. And since at our first approach to something unknown all that we need is the assistance of provisional ideas, I shall give prefer-

ence in the first instance to hypotheses of the crudest and most concrete description.[28]

A symphony of metaphors, *The Interpretation of Dreams* offers, alongside some brief comparisons and isolated brilliant analogies, two major Freudian themes: the unconscious as a text and the unconscious as an optical device.[29]

The dream product, despite its obvious visuality, is a narrative and not the succession of plastic scenes. "A dream is a picture-puzzle . . . and our predecessors in the field of dream-interpretation have made the mistake of treating the rebus as a pictorial composition."[30] It is a language for which each dreamer invents the grammar, to the point where the dream, and his dream book, seem to Freud to be untranslatable. Psychic writing, the writing of the unconscious, is original, not phonetic but close to hieroglyphics and Chinese writing, with pictographic, ideogrammatic, and phonetic elements.[31] But there is no original, unique, final text, even if Freud intends to treat the least detail of a dream as though it were Holy Writ.[32] If there is a lost manuscript of memory, it cannot be rediscovered intact but only distorted, reworked, transformed, reconstructed.[33] Despite his conviction that the apparatus of the soul is a writing machine, Freud cannot demonstrate this fully except in "A Note upon the 'Mystic Writing Pad,'" (1925c),[34] where the image of the unconscious as a system of inscriptions reigns supreme.

Alongside the textual metaphor, optical analogies also arise insistently. The eye has always played a decisive role for Freud. From 1876 to 1886, during the first ten years he devotes to laboratory research, he scrutinizes, observes, and looks, in particular through a microscope. He even came close to becoming famous, as a young man, for discovering the anesthetic properties of cocaine in eye surgery; a trip to see his fiancée prevented him from publicizing his results. By the time he returned his friend Köller had used them instead, though Freud never held this lost opportunity against Martha.

When he becomes a psychoanalyst, he stresses the role of inner vision and makes the absence of the gaze a precept of psychoanalytic treatment. He finds the associations of his patients easier to use when they are in the form of images, not ideas, and that "hysterical patients, who are as a rule of a 'visual' type, do not make such difficulties for the analyst as those with obsessions."[35]

To corroborate Freud's passion for seeing, all we have to do is list, without further commentary and in random order, the visual books of his childhood; Goethe's studies of vision; his father's glaucoma; Moses' wrathful eye; the house at Bellevue, where the secret of dreams was revealed; Oedipus becoming blind and Narcissus blinded by his own image; Freud's dream of the myopic son and the dream of Rome that can be seen only from afar; the fright caused by the sight of Medusa's head; the difficulty in seeing Athens with his own eyes; and so forth. Freud never stops obeying the paradoxical injunction "You are requested to close the eyes/an eye."

Optical instruments appear in the seventh chapter of *The Interpretation of Dreams*, where Freud speaks of regression and tries to spell out the idea of a topography of the soul that would have nothing to do with any anatomic localization. He thinks of the lenses of a telescope or camera producing a virtual world: "Psychical locality will correspond to a point inside the apparatus at which one of the preliminary stages of an image comes into being. In the microscope and telescope, as we know, these occur in part at ideal points, regions at which no tangible component of the apparatus is situated."[36] Later he will again take up this optical comparison to explain that every psychic act begins by being unconscious and can either remain so or evolve into consciousness, just as every photograph must first be turned into a negative; only those that pass the test being acceptable for making into positives.[37]

In 1910 he explains to his opthalmologist colleagues that people afflicted with hysterical blindness are not blind except when it comes to consciousness: in the unconscious, they see. At the end of his paper, he mentions a legend that connects the eye to the genital and the gaze to castration: in the story of Lady Godiva, everyone in town hid behind closed windows while she rode through the streets naked. The only man who spied on her was punished with blindness.[38]

The anxiety about being deprived of one's eyes is also at the center of his analysis of E. T. A. Hoffmann's "The Sandman," in which he shows that the horror of losing one's eyesight is a substitute for castration anxiety, and that it is closely connected with the death of the father.[39]

> Don Quixote continued on his way, which was none other than the one his horse wanted, for he believed that this was the essence of adventures.
> —Cervantes, *Don Quixote*[40]

From parallels to approximations, from detours to analogies, Freud makes his way along the tangled threads of his associations. He goes from personal images, to intimate resonances, to cultural sources that may be shared by all, so as to give form to highly abstract notions, often speculative ones. The singular unconscious in which his theory is rooted opens out onto the universal through sequences of metaphors: the Bible; Greek antiquity; Western literature with its myths and civilizing heroes; references to animals (horse, camel, polar bear, whale), plants, and minerals; and also to politics, economics, and the military (defense, resistance); humor; the sciences (biology, physics, analytic chemistry, mechanics); painting, architecture, and decoration; medicine; law; sometimes music or even daily objects (the mystic writing pad, an item recently displayed in a department store, the telephone); geography (cities, oceans, mountains, jungle, or the "dark continent"); journeys on foot, on horseback, by boat or train; and, of course, always archeology and writing.

Rapid or prolonged, in motion or static, rooted in the soil of erotic or aggressive drives, Freud's metaphors extend over the entire field of human activities, always in transformation, in evolution, infinitely unfolding to model the endless metamorphoses of the unconscious, which he seeks without ever being able to reach it: "In psychology we can only describe things by the help of analogies. There is nothing peculiar in this; it is the case elsewhere as well. But we have constantly to keep changing these analogies, for none of them lasts us long enough."[41]

In the account of the Dora case, for example,[42] as he goes along Freud mentions the work of the archeologist, Goethe's *Faust*, a river image, the Church Fathers, writing, Schnitzler, the Greek people, and then, once more, the riverbed and archeology. He goes on to refer to the Gospels and the myth of Oedipus. Medea and Creusa are evoked along with contemporary figures: the entrepreneur and the capitalist. And, at the end, the devil, Charcot, and the textual metaphor conclude the narrative.

Freud approaches his object as a photographer would, varying the angles, modifying the framing, and adding perspectives in the attempt to seize a bit of truth beyond appearances. The unconscious is inexhaustible. One association is echoed by the next or revives an earlier one; one image refers to another, diffracted and multiplied as on the edges of a Venetian mirror. Freud does not renounce his analogies but instead transforms them, piling up comparisons. On occasion, he is not afraid to pursue the development of his bold metaphorical imagination to the point of absurdity. "[W]e must always be prepared to drop our conceptual scaffolding if we feel that we are in a position to replace it by something that approximates more closely to the unknown reality," he states.[43]

He follows this recommendation up to the end, although he is especially attached to certain of his metaphors, in particular the archeological comparison, and gives it up only unwillingly. Thus, after likening the past of the soul to the Eternal City, he recognizes the limitations of his analogy: "There is clearly no point in spinning our phantasy any further, for it leads to things that are unimaginable and even absurd." Yet he does not give up the comparison without defending it once again, even *a contrario*: "Our attempt seems to be an idle game. It has only one justification. It shows us how far we are from mastering the characteristics of mental life by representing them in pictorial terms."[44]

Never giving anything up is surely one of Freud's character traits.

Optical, textual, geographical, or archeological: Freud's metaphors are attached to the body: the gaze, the hand, the foot, and always the genital. Traces on the soil, in earth or water, on paper, wax, stone. Fleeting traces in search of an inscription of eternity, ephemeral sensations for an indelible memory. Paths blazed, body on the march: metaphorical writing surveys, digs, penetrates, goes astray, and abandons itself to the rigorous play of creative fantasy.

Though Freud, like Moses, obeys an interdiction against representation, though he hopes to resist the blinding seductions of the visible so as to privilege the life of the mind over the perceptions of the senses, throughout all his experience of writing about the unconscious he nevertheless pursues the dream of making this unknown, "unseen"[45] knowledge of the soul figurable, perceptible, almost palpable. His gaze turned inward, with the invisible eyes of words, Freud feels his way tentatively and blindly, sketching for us the paths toward revelation.

Metaphor, metamorphosis, transference, displacement, journey: Freud names the metaphorical course of the human odyssey.

NOTES

1. Poe 1845, p. 194.
2. Gardiner 1971, p. 193.
3. Goetz 1976, p. 223 (trans. S. F.).
4. Reik 1940, p. 28.
5. Sachs 1944, p. 110.
6. Jones 1957, p. 219.
7. Nunberg and Federn 1962, pp. xxvi–xxvii (emphasis in original).
8. Goetz 1976, p. 220 (trans. S. F.).
9. Plato, p. 132.
10. Freud 1900, pp. 317–318.
11. Cf. Freud 1911b.
12. Lacoste 1981, 1990.
13. Sophocles 1954b, p. 142.
14. Pontalis 1990, p. 95.
15. Cf. Freud 1914d.
16. Letter to Ferenczi of July 31, 1915 (Freud and Ferenczi 1996, p. 74).
17. Freud 1890, p. 283.
18. Freud 1916–1917, p. 17.
19. Freud 1916–1917, p. 20.
20. Freud 1920c, p. 60.
21. Freud uses this quotation in the introduction to "Creative Writers and Daydreaming" (1907b, p. 143).

22. "With neurotics it is though we were in a prehistoric landscape—for instance in the Jurassic. The great saurians are running about; the horsetails grow as high as palms" (Freud 1938c, p. 299).

23. For this metaphor, see Urtubey 1983.

24. On the role of the Bible in Freud's works and correspondence, see Pfrimmer 1981.

25. Freud 1893–1895, p. 291.

26. In Freud 1954, p. 197–200.

27. Freud and Abraham 1965, p. 284.

28. Freud 1900, p. 536.

29. On this double metaphor, see Derrida 1967.

30. Freud 1900, p. 278.

31. Freud takes up this idea again in "The Claims of Psycho-Analysis to Scientific Interest" (1913c).

32. Freud 1900, p. 514.

33. See Baudry 1968.

34. Freud 1925c.

35. Freud 1883–1895, p. 280.

36. Freud 1900, p. 536.

37. Freud 1912.

38. Freud 1910d.

39. Freud 1919a.

40. Cervantes 1605–1615, p. 69.

41. Freud 1926a, p. 195.

42. Freud 1905b.

43. Freud 1900, p. 61.

44. Freud 1929, pp. 70–71.

45. Jacques Derrida develops this notion in *Memoirs of the Blind* (1990).

10

The Friend

To introduce a detailed account of Freud's friendships, one would have to begin with "Once upon a time."[1]

Still answering to the royal name Sigismund, Freud likes to acknowledge the ties linking him to his friends Silberstein, Fluss, and Rosanès. This was around a hundred and twenty years ago. But how can we, now, untangle the threads that bound him so closely, beyond fate and necessity, to so many friendships won? For, from these first intimates, he goes on to join tarot players, university colleagues, brothers in B'nai B'rith, the Wednesday Evening disciples, several idealists, great writers, a Berlin mentor, a vigorous Swiss, an archeologist in Rome, a Parisian café singer, and a real princess. And to complete the catalog—since in this earthly world a square is not a circle—some dogs.

It is for a golden-haired chow that Freud finds himself humming an aria from *Don Giovanni* that he knows well, although he is in no way a musician: "A bond of friendship unites us both" (*Così saremo amici*).[2]

Cicero, Aristotle, Spinoza, and Montaigne extolled friendship as a rare pleasure granted only to the wisest and most virtuous of men. Freud does not hesitate to reveal this scandalous truth of the unconscious: one and the same person can arouse both love and hate in us, friendship and enmity. But at the end of his life—as though he had never ceased to aspire to some peaceful bond—with Topsy, Lun, Jo-fi, and Wolf, his canine brothers, he finally admits that he can enjoy an unalloyed inclination, free of ambivalence and the "almost unbearable" conflict with civilization.

Already as an adolescent Freud recognizes in himself an unquestionable affinity with these animals, since, in his dialogues with his fellow student Eduard Silberstein, he borrows the name of a dog imagined by Cervantes.[3] They are Scipio and Berganza, suddenly endowed with the extraordinary grace of speech and reason. Did Freud know, at that time, the treatise of Cicero in which Scipio and Laelius represent eternal friendship? And did he know that Cervantes, for whom he learned Spanish, wrote a book called *Persiles and Sigismond* shortly before he died?

Of the two dogs placed onstage by the poet, Berganza is the one who recites his adventures, and Scipio the one who listens and comments. Freud, of course, chooses the pseudonym of the faithful Scipio. Freud-Scipio and Silberstein-Berganza form a learned society of two, the Academia Castellana (AC), with the purpose of composing a secret mythology and witty writings. The AC prefigures all the brotherhoods to which Freud will later belong: the Bund, B'nai B'rith, the "Congress" with Fliess, the Wednesday Evenings, and the Secret Committee. Since ritual is appropriate in friendship, there are always the gestures and tokens of closeness and fraternal intimacy as well as signs of fetishization: the choice of secret names, a shared language, the solemn distribution of rings, the gifts of ancient objects or money, shared journeys, and the regular exchange of letters and offprints. But friendship is also nourished by common aspirations and values.

The two adolescents discover in Cervantes heroic figures with whom to identify in their search for ideals. Following the example of the Dog Conversation, they find in their friendship the strength to confront the struggles of existence: "We became friends at a time when one doesn't look upon friendship as a sport or an asset, but when one needs a friend with whom to share things."[4]

When circumstances draw them apart, Freud immediately suggests to Silberstein that they exchange letters, every Sunday, comprising "an entire encyclopedia of the past week"[5] and guided solely by the love of truth. Already we have the promise to tell everything. He sends his friend "a biblical study," but it never arrives, and Freud cannot get over the loss of this work, "biblically naive and forceful, so melancholy and so gay," that he is, he says, "as proud of as of my nose or my maturity.[6]

Silberstein is thus assigned the role that will subsequently be taken by Fliess: his first and best audience. To get underway on the road to creation, Freud can never do without an Other. His work emerges only from open space and the support of friendship. And the work bears the mark of its origin: the uninterrupted dialogues with the friend and the correspondent.

After the AC and the dog conversations, Freud integrates into his theoretical writings a fictive dialogue with the reader and the latter's presumed objections.[7] This stylistic trait is not just a particular mode of exposition and communication but also an inner need, the need to address an interlocutor in order to give form to the often literary intuitions of his imagination in a construct that will conform to scientific tradition.

Thus the wish to converse with the friend extends into the writing of the oeuvre. Whereas for Montaigne it is in true friendship that the souls of friends form a seamless whole,[8] for Freud, on the contrary, it is as though the seam must always remain visible to bind the work to friendship without which it could not have been written. Freud must have a friend in order to live and write.

From the *Studies on Hysteria* written with Josef Breuer, "dearest friend and best loved of men,"[9] to "A Disturbance of Memory on the Acropolis" dedicated to Romain Rolland, his adored friend,[10] the work is woven on the busy loom of his uninterrupted friendships. The texts arise from times of joy (the *Gradiva* during the idyll with Jung) as well as times of heartbreak ("On Narcissism: An Introduction" and the "Moses of Michelangelo" after the rupture with the successor known as "Joshua").

From the time of the first elective affinities, he wants friendship to be set down in writing. He never gives up the wish to live with the friend and share words offered and, when he awaits them, received.

It is no wonder, then, that on the long list of his friendships there are so many writers: Stefan and Arnold Zweig, Arthur Schnitzler, Thomas Mann, Romain Rolland, and also Lou Andréas-Salomé, the prolix Princess Bonaparte, and even the singer Yvette Guilbert, who dedicates several autobiographical volumes to him.

Although friendship is written about and gives rise to the writing of the oeuvre, feelings of friendship—the drives that animate it, the inhibition it calls for—remains almost entirely private and intimate. Over the course of more than forty years of psychoanalytic reflection, barely a few paragraphs touch on it, and then as if by accident. There is a striking contrast between the profusion of friendships in Freud's daily life and the discreet role he reserves for them in his theory.

Maurice Blanchot, unwilling to say that Georges Bataille had disappeared but agreeing to accompany this friendship into oblivion, was able to recognize "the common strangeness that does not allow us to speak of our friends but only to speak to them, not to make them a theme of conversations (or articles)."[11] But since Freud, despite his talent as a writer and his wish to be one, did not choose as the sole basis for his undertaking the absolute arbitrariness of the writer, how can we understand this silence on his part?

Surely we may conclude that the places where Freud is silent, his black continents, the subjects that resist articulation, tell us about him more accurately than any other autobiographical utterance. The areas in which the upheavals of his joys and his writing are stored up can be named: Judaism, femininity, friendship. They often enhance one another reciprocally. But, above all, this theoretical silence is in accord with the paradoxes of his practice of friendship and thereby reveals to the point of absurdity the space of excess that it occupies for him. *A scent of friendship.* . . .

As a young man, Freud believed that he was afflicted with a painful weakness in this matter: "I consider it a great misfortune that nature has not granted me that indefinite something which attracts people."[12]

And in the evening of his life he acknowledges another failing in himself, confiding to Marie Bonaparte that he is not a good judge of people: he trusts them and is then disappointed.[13]

And Freud *was* disappointed. The history of his friendships is strewn with sudden dazzlements followed by rancor, bitterness, accusations, quarrels, and ruptures. He is a man of enthusiasm and ardor. And yet he does not combine violence with love but instead friendship with passion.

Even though his married life plays out in pastel tones, he tries his hand at a psychology of romance, as we know from several fragments. But when it comes to feelings of friendship, so much more present and invested in his actual reality, Freud does not elaborate a theory.[14] When by chance we find the word "friendship" in a text, it is always slipped into some list between "the affective bonds of marriage" and "the tenderness between parents and children." The word never achieves autonomy. Mentioned among other "social instincts," friendship is one of the forms of "aim-inhibited" love, a term that is more descriptive than rigorous from the metapsychological standpoint. In *Civilization and Its Discontents*, he sets off the word in quotation marks at the same time that he uses it in the plural, thereby denying it the force of exclusivity:

> Both—fully sensual love and aim-inhibited love—extend outside the family and create new bonds with people who before were strangers. Genital love leads to the formation of new families, and aim-inhibited love to "friendships" which become valuable from a cultural standpoint because they escape some of the limitations of genital love, as, for instance, its exclusiveness.[15]

Nevertheless, it is in the masculine singular, repeated twice, that Freud declines the noun of his own bonds of friendship, and, when the plural follows, no one is any longer the one and only for him; from now on, he will offer himself as the one and only for everyone.

Before taking the form of Lou, Marie Bonaparte, or Yvette Guilbert, friendship in the feminine haunts his relationships with men. His Judaism, too, is part of the mix.

At the beginning of the century, Freud sends Fliess a letter in which he tries to understand what attaches him so powerfully to the friend who made it possible for him to conquer the unconscious. At the same time, he reveals to him the two major biblical identifications that dwell within him in his solitary struggle:

> [T]here can be no substitute for the close contact with a friend which a particular—almost a feminine—side of me calls for. . . .
> [I]t will be a fitting punishment for me that none of the unexplored regions of the mind in which I have been the first mortal to set foot will ever bear my name or submit to my laws. When breath threatened to fail me in the struggle, I prayed the angel to desist, and that is what he has done since then. But I have not turned out to be the stronger, though since then I have been noticeably limping. Well, I really am forty-four now, a rather shabby old Jew. . . .[16]

Between Freud and Fliess there is love/passion. They share the same fantasy of bisexuality, the fruit of an envy of the feminine. Almost at the same moment, they announce to one another the pregnancies of their wives. If Freud's child had been a son, he would have called him Wilhelm. But it will be Anna. Here we may recall that he believed his friends and his children were revenants. This underlying feminine element will bring about a bruising rupture when Fliess accuses Freud of not having respected his priority in the theorization of bisexuality. His "narcissistic" and "homosexual" double also wanted to be recognized in his original fecundity.

With Jung, on the other hand, the feminine was removed from their friendly passion, even denied, and assigned to Ferenczi, about whom Freud complains to his virile friend: "He has been too passive and receptive, letting everything be done for him like a woman, and I really haven't got enough homosexuality in me to accept him as one."[17] Judaism also plays a role in the relations with Jung, the sacred successor and prince royal: "If I am Moses, then you are Joshua and will take possession of the promised land of psychiatry, which I shall only be able to glimpse from afar."[18] When the break occurred,

Freud wrote "The Moses of Michelangelo," describing how the prophet mastered his anger in the face of his people's betrayal.

Friendship and Judaism often overlap, and what is only the sign of an epoch and a milieu lends the circles of friends and early figures in psychoanalysis a touch of endogamy: during his studies, he meets with his friends in the Bund each week to converse or play cards or chess in the Kurzweil café. Present are Eli Bernays, the brother of Freud's future wife (and the future husband of his sister Anna); Ignaz Schönberg, Minna Bernays's erstwhile fiancé; and the brothers Richard, Alfred, and Emil Fluss, who, like Freud, hailed from Freiberg. Breuer and Hammerschlag, his paternal supports, live in the same building and marry the former's son to the latter's daughter. Anna O., Breuer's famous patient (whose real name was Bertha Pappenheim), was an old friend of Martha's. The Emma/Irma of the injection dream is simultaneously Freud's patient and, unfortunately, Fliess's, and all the while a friend of the Freud family. Wilhelm Fliess marries Ida Bondy, an acquaintance of Breuer's; Oscar Rie, Freud's tarot partner, longtime friend, and pediatrician to the Freud children, marries Ida Fliess's sister, and so forth. When, in order to emerge from his isolation, Freud becomes a member of the liberal Jewish association B'nai B'rith, he is soon joined by his brother Alexander and also by his card partners Oscar Rie and Leopold Konigstein, to be followed by Theodor Reik and Edward Bibring. In the "secret committee" formed by Freud's closest friends are Karl Abraham, Sandor Ferenczi, Otto Rank, Hanns Sachs, and Ernest Jones (who was called the *shabbes goy*).

No doubt the choice of friends, like romantic choice, is guided by the incestuous features of one's first loves.

In a Vienna where Freud is not one of the majority, he must wait a long time before he is recognized outside this small Jewish circle in which psychoanalysis was born. Beyond the singularity of his discovery, Freud wants to be the father of a Western oeuvre. Jung, and the Swiss with him, carry the hope of such an opening. After Josef Breuer,

Josef Paneth, Ernst Fleischl von Marxow,[19] and Wilhelm Fliess, Carl Gustav Jung is set aside in turn.

As in his *non vixit* dream, Freud lost his friends/rivals, some through death, others through the disappearance of the friendship:

> I have already shown how my warm friendships as well as my enmities with contemporaries went back to my relations in childhood with a nephew who was a year my senior; how he was my superior, how I learned to defend myself against him, how we were inseparable friends, and how, according to the testimony of our elders, we sometimes fought with each other and—made complaints to them about each other. All my friends have in a certain sense been reincarnations of this first figure.[20]

Behind all the revenants (and Jung is their last, passionate avatar), behind the screen memory of his nephew John, lies Julius, buried deep in his guilty memory: the younger brother who died after having deprived him of his mother's exclusive love for six months when Freud was 2. To escape survivor guilt, to be free of the painful fraternal rivalry that each new friendship reawakens, there is no way out but to stop loving the brothers/friends. From now on, he is the father—a father who is always in search of sons.

In 1910 Freud writes to Jung:

> I am merely irritated now and then—I may say that much, I trust—that you have not yet disposed of the resistances arising from your father-complex, and consequently limit our correspondence so much more than you would otherwise. Just rest easy, dear son Alexander, I will leave you more to conquer than I myself have managed, all psychiatry and the approval of the civilized world, which regards me as a savage![21]

Jung refuses this seductive proposition and replies in no uncertain terms: "If ever you should rid yourself entirely of your complexes and stop playing the father to your sons, and instead of aiming continually at their weak spots take a good look at your own for a change, then I will mend my ways and at one stroke uproot the vice of being of two minds about you. . . . No doubt you will be outraged by this peculiar token of friendship. . . ."[22]

But, as after a squabble with John, Freud still thinks: "I was the stronger and remained in possession of the field."[23] No one is irreplaceable, as he tries to persuade Binswanger:

> I am completely indifferent. Warned by earlier experiences, and proud of my elasticity, I withdrew my libido from him months ago, at the first signs, and I miss nothing now. Also, this time things are easier for me, for I can redistribute the quantity of libido that has been set free in new places, such as with you, Ferenczi, Rank, Sachs, Abraham, Jones, Brill, and others.[24]

This divided friendship, suddenly plural, judiciously allocated as though to lower the affective stakes and the risk of betrayal,[25] no longer carries the dream of an exclusive bond with the other. Despite his wish for a nonconflictual relationship, a friendly solidarity without oedipal rivalry and destructive envy, ambivalence and omnipotence get the upper hand. It is cruel, Aristotle writes, that the wish for friendship arises quickly but friendship itself does not.[26]

Freud no longer admits to anyone what he wrote to Fliess at the time of his strongest transferential friendship:

> Your kind should not die out, my dear friend; the rest of us need people like you too much. How much I owe you: solace, understanding, stimulation in my loneliness, meaning to my life that I gained through you, and finally even health that no one else could have given back to me. It is primarily through your example that intellectually I gained the strength to trust my judgment [and] to face with lofty humility all the difficulties that the future may bring. For all that, accept my humble thanks![27]

But friendship, supposedly a consolation in solitude, is never anything but a lie in the clear light of day. It must be mourned. As he grows older, Freud discovers a beautiful friendship with a few rare beings, beyond the dreams of transparency with a double, in acceptance of the joy of the incomprehensible.

But first comes the time of the "analytic fraternity." Freud's disciples, though they may be called friends, never lose their original status as pupils and ambassadors of his work. Freud offers them intaglios from his collection of antiquities as a sign of alliance more than as a token of friendship. For a long time his personal and theoretical preoccupations had been inscribed in the lineage of sons: Oedipus, Hamlet, Hannibal, Joseph. Now it is the figure of the father that concerns him, and Moses haunts him right up to the end of his life. Like the biblical hero, he himself is now a founding father. And, like him, he is a lawgiver, a leader of men.

He thereby finds himself safe from competition and rivalry with his equals, but being a master hardly keeps him from experiencing disappointments and ruptures. Freud often sees an analogy between the sons of the primal horde and some of his pupils as they await the death of the primal father.

His most harmonious, most faithful, most lasting friendships are to be found where one would surely least expect them, with women. The precious friend of whom he dreams in his youth is what he hopes to find, together with a housekeeper and a cook, in the charming form of a lover, his cherished fiancée Martha: his princess, his Dulcinea, his Cordelia.[28] He does not hide this aspiration from her: "I am going to be very frank and confidential with you, as is right for two people who have joined hands for life in love and friendship. . . . Nor shall I always be very affectionate; sometimes I will be serious and outspoken, as is only right between friends and as friendship demands. . . . And you will understand me when I say that even for a beloved girl there is still one further step up: to that of friend."[29]

Freud, who has not abandoned the values of his adolescence, idealizes Martha as Cervantes' hidalgo does his Dulcinea. And throughout his life he will choose to renounce the world of sense perception in order to accomplish an ideal of abstraction. Thus friendship—with its need for disembodiedness, especially highlighted in friendship with women—fully corresponds to his aspiration and presents itself as one of the most *sublime* forms of love.

Separated from Martha during the four years preceding their marriage, and bound to her by a love that is as ardent as it is platonic, Freud speaks to her as a lover and a friend. As earlier with Silberstein and later with Fliess, Martha receives letters in which Freud confides his scientific projects, works out new ideas, and begins to trace the pathways of his inner journey. He holds his fiancée's intellectual ability in high esteem, and the words he sends her anticipate those he will write thirty years later to Lou Andréas-Salomé, his second female correspondent, the "understander": "[Y]ou write so intelligently and to the point that I am just a little afraid of you. I think it all goes to show once more how quickly women outdistance men. Well, I am not going to lose anything by it."[30]

Since, in the rare cases where friendship is mentioned in his theoretical writing, Freud always speaks of the affectional bonds in marriage that arise from sexual attraction, we may imagine that, when the union of Martha and Sigmund takes place, their feelings of friendship are not diminished but continue alongside their conjugal intimacy.

After the birth of their six children, their sexual relations seem to dwindle and perhaps even to stop, probably for reasons of contraception. Freud had hoped that Wilhelm Fliess would discover the secret of the female cycle, which would have permitted a sex life without constraint or an undesired conception. "We are now living in abstinence, and you know the reasons for this as well," he admits to his friend in 1893.[31] Shortly thereafter, in a paper on anxiety neurosis that has an autobiographical resonance, Freud condemns coitus interruptus, which he holds responsible for anxiety and neurasthenia.[32] In 1908, he explains that sexual intercourse is restricted even in marriage, and here we can sense his own disappointment: "After three, four, or five years, the marriage becomes a failure in so far as it has promised the satisfaction of sexual needs. For all the devices hitherto invented for preventing conception impair sexual enjoyment, hurt the fine susceptibilities of both partners, and even actually cause illness."[33]

In this same paper, he admits that abstinence calls for all the strength of a human being, and that mastery via sublimation is possible for only some people. No doubt he counts himself among the latter and channels his sexual energy into psychoanalytic theory.

In 1915 he declares to James Putnam that he is in favor of a much freer sex life than that permitted by society, and in particular by American puritanism, even though he admits that, for his part, "I have made little use of such freedom, except in so far as I was convinced of what was permissible for me in this area."[34] What did he mean by this? Is he alluding to masturbation, "the one great habit that is a 'primary addiction,'"[35] or to some inclination toward his sister-in-law?

For Minna Bernays, who remained single after mourning Ignaz Schönberg, had moved in with her sister and brother-in-law after the birth of their last child. It is said that Freud found in her a valued companion in conversations and travel. Some think that what went on between them was more than friendship or platonic love. Yet it does not seem very surprising that a man of high ethical standards, capable of vigorous sublimation of the passions, could have lived much of his sexual life in abstinence and have been able to transform his aptitude for love into a thirst for knowledge.

As is the case for the most official facets of his life, documents, if they exist, remain hidden in archives. Will we, like over-curious children, have to keep waiting for a long time at the door of the parents' bedroom, or will we finally, as primary heirs, come to know at least the catalogue of family riches?[36]

In his office laden with books and ancient figurines—which he sometimes invites to his desk like Don Giovanni and the statue of the Commandant—Freud hangs the portraits of the friendly conquests of his mature years: two photos of Marie Bonaparte, one of Lou Andréas-Salomé, and a portrait of the singer Yvette Guilbert, immortalized by Toulouse-Lautrec. In counterpoint to the tumult of constantly rebellious sons, these sisters, these daughters, these faithful women friends bring him calm and consolation. Freud had demanded friendship from Fliess and Jung; he required this from his disciples, both toward him and, if possible, also among themselves. But Lou comes on her own and offers to dedicate herself to his cause.

The adherence of this woman writer, the friend of poets and philosophers, is immediately interpreted by Freud as a good omen. He is won over by her fine perception of the most complex mechanisms of the unconscious and savors her detailed commentaries on his works. He even finds in her the qualities of a visionary and an innovator: "It is quite evident . . . how you anticipate and complement me each time, how you strive prophetically to unite my fragments into a structural whole."[37]

Their mutual admiration, esteem, and friendship persist until Lou's death, two and a half years before Freud's. For a quarter of a century, they keep on inventing an encounter in writing. As time goes on, they exchange words and laments. "Well, I have got this off my chest, since we both seem prevented from meeting. The number of things one has to renounce!"[38] And Lou, in a more optimistic mood: "[In the last resort we shall only be able to hobble on crutches to meet each other. Well, I for my part look forward eagerly to this hobble!"[39] But the meetings are rare, and so they send one another their photographs and especially their offprints. One winter Freud offers her a bit of money so that she can repair an old fur coat. In a small section, chiseled like a precious stone, in *The Psychopathology of Everyday Life*, he tells how, thanks to a slip, he understood that he was getting ready to send, for the second time, a little gem to a friend, Lou, to be mounted in a ring.[40]

When Freud and Lou meet in Weimar, in 1911, they are 55 and 50 years old. Although they do not grow old together, at least they get on in years at the same time and confide to one another the inner transformations that accompany aging. "A crust of indifference is slowly creeping up around me," Freud writes to Lou. "The change taking place is perhaps not very noticeable; everything is as interesting as it was before, neither are the ingredients very different; but some kind of resonance is lacking; unmusical as I am, I imagine the difference to be something like using the pedal [of a piano] or not."[41]

This is the same Freud who constantly states that he is as much a stranger to music as to mysticism but knows Mozart's operas almost by heart and likes to use musical metaphors throughout his correspondence. Thus, still to his friend Lou: "I strike up a—mostly very simple—melody; you supply the higher octaves for it; I separate the one from the other and you blend what has been separated into a higher unity; I silently accept the limits imposed by our subjectivity, whereas you draw express attention to them. Generally speaking we have understood each other and are at one in our opinions."[42]

Freud speaks of music; Lou replies in terms of pastries. When she receives the *Introductory Lectures on Psycho-Analysis*, she writes: "[A]fter my enjoyment of the book as a whole I picked out the freshest and plumpest plums from the cake."[43] Because they accept a margin of disagreement and of the unknown between them, despite the differences in their temperaments and world views their friendship never clouds over for twenty-five years. There is no irritation, no touchiness, but a constant gratitude of one toward the other and a joy in writing that is always quivering with affect and with sensuality. Lou was the only sister among five boys, but Freud always attributed six to her. Did he count himself among them?

Fifteen years after Louise von Salomé another great lady, descended from the nobility of the czars, asks to be received by the old Jewish master of Vienna. He warns her right from her first visit, on September 30, 1925, that, since he is getting on in years and is no longer in good health, she should not get too attached. With that, Marie Bonaparte, Princess of Greece, bursts into tears and tells him that she loves him. "To hear that when you are seventy!" Freud replies.[44] He has just met the good fairy of his old age. Of all his analytic children, she is the most fervent disciple. When she met Niels Bohr, who explained the theories of the atom to her, she writes to Freud: "Modem physicists are simultaneously metaphysicians. The oedipus complex is less hypothetical."[45]

She has the necessary money, energy, and prestige to fulfill her dreams, along with an inexhaustible wish to win the love and approval of the last of her chosen fathers and masters. With her, Freud can finally believe that he will not be disappointed: "I think that with you I am not mistaken."[46] For fourteen years she is a princess of fantasies come true and, at the same time, a skilled and effective diplomat, one who, at the moment when Europe is tipping over into horror, can save an old man and his relatives.

Marie Bonaparte gives him the best cigars and superb ancient objects, thereby fulfilling his two most basic passions. To her Viennese empire the last of the Bonapartes, a descendant of Napoleon, attaches her Parisian fief. Against Freud's will, to be sure, she buys back and preserves the precious letters to Fliess that witness the birth of psychoanalysis. To mitigate his suffering from cancer, she sends him her physician, Dr. Schur, and, through him, accompanies Freud up to the threshold of death. And even beyond, since it is the Greek krater she gives him for his sixty-fifth birthday that receives his body when it has been reduced to ashes.

From the Viennese couch to the London exile, their friendship is formed around suffering and death but also, always, the life instincts. Until the moment when he fades away, Freud knows, despite his profound pessimism, how to attach himself to people and be attentive to them. He confides to Jones that, as one grows older, one still wants a bit of love and friendship from those close to one.[47] And to the poet H. D. (Hilda Doolittle), who had sent him a bouquet of white gardenias for his eightieth birthday, he writes: "Life at any age is not easy, but spring is beautiful and so is love."[48]

The discussion of Freud's friendships would be incomplete without a brief mention of the salons in the Hotel Bristol in Vienna, where Freud and Martha go to have tea in the company of Yvette Guilbert and her husband during the Parisian singer's annual tours. On the advice of Mme. Charcot, Freud had let himself be seduced by the charm of this voice when he was in Paris for the second time in 1889. The coincidences of the little history of psychoanalysis enable him to meet her. For one of Guilbert's nieces, Eva Rosenfeld, came to Vienna in 1924 to study psychology; she met Anna Freud and her father, with whom she undertook an analysis in 1929. In 1926, she told her aunt how much Freud had admired her over the years, and thus, beginning in 1927, he missed no opportunity to hear her sing when she came to Vienna, and to chat with her. The last time he leaves the house, in October 1938 in London, it is once again Yvette Guilbert he goes to hear sing *Le Fiacre*, *La Pocharde*, and *Elle avait le nombril en forme de cinq*.[49]

When Freud stops in Paris on his way into exile, Marie Bonaparte gives a reception in his honor and invites Yvette Guilbert, who, in this dark hour, is able to provide a momentary diversion with her lively songs for an old man who once, in other Parisian salons, had dreamed of glory. To achieve it, he had dedicated his life to understanding the most unseemly part of humankind. Guilbert, with a seductiveness full of intelligence and innocence, had done the same in her own way. They met face to face, like two real people, and "the magic spell"[50] of their friendship surely had to do with the fact that she did not belong to psychoanalytic circles.

At each period of his life, Freud keeps a few rare friends who have nothing to do with his analytic work and concerns. Little has come to light about them, apart from some scattered traces in the correspondences and the dates that mark the long duration of these faithful friendships. Thus Emmanuel Löwy, the professor of archeology who makes Freud dream of Rome as early as 1896, gives him a Dürer etching when he turns 80, and Freud recalls his old friend's birthday as well: "But it is difficult to find him a present. I have nothing but the collected works, but with his poor eyesight he can hardly read anymore."[51]

Learning that his friend Oscar Rie has died, Freud writes: "It is an inevitable lot to see one's old friend die; enough if one is not condemned to outlive the young ones."[52]

The ideal of friendship is to share everything. Everything except sex. When Lou dies, Freud acknowledges that he admired her a lot, loved her as a friend, and was very attached to her, but "without a trace of sexual attraction."[53]

In the fourth chapter of *Group Psychology and the Analysis of the Ego*, he unambiguously affirms the convergence of all the forms of love—including friendship—and their basis in sexuality. He makes no distinction between the love that leads to sexual union and other kinds of love, such as self-love, the love one feels for one's parents and children, and friendship, feelings that are aim-inhibited and yet retain enough of their originally sexual nature that their identity is unmistakable.

Friendship, he writes, is grounded in two contradictory movements. On the one hand, sexual desire is never completely absent from it, since total desexualization would bring about the disappearance of the sex drive and with it the very feelings of friendship. For, although friendship is inhibited with regard to its sexual aim, it is nourished by the libidinal urge and cannot exist without it. On the other hand, affective life remains marked by the original inhibition of the genital sex drive. This hindrance leads to an increase in psychic participation and the idealization of the object. Freud finds here the cement of lasting relations among people, since no discharge reduces its binding force:

> The social instincts belong to a class of instinctual impulses which need not be described as sublimated, though they are closely related to these. They have not abandoned their directly sexual aims, but they are held back by internal resistances from attaining them; they rest content with certain approximations to satisfaction and for that very reason lead to especially firm and permanent attachments between human beings. To this class belong in particular the affectionate relations between parents and children, which were originally fully sexual, feelings of friendship, and the emotional ties in marriage which had their origin in sexual attraction."[54]

If friendship occurs in everyone's experience or aspirations as the presumed, or lived, source of unique pleasures, this is because the renunciation of earthly nourishments is always credited with a spiritual supplement, an unmatched enjoyment.

In perpetually deferring the sexual aim, friendship—that disembodied love—promises a surplus of pleasure. Sharing everything with the friend but not putting anything into effect sexually leads to a preference for fantasy over reality, affects over perception, internal psychic satisfactions over object relations. And it often leads to a choice of absence over presence, since absence increases psychic participation even more. Thus the exchange of letters with the faraway friend makes use of that stronger mobilization of fantasies, feelings, and imaginary feelings and representations. Absence magnifies and heightens friendship.[55] Like the work of thought, friendship is called upon to sketch a face in absentia. Often it idealizes and does not suffer the disappointment that wounds the tyrannical demands of the ego ideal. Here we can sense its rootedness in narcissism and its legacy of the symbiotic experience with the first love object.[56] Friendship seeks to reproduce an intimate encounter, no longer of skin to skin but of "saying to saying": words, listening, writing, and silence.

Between friends there is no touching, or only a little, but there is speaking and falling silent, sometimes joined together in a warm silence. It is surely no coincidence that, under Freud's pen, we find mention of both music and dogs; doesn't friendship always grow from the drive-soil of the nonverbal? And, despite the inhibition of sensuality, the body tends to reappear, at least in discourse. Thus, from Fliess to Zweig, Freud insistently discusses his cardiac episodes, his sinus infections, the pieces of his jaw that are coming loose. It is as though the presence of the body in words tended to compensate for the silence of gestures, and that he could not form bonds to the Other without the real or fantasized vehicle of the body.

But who is this Other that our desire for closeness calls by the name of friend, if it is not first of all our own face discovered in another mirror? And how to encounter the Other, the *alter*, when it is through him alone that our confusions and opacities can be cleared up, and through him, too, that we constantly pursue our old rainbows? The friend serves as an alibi for our ceaseless repetitions, at the same time as he opens up for us an always possible space for a new inner disposition, a new game to help us decipher and interpret in a different way the score of our imaginary music.[57]

In the mansion of friendship there is, undoubtedly, always an element of self-forgetting. To love is also to be willing to be taken away from oneself, to give up one's dreams of transparent fusion. But an even greater proof of friendship is the unconditional acceptance of the mystery of the Other, his radical alterity, his incomprehensible difference. Freud writes to Romain Rolland in the evening of his life,

"[A]ware that I am unlikely to see you again, I may confess to you that I have rarely experienced that mysterious attraction of one human being for another as vividly as I have with you; it is somehow bound up, perhaps, with the awareness of our being so different."[58]

Since the entire European tradition sees the will to know as a legitimate passion, there is wisdom in daring not to understand.

NOTES

1. This chapter is a revised version of Flem 1983b.
2. Act I, Scene 4. Letter to Marie Bonaparte of December 6, 1936 (Freud 1960, p. 434, where the following quotation is also to be found).
3. Cervantes 1615.
4. Letter to Martha of February 7, 1884 (Freud 1960, p. 96).
5. Letter of September 4, 1874 (Freud 1992, p. 57).
6. Letter of July 24, 1873 (Freud 1992, p. 26).
7. See Gedo and Wolf 1976.
8. Montaigne 1580, Book I, Chapter 28.
9. Letter to Breuer of May 3, 1889 (Freud 1960, p. 226).
10. "When men like you whom I have loved from afar express their friendship for me, then a particular ambition is gratified. I enjoy it without questioning whether or not I deserve it; I relish it as a gift." (Letter to Romain Rolland of May 13, 1926, in Freud 1960, p. 370).
11. Blanchot 1971, p. 328 (trans. S. F.).
12. Letter to Martha of January 27, 1886 (Freud 1960, p. 199).
13. Bertin 1982, p. 361.
14. This theoretical lack is found throughout the psychoanalytic literature. Bergler (1946) offers some reflections, and Khan (1991) discusses the role of friendship in the self-experience of Montaigne, Rousseau, and Freud. In his view, special friendship became necessary to fill the void created by the absence of God.
15. Freud 1929, p. 103. In this connection see Granoff 1976.
16. Letter of May 7, 1900 (Freud 1954, pp. 318–319).
17. Letter of September 24, 1910 (Freud and Jung 1974, p. 353).
18. Letter of January 17, 1909 (Freud and Jung 1974, pp. 196–197).
19. "I admire and love him with an intellectual passion, if you will allow such a phrase. His destruction will move me as the destruction of a sacred and famous temple would have affected an ancient Greek. I love him not so much as a human being, but as one of Creation's precious achievements" (Freud 1955, p. 271).
20. Freud 1900, p. 483.
21. Letter of March 6, 1910 (Freud and Jung 1974, p. 300).
22. Letter of December 18, 1912 (Freud and Jung 1974, p. 535).

23. Freud 1900, p. 483.

24. Letter of July 29, 1912, cited in Schur 1972, p. 264.

25. Does he have him in mind when he writes: "Thus we have people all of whose human relationships have had the same outcome: such as . . . the man whose friendships all end in betrayal by his friend" (1920c, p. 22).

26. *Nichomachean Ethics* VIII.iii.9.

27. Letter of January 1, 1896 (Freud and Fliess 1985, p. 158).

28. Letter to Martha of April 19, 1884 (Freud 1960, p. 105).

29. Letter of September 25, 1882 (Freud 1960, pp. 28–30).

30. Letter to Martha of October 6, 1883 (Freud 1960, p. 67).

31. Letter to Fliess of August 20, 1893 (Freud and Fliess 1985, p. 54).

32. Freud 1895b.

33. 1908b, p. 194.

34. Putnam 1971, p. 189.

35. Letter to Fliess of December 22, 1897 (Freud 1954, p. 238). Freud goes on to say that alcohol, morphine, and tobacco are substitutes for masturbation. In "'Civilized' Sexual Morality and Modern Nervous Illness" (1908b), he explains that masturbation in no way corresponds to the ideal requirements of sexual morality.

36. We can see on the map of Berggasse that, by virtue of an odd arrangement of the rooms in their apartment, Minna had to go through her sister's marital bedroom to reach her own room. Thanks to the International Association for the History of Psychoanalysis and its president, Alain de Mijolla, we may hope that the veil will gradually be lifted and the Freud Archives opened to critical study and reflection.

37. Letter of July 13, 1917 (Freud and Andréas-Salomé 1985, pp. 60–61).

38. Letter of May 13, 1924 (Freud and Andréas-Salomé 1985, p. 135).

39. Letter of August 25, 1919 (Freud and Andréas-Salomé 1985, p. 100).

40. Freud 1901, p. 168.

41. Letter of May 10, 1925 (Freud and Andreas-Salomé 1985, p. 154).

42. Letter of March 33, 1930 (Freud and Andréas-Salomé 1985, p. 185).

43. Letter of June 14, 1917 (Freud and Andréas-Salomé 1985, p.56).

44. Bertin 1982, p. 154.

45. Letter of October 20, 1932, cited in Schur 1972, p. 439.

46. Bertin 1982, p. 154.

47. Jones 1957, p. 206.

48. Letter of May 24, 1936 (Doolittle 1956, p. 194).

49. Steel 1982.

50. Letter to Guilbert of October 24, 1938 (Freud, 1960, p. 452).

51. Letter to Martin Freud of August 16, 1937 (Freud, 1969, pp. 437–438).

52. Letter to Marie Bonaparte of September 18, 1931, cited in Schur 1972, p. 430.

53. Jones 1957, p. 213.

54. Freud 1921, pp. 138–139.

55. See Olender 1978, 1980.

56. See Anzieu 1981, 1985.

57. Just as there is more than one kind of therapeutic friendship, more than one analyst appreciates patients who may become friends. Freud himself (1937b) notes that some of the good relationships that form between analysts and their present and former patients are not transferences but are based on objective grounds.

58. Letter written sometime in May 1931 [no date] (Freud 1960, p. 406).

References

Anzieu, D. (1959). *L'Auto-analyse de Freud et la Découverte de la Psychanalyse.* Paris: PUF.

——— (1970). Freud et la mythologie. *Nouvelle Revue de Psychanalyse* 1:114–145.

——— (1981). *Le Corps de l'Oeuvre.* Paris: Gallimard.

——— (1985). *The Skin Ego: A Psychoanalytic Approach to the Self.* New Haven and London: Yale University Press, 1989.

Arendt, H. (1938). *Rahel Varnhagen: The Life of a Jewess*, trans. R. Winston. Baltimore, MD: Johns Hopkins University Press, 1997.

Aristotle. *Nichomachean Ethics*, trans. D. Ross. Oxford, U.K.: Oxford University Press, 1998.

Bakan, D. (1964). *Sigmund Freud and the Jewish Mystical Tradition.* London: Free Association, 1991.

Baudry, J.-L. (1968). Freud et la "création littéraire." *Tel Quel. Théorie d'Ensemble.* Paris: Seuil.

——— (1984). *Proust, Freud et l'Autre.* Paris: Minuit.

Bergler, E. (1946). Psychology of friendship and acquaintanceship. In *Selected Papers*, pp. 35–47. New York: Grune & Stratton, 1969.

Bernfeld, S. (1951). Freud and archeology. *American Imago* 8:35–51.

Bertin, C. (1982). *Marie Bonaparte. A Life.* New York: Harcourt.

Binswanger, L. (1970). *Analyse Existentielle et Psychanalyse Freudienne.* Paris: Gallimard.

Blanchot, M. (1971). *L'Amitié.* Paris: Gallimard.

Blanton, S. (1971). *Diary of an Analysis with Sigmund Freud*, ed. M. Blanton. New York: Hawthorne.

Boorstin, D. J. (1983). *The Discoverers. A History of Man's Search to Know His World and Himself.* New York: Random House.

Börne, L. (1823). *Gesammelte Schriften*, Bd. 1. Leipzig: Hesse, 1925.

Breuer, J., and Freud, S. (1893–1895). *Studies on Hysteria. Standard Edition* 2.

Carotenuto, A. C. (1984). *A Secret Symmetry. Sabina Spielrein between Freud and Jung*, trans. J. Shepley, A. J. Pomeranz, and K. Winston. New York: Pantheon.

Certeau, M. de (1975). *The Writing of History.* New York: Columbia University Press, 1992.

——— (1987). *Histoire et Psychanalyse entre Science et Fiction.* Paris: Gallimard.

Cervantes, M. de (1605–1615). *Don Quixote*, trans. S. Putnam. New York: Modern Library, 1998.

——— (1615). *The Exemplary Novels*, ed. and trans. B. W. Ife. London: Aris and Phillips, 1992.

Chamisso, A. von (1813). *Peter Schlemihl*, trans. P. Wortman. New York: Fromm, 1993.

Chemouni, J. (1988). *Freud et le Sionisme.* Paris: Solin.

Dante. *The Divine Comedy of Dante Alighieri*, trans. A. Mandelbaum. New York: Bantam, 1986.

David, C. (1982). Pulsation, travail de pensée, pensée en travail. *Nouvelle Revue de Psychanalyse* 25:59–69.

Derrida, J. (1967). Freud and the scene of writing. In *Writing and Difference*, trans. A. Bass, pp. 115–141. Chicago: University of Chicago Press, 1978.

——— (1990). *Memories of the Blind*, trans. P.-A. Brault and M. Naas. Chicago: University of Chicago Press, 1993.

Detienne, M. (1981). *The Creation of Mythology*, trans. M. Cook. Chicago: University of Chicago Press, 1986.

Doolittle, H. (1956). *Tribute to Freud.* New York: Norton.

Engelman, E. (1998). *Sigmund Freud, Vienna IX, Berggasse 19.* New York: Universe, 1998.

Flem, L. (1982). L'archéologie chez Freud. *Nouvelle Revue de Psychanalyse* 26:59–74.

——— (1983a). Freud entre Athènes, Rome et Jérusalem. La géographie d'un regard. *Revue Française de Psychanalyse* 2:80–97.

——— (1983b). L'amour de l'amitié, ou *Der Freund Freud. Nouvelle Revue de Psychanalyse* 28:138–165.

——— (1986). *La Vie Quotidienne de Freud et ses Patients.* Paris: Hachette.

Fourton, J. (1981). Freud avec Börne ou "L'art de devenir un écrivain original en trois jours." *Littoral* 2:151–154.

Freud, E., Freud, L., and Grubrich-Simitis, I., eds. (1978). *Sigmund Freud:*

His Life in Pictures and Words, trans. C. Trollope. St. Lucia, Queensland: University of Queensland Press.

Freud, M. (1957). *Glory Reflected. Sigmund Freud, Man and Father*. New York: Jason Aronson, 1983.

———— (1967). Who was Freud? In J. Fraenkel, *The Jews of Austria. Essays on Their Life, History, and Destruction*, pp. 317–343. London: Valentine Mitchell.

Freud, S. (1877a). Über den Ursprung der hinteren Nervenwurzeln in Rückenmark von Ammocoetes (Petromyzon Planeri). *Sitzungsberichte der kaiserlichen Akademie der Wissenschaften* [Wien]. Mathematisch-Naturwissenschaftliche Klasse 75, III. Abteilung 15–27.

———— (1877b). Beobachtungen über Gestaltung und feineren Bau der als Hoden beschriebenen Lappenorgane des Aals. *Sitzungsberichte der kaiserlichen Akademie der Wissenschaften* [Wien]. Mathematisch-Naturwissenschaftliche Klasse 75, I. Abteilung 419–430.

———— (1878). Über Spinalganglien und Rückenmark des Petromyzon. *Sitzungsberichte der kaiserlichen Akademie der Wissenschaften* [Wien]. Mathematisch-Naturwissenschaftliche Klasse 78, III. Abteilung 81–167.

———— (1885). Contribution to the knowledge of the effect of cocaine. In *Cocaine Papers*, ed. R. Byck, pp. 97–104. New York: Stratton, 1974.

———— (1891). *On Aphasia. A Critical Study*, trans. E. Stengel. New York: International Universities Press, 1953.

———— (1892). Letter to J. Breuer. *Standard Edition* 1:147–148.

———— (1893). Charcot. *Standard Edition* 3:9–23.

———— (1894). Preface and footnotes to the translation of Charcot's "Tuesday lectures." *Standard Edition* 1:129–143.

———— (1895a). *Project for a Scientific Psychology. Standard Edition* 1:289–397.

———— (1895b). On the grounds for detaching a particular syndrome from neurasthenia under the description "anxiety neurosis." *Standard Edition* 3:385–415.

———— (1896a). The aetiology of hysteria. *Standard Edition* 3:187–221.

———— (1896b). The psychological mechanism of forgetfulness. *Standard Edition* 3:287–300.

———— (1899). Screen memories. *Standard Edition* 3:299–322.

———— (1900). *The Interpretation of Dreams. Standard Edition* 4, 5.

———— (1901). *The Psychopathology of Everyday Life. Standard Edition* 6.

———— (1905a). *Three Essays on the Theory of Sexuality. Standard Edition* 7:123–243.

———— (1905b). Fragment of an analysis of a case of hysteria. *Standard Edition* 7:1–122.

—— (1905c). *Jokes and Their Relation to the Unconscious. Standard Edition* 8.

—— (1905d). Psychical (or mental) treatment. *Standard Edition* 7:281–302.

—— (1907a). *Delusions and Dreams in Jensen's "Gradiva." Standard Edition* 9:1–95.

—— (1907b). Creative writers and day-dreaming. *Standard Edition* 9:141–154.

—— (1908a). Family romances. *Standard Edition* 9:235–241.

—— (1908b). "Civilized" sexual morality and modern nervous illness. *Standard Edition* 9:177–204.

—— (1909). Notes upon a case of obsessional neurosis. *Standard Edition* 10:151–249.

—— (1910a). *Five Lectures on Psycho-Analysis. Standard Edition* 11:1–55.

—— (1910b). Leonardo da Vinci and a memory of his childhood. *Standard Edition* 11:57–137.

—— (1910c). A special type of choice of object made by men. *Standard Edition* 11:163–176.

—— (1910d). The psycho-analytic view of psychogenic disturbance of vision. *Standard Edition* 11:209–218.

—— (1911a). "Great Is Diana of the Ephesians." *Standard Edition* 12:242–244.

—— (1911b). The significance of sequences of vowels. *Standard Edition* 12:341.

—— (1912). A note on the unconscious in psycho-analysis. *Standard Edition* 12:255–266.

—— (1913a). On beginning the treatment. *Standard Edition* 12:121–144.

—— (1913b). The theme of the three caskets. *Standard Edition* 12:289–301.

—— (1913c). The claims of psycho-analysis to scientific interest. *Standard Edition* 13:163–190.

—— (1914a). On the history of the psycho-analytic movement. *Standard Edition* 14:3–66.

—— (1914b). Some reflections on schoolboy psychology. *Standard Edition* 13:239–244.

—— (1914c). From the history of an infantile neurosis. *Standard Edition* 17:1–122.

—— (1914d). The Moses of Michelangelo. *Standard Edition* 13:209–236.

—— (1916a). A mythological parallel to a visual obsession. *Standard Edition* 14:337–338.

—— (1916b). Some character types met with in psycho-analytic work. *Standard Edition* 14:309–333.

———— (1916–1917). *Introductory Lectures on Psycho-Analysis. Standard Edition* 15, 16.

———— (1917a). A childhood recollection from *Dichtung und Wahrheit. Standard Edition* 17:145–156.

———— (1917b). The taboo of virginity. *Standard Edition* 11:191–208.

———— (1919a). The "uncanny." *Standard Edition* 17:217–256.

———— (1919b). "A child is being beaten." *Standard Edition* 17:175–204.

———— (1920a). The psychogenesis of a case of homosexuality in a woman. *Standard Edition* 18:202–231.

———— (1920b). A note on the prehistory of the technique of analysis. *Standard Edition* 18:263–265.

———— (1920c). *Beyond the Pleasure Principle. Standard Edition* 18:1–64.

———— (1921). *Group Psychology and the Analysis of the Ego. Standard Edition* 18:65–143.

———— (1922). Medusa's head. *Standard Edition* 18:273–274.

———— (1923). *The Ego and the Id. Standard Edition* 19:1–59.

———— (1924). *An Autobiographical Study. Standard Edition* 20:1–70.

———— (1925a). The resistances to psycho-analysis. *Standard Edition* 19:211–222.

———— (1925b). On the occasion of the opening of the Hebrew University. *Standard Edition* 19:292.

———— (1925c). A note upon the "mystic writing pad." *Standard Edition* 19:225–232.

———— (1926a). *The Question of Lay Analysis. Standard Edition* 20:177–250.

———— (1926b). *Inhibitions, Symptoms, and Anxiety. Standard Edition* 20:77–176.

———— (1927a). Fetishism. *Standard Edition* 21:147–157.

———— (1927b). Humor. *Standard Edition* 21:159–166.

———— (1927c). *The Future of an Illusion. Standard Edition* 21:1–56.

———— (1929). *Civilisation and Its Discontents. Standard Edition* 21:57–145.

———— (1930). Address delivered in the Goethe House at Frankfurt. *Standard Edition* 21:208–212.

———— (1933). *New Introductory Lectures on Psycho-Analysis. Standard Edition* 22:1–182.

———— (1936a). Letter to Georg Hermann. *Revue Internationale de l'Histoire de la Psychologie* 2:261–262, 1989.

———— (1936b). A disturbance of memory on the Acropolis. *Standard Edition* 22:237–248.

———— (1937a). Constructions in analysis. *Standard Edition* 23:255–269.

———— (1937b). Analysis terminable and interminable. *Standard Edition* 23:209–254.

———— (1938a). *An Outline of Psycho-Analysis. Standard Edition* 23:139–207.

———— (1938b). Some elementary lessons in psycho-analysis. *Standard Edition* 23:279–286.

———— (1938c). Findings, ideas, problems. *Standard Edition* 23:299–300.

———— (1939). *Moses and Monotheism. Standard Edition* 23:1–137.

———— (1954). *The Origins of Psychoanalysis. Letters to Wilhelm Fliess*, trans. E. Mosbacher and J. Strachey. New York: Basic Books.

———— (1960). *Letters of Sigmund Freud*, ed. E. L. Freud. New York: Basic Books.

———— (1974). *Cocaine Papers*, ed. R. Byck. New York: Stratton.

———— (1984). *S. Freud Présenté par Lui-Même.* Paris: Gallimard.

———— (1985). *The Complete Letters of Sigmund Freud to Wilhelm Fliess, 1887–1904*, trans. J. M. Masson. Cambridge, MA: Harvard University Press.

———— (1990). *Lettres de Jeunesse.* Paris: Gallimard.

———— (1992). *The Letters of Sigmund Freud to Eduard Silberstein, 1871–1881*, ed. W. Boehlich, trans. A. J. Pomerans. Cambridge, MA: Harvard University Press.

Freud, S., and Abraham, K. (1965). *A Psycho-Analytic Dialogue. The Letters of Sigmund Freud and Karl Abraham, 1907–1926*, ed. H. C. Abraham and E. L. Freud, trans. B. Marsh and H. C. Abraham. New York: Basic Books.

Freud, S., and Andréas-Salomé, L. (1985). *Sigmund Freud and Lou Andréas-Salomé. Letters*, ed. E. Pfeiffer, trans. W. Robson-Scott and E. Robson-Scott. New York: Norton.

Freud, S., and Ferenczi, S. (1996). *The Correspondence of Sigmund Freud and Sándor Ferenczi*, vol. 2, ed. E. Falzeder and E. Brabant, trans. P. Hoffer. Cambridge, MA: Harvard University Press.

Freud, S., and Jones, E. (1993). *The Complete Correspondence of Sigmund Freud and Ernest Jones, 1908–1939*, ed. A. Paskauskas. Cambridge, MA: Harvard University Press.

Freud. S. and Jung, C. G. (1974). *The Freud/Jung Letters. The Correspondence between Sigmund Freud and C. G. Jung*, ed. W. McGuire, trans. R. Mannheim and R. F. C. Hull. Cambridge, MA: Harvard University Press.

Freud, S. and Pfister, O. (1963a). *Psycho-Analysis and Faith. The Letters of Sigmund Freud and Oskar Pfister*, ed. E. L. Freud and H. Meng, trans. E. Mosbacher. New York: Basic Books.

———— (1963b). *Sigmund Freud, Oskar Pfister. Briefe, 1909–1937.* Frankfurt am Main: Fischer.

Freud, S. and Zweig, A. (1970). *The Letters of Sigmund Freud and Arnold Zweig*, ed. E. L. Freud. New York: Harcourt Brace.

Gardiner, M., ed. (1971). *The Wolf Man. With the Case of the Wolf Man by Sigmund Freud and a Supplement by Ruth Mack Brunswick.* New York: Basic Books.

Gay, P. (1987). *A Godless Jew. Freud, Atheism, and the Making of Psychoanalysis*. New Haven, CT: Yale University Press.

Gedo, J. and Wolf, E. (1976). The "Ich" letters and Freud's *Novelas Ejemplares*. *Psychological Issues* 9:71–111.

Goethe, J. W. von (1789). *Italian Journey*, trans. W. H. Auden. San Francisco: North Point, 1982.

———— (1808–1832). *Faust*, trans. W. Arndt. New York: Norton, 1976.

Goetz, B. (1976). Souvenirs sur S. Freud. In *Freud, Jugements et Témoignages*, ed. R. Jaccard, pp. 213–223. Paris: PUF.

Goldschmidt, G.-A. (1988). *Quand Freud Voit la Mer. Freud et la Langue Allemande*. Paris: Buchet-Chastel.

Gomperz, T. (1896–1902). *Greek Thinkers. A History of Ancient Philosophy*, trans. L. Magnus and G. G. Berry. London: Thoemmes, 1997.

Goux, J.-J. (1978). *Les Iconoclastes*. Paris: Seuil.

Graf, M. (1942). Reminiscences of Professor S. Freud. *Psychoanalytic Quarterly* 11:465–476.

Granoff, W. (1976). La bisexualité à l'abri dans l'amitié. In *La Pensée et le Féminin*, pp. 53–73. Paris: Minuit.

Green, A. (1980). Le mythe: un objet transitionnel. In *Le Temps de la Réflexion*, pp. 99–131. Paris: Seuil.

Grubrich-Simitis, I., ed. (1986). *Vue d'Ensemble des Névroses de Transfert. Un Essai Métapsychologique. Edition Bilingue d'un Manuscrit Retrouvé*. Paris: Gallimard.

Haddad, G. (1981). *L'Enfant Illégitime. Sources Talmudiques de la Psychanalyse*. Paris: Hachette.

Heine, H. (1930). *The Journey to Italy*, trans. C. G. Cleland. New York: Marsilio, 1998.

Herzl, T. (1896). *The Jewish State*. New York and London: Dover, 1989.

Holt, R. (1965). Freud's cognitive style. *American Imago* 22:87–96.

Jensen, W. (1903). *Gradiva*, trans. H. M. Downey. Los Angeles, CA: Sun & Moon, 1987.

Jones, E. (1949). *Hamlet and Oedipus*. New York: Norton.

———— (1953). *The Life and Work of Sigmund Freud. Vol. 1. The Formative Years and the Great Discoveries, 1856–1900*. New York: Basic Books.

———— (1955). *The Life and Work of Sigmund Freud. Vol. 2. Years of Maturity, 1901–1919*. New York: Basic Books.

———— (1957). *The Life and Work of Sigmund Freud. Vol. 3. The Last Phase, 1919–1939*. New York: Basic Books.

Kahn, L. (1986). Une ruine en son absence. *L'Ecrit du Temps* 11:15–25.

Khan, M. (1991). *Hidden Selves. Between Theory and Practice*. New York: International Universities Press.

Klein, D. B. (1985). *Jewish Origins of the Psychoanalytic Movement*. Chicago: University of Chicago Press.

Krüll, M. (1983). *Sigmund, Fils de Jacob*. Paris: Gallimard.

Knoepfmacher, H. (1979). Freud and the B'nai B'rith. *Journal of the American Psychoanalytic Association* 27:440–453.

Lacoste, P. (1981). *Il Ecrit. Une Mise en Scène de Freud*. Paris: Galilée.

——— (1990). *L'Etrange Cas du Professeur M. Psychanalyste à l'Ecran*. Paris: Gallimard.

Lacoue-Labarthe, P., and Nancy, J.-L. (1981). *Les Fins de l'Homme. A Partir du Travail de Jacques Derrida*. Paris: Galilée.

Lacouture, J. (1988). *Champollion. Une Vie de Lumières*. Paris: Livres de Poche, 1991.

Laister, M. (1889). *Das Rätsel von der Sphinx*. Berlin: Hertz.

Laplanche, J., and Pontalis, J.-B. (1985). *Fantasme Originaire, Fantasme des Origines, Origine du Fantasme*. Paris: Hachette.

Levinas, E. (1981). Quelques vues talmudiques sur le rêve. In *La Psychanalyse est-elle une Histoire Juive?*, pp. 114–128. Paris: Seuil.

Lévy-Valensi, E. A. (1971). *Les Voies et Pièges de la Psychanalyse*. Paris: Editions Universitaires.

Loraux, N. (1989). *The Experiences of Tiresias*, trans. P. Wissing. Princeton, NJ: Princeton University Press.

Mahoney, P. J. (1987). *Freud as a Writer*. New Haven, CT: Yale University Press.

——— (1989). *On Defining Freud's Discourse*. New Haven, CT: Yale University Press.

Mann, T. (1936). Freud and the future. In *Essays of Three Decades*, trans. H. T. Lowe-Porter, pp. 205–236. New York: Knopf, 1947.

Maspero, G. (1900). *Ruines et Paysages d'Egypte*. Paris: Payot, 2000.

Mijolla, A. de (1981). *Les Visiteurs du Moi. Fantasmes d'Identification*. Paris: Les Belles Lettres.

Montaigne, M. de (1580). *The Complete Essays of Montaigne*, trans. D. M. Frame. Stanford, CA: Stanford University Press, 1989.

Muschg, W. (1930). Freud écrivain. In *Freud. Jugements et Témoignages*, ed. R. Jaccard, pp. 159–209. Paris: PUF, 1976.

Nunberg, H., and Federn, E., eds. (1962). *Minutes of the Vienna Psychoanalytic Society, Vol 1: 1906–1908*, trans. M. Nunberg and H. Collins. New York: International Universities Press.

——— (1967). *Minutes of the Vienna Psychoanalytic Society, vol 2: 1908–1910*, trans. M. Nunberg and H. Collins. New York: International Universities Press.

——— (1974). *Minutes of the Vienna Psychoanalytic Society, vol 3: 1910–1911*, trans. M. Nunberg and H. Collins. New York: International Universities Press.

Olender, M. (1978). De l'absence de récit. In *Le Récit et ses Représentations*, pp. 175–180. Paris: Payot.

——— (1980). Une magie de l'absence. In *La Séduction*, pp. 109–118. Paris: Aubier.

——— (1990). Aspects of Baubo: ancient texts and contexts. In *Before Sexuality. The Construction of Erotic Experience in the Ancient World*, ed. F. Zeitlin, pp. 83–114. Princeton, NJ: Princeton University Press.

Pfrimmer, T. (1981). *Sigmund Freud, Lecteur de la Bible*. Thesis presented in January to the Theological Faculty of Strasbourg.

——— (1982). *Sigmund Freud, Lecteur de la Bible*. Paris: PUF.

Philippson, L. (1858). *Die israelitische Bibel, enthaltend den heiligen Urtext, die deutsche Übertragung, mit Erläuterung und Einleitungen*. Leipzig: Baumgärtner.

Plato. *Plato's Phaedo*, trans. R. Hackforth. Cambridge, UK: Cambridge University Press, 1967.

Poe, E. A. (1845). The purloined letter. In *Poe. Selected Works*, pp. 192–210. New York: Vintage, 1991.

Poliakov, L. (1968). *History of Anti-Semitism: From Voltaire to Wagner*. New York: Vanguard, 1976.

Pontalis, J.-B. (1982). L'archéologie chez Freud. *Nouvelle Revue de Psychanalyse* 26: 30–48.

——— (1990). *La Force d'Attraction*. Paris: Seuil.

Prokhoris, S. (1988). *La Cuisine de la Sorcière*. Paris: Aubier.

Proust, M. (1913). *Du Côté de Chez Swann*. Paris: Pleiade.

Putnam, J. J. (1971). *James Jackson Putnam and Psychoanalysis*, ed. N. G. Hale. Cambridge, MA: Harvard University Press.

Reik, T. (1940). *Thirty Years with Freud*, trans. R. Winston. New York: International Universities Press, 1949.

Robert, M. (1974). *From Oedipus to Moses: Freud's Jewish Identity*, trans. R. Mannheim. New York: Doubleday.

Rosolato. G. (1978). *La Relation d'Inconnu*. Paris: Gallimard.

Roustang, F. (1977). Du chapitre VII. *Nouvelle Revue de Psychanalyse* 16:65–95.

Ruitenbeek, H. M., ed. (1973). *Freud as We Knew Him*. Detroit, MI: Wayne State University Press.

Sachs, H. (1944). *Freud, Master and Friend*. Cambridge, MA: Harvard University Press.

Schliemann, H. (1880). *Ilios: The City and Country of the Trojans*. London: Murray.

Schnapp, A. (1982). Archéologie et tradition académique en Europe au XVIIIe et XIXe siècles. *Annales ESCS* 6:760–777.

Schnitzler, A. (1927). The prophecy. In *Little Novels*, trans. E. Sutton, pp. 79–120. New York: Simon & Schuster, 1957.

Scholem, G. (1977). *From Berlin to Jerusalem*. New York: Schocken, 1987.

———— (1978). *Fidelité et Utopie. Essais sur le Judaisme Contemporain*. Paris: Calman-Lévy.

Schönau, W. (1968). *S. Freuds Prosa: Literarische Elemente Seines Stils.* Stuttgart: Metzler.

Schorske, C. E. (1981). *Fin-de-Siècle Vienna: Politics and Culture.* New York: Random House.

Schotte, J. (1930). Introduction à la lecture de Freud écrivain. In *Freud: Jugements et Témoignages*, ed. R. Jaccard, pp. 159–209. Paris: PUF.

Schur, M. (1972). *Freud: Living and Dying.* New York: International Universities Press.

Schwab, R. (1950). *The Oriental Renaissance*, trans. G. Patterson Black, V. Reinking, and E. Said. New York: Columbia University Press, 1984.

Shakespeare, W. (1609). *Macbeth*. In *The Riverside Shakespeare*, vol. 5, ed. G. White, pp. 446–509. Boston: Houghton Mifflin, 1983.

Simon, E. (1957). S. Freud, the Jew. *The Leo Baeck Institute Yearbook* 2:270–305.

Sophocles. *Ajax*, trans. R. C. Jebb. Amsterdam: Hokkert, 1967.

———— *Oedipus the King*, trans. D. Grene. In *Sophocles I. Three Tragedies*, ed. D. Grene and R. Lattimore, pp. 9–76. Chicago: University of Chicago Press, 1954.

———— *Oedipus at Colonus*, trans. R. Fitzgerald. In *Sophocles I. Three Tragedies*, ed. D. Grene and R. Lattimore, pp. 77–155. Chicago: University of Chicago Press, 1954.

Spector, J. J. (1976). Freud, collectionneur d'art. In *Freud, Jugements et Témoignages*, ed. R. Jaccard, pp. 79–89. Paris: PUF.

Stanley, H. M. (1872). *How I Found Livingstone in Central Africa*. London and New York: Dover, 2002.

———— (1881). *Through the Dark Continent*. London and New York: Dover, 1988.

Starobinski, J. (1954). Hamlet et Freud. In E. Jones, *Hamlet and Oedipus*, pp. vii–xl. New York: Anchor, 1967.

Steel, D. (1982). L'amitié entre Sigmund Freud et Yvette Guilbert. *La Nouvelle Revue Française* 352:84–92.

Stekel, W. (1950). *The Autobiography of Wilhelm Stekel*, ed. E. Gutheil. New York: Liveright.

Trosman, H., and Simmons, R. (1973). The Freud library. *Journal of the American Psychoanalytic Association* 21:646–687.

Urtubey, L. de (1983). *Freud et le Diable*. Paris: PUF.

Vernant, J.-P., and Vidal-Naquet, P. (1972). *Myth and Tragedy in Ancient Greece*, trans. J. Lloyd. London and New York: Zone, 1990.

Wolf, E. (1976). Saxa Loquuntur. Artistic aspects of Freud's "The aetiology of hysteria." *Psychological Issues* 9:208–228.

Wortis, J. (1954). *Fragments of an Analysis with Freud*. New York: Simon & Schuster.

Yerushalmi, Y. H. (1989). Freud on the "historical novel." From the manuscript draft (1934) of *Moses and Monotheism*. *International Journal of Psycho-Analysis* 70:375–395.

Index